Reframing Decadence

REFRAMING DECADENCE

C. P. Cavafy's Imaginary Portraits

PETER JEFFREYS

CORNELL UNIVERSITY PRESS
ITHACA AND LONDON

First published 2015 by Cornell University Press

Printed in the United States of America

Library of Congress Cataloging-in-Publication Data

Jeffreys, Peter, author.
    Reframing decadence : C.P. Cavafy's imaginary portraits /
Peter Jeffreys.
        pages cm
    Includes bibliographical references and index.
    ISBN 978-0-8014-4708-2 (cloth : alk. paper)
    1. Cavafy, Constantine, 1863–1933—Criticism and interpretation.
    2. Decadence in literature. I. Title.
    PA5610.K2Z7256   2015
    889.1′32—dc23   2015010882

Cornell University Press strives to use environmentally responsible suppliers and materials to the fullest extent possible in the publishing of its books. Such materials include vegetable-based, low-VOC inks and acid-free papers that are recycled, totally chlorine-free, or partly composed of nonwood fibers. For further information, visit our website at www.cornellpress.cornell.edu.

Cloth printing   10 9 8 7 6 5 4 3 2 1

For my parents, Irene and George

Contents

Prologue

"Dangerous Thoughts"

After his memorable encounter with C. P. Cavafy in 1927, the Greek novelist Nikos Kazantzakis recorded his impressions of the poet in a verbal portrait that mischievously casts upon him the effete aura of decadence: "Now as I see him for the first time this evening and hear him, I feel how wisely such a complex, heavy-ladened soul of sanctified decadence succeeded in finding its form in art—a perfect match—in order to be saved." For Kazantzakis, Cavafy possesses all the formal traits of an "exceptional man of decadence": "wise, ironic, hedonistic—a charmer with a vast memory. . . . Seated in a soft armchair, he looks out the window, waiting for the barbarians to arrive. He holds a parchment with delicate encomia written in calligraphy, dressed in his best, made up with care, and he waits. But the barbarians do not arrive, and by evening he sighs quietly, and smiles ironically at the naiveté of his own soul which still hopes" (1965, 79). Although Kazantzakis likely intended these slightly irreverent comments to be read more for their dramatic effect than for their critical astuteness, his unsparing use of the word "decadence" (παρακμή) throughout his account conveys as much about Cavafy's poetics as it does about the aging poet's vanity. Indeed, Kazantzakis's portrait perceptively identifies Cavafy's literary descent from the decadent tradition, a central dimension of his poetics that forms the subject of this book. Not only did Cavafy write under the intoxicating spell of *décadisme* during his early years, but he would remain a devout votary of this loosely defined but unmistakably influential movement, the "common denominator" of all literary trends that emerged during the last two decades of the nineteenth century, as Jean Pierrot (1981, 7) maintains. Cavafy's literary genealogy is firmly rooted in the "dangerous thoughts" of fin de siècle decadence, a source of subject matter and imagery that constitutes an overarching literary strategy that enabled him to transgress and transcend moral and aesthetic boundaries; his poem "Dangerous Thoughts" (1911),[1] which offers an imaginary portrait of the youth Myrtias who willingly succumbs to "audacious erotic desires" and "lascivious impulses," serves as one of the best illustrations of this decadent temperament. Cavafy cultivated this distinct cosmopolitan aesthetic throughout his poetic career, and thus it is no coincidence that the cunning Kazantzakis chose this tainted but highly fitting category to characterize the enigmatic personality of the Alexandrian poet.

Today, nearly a century after Kazantzakis penned his lines, the paradigm of economic, military, social, and cultural decline has once again become the undeniable historical reality for many Western nations. From Niall Ferguson's provocative recasting of the Spenglerian narrative in *Civilization: The Rest and the West* (2011) to Hanif Kureishi's contemporary reprisal of it in his short story "The Decline of the West" (2010), we are regularly reminded of the cyclical inevitability of cultural decline. The timeliness, therefore, of a comprehensive reappraisal of the most widely read modern Greek poet—one that aims to realign him with the decadent tradition—requires little by way of justification. As a poet who has profoundly explored the themes of failure, decline, and defeat from various literary angles, Cavafy has a cultural relevance that has been gradually expanding to a newer and wider contemporary readership beyond his traditional base of diaspora Greeks, classicists, and gays. This has as much to do with the current decline-obsessed zeitgeist as it does with Cavafy's cosmopolitan appeal. A telling illustration of this appeal is a statement that appeared in the *New Yorker* defining the cultural pose of the suave über-European "drinking Burgundy wine, listening to Sibelius, and reading

Cavafy" (Buruma 2011, 39). Implied in this highly sophisticated defini-tion is the impending onslaught of some looming disaster awaiting those who assume such precious poses (in this instance, Belgian politicians in denial of the growing decay of their urban centers and the rise of Flem-ish nationalism). That Cavafy's name presently resonates so unmistak-ably with the poetics of decline is a complex and fascinating phenomenon, one that requires more than a predictable gloss referencing his signature poem "Waiting for the Barbarians." Rather, it calls for an engaged study of the extensive and pervasive decadent thematics that inform so much of Cavafy's poetry. Even though he brilliantly rehabilitated and subtly in-fused many of the central tropes of decadence in his work, numerous read-ers and critics maintain quite mistakenly that Cavafy moved well beyond decadence into different poetic modes altogether. One aim of this book is to address this misperception by firmly establishing Cavafy's decadent pedigree and elucidating how the decadent lineage remained an enduring part of his creative repertoire.

Although the concept of literary decadence remains highly contested and continues to resist any precise definition, as a critical term it encom-passes Cavafy's poetics more effectively than does the literary category symbolism or realism. Several early Greek critics—namely, Alkis Thrylos, Tellos Agras, Panos Karavias, and Timos Malanos—were eager to con-nect Cavafy with decadent literary trends. Despite the initial influence of this critical consensus, Cavafy's association with the decadent movement underwent a curious reappraisal and revision, a fact that is not surprising considering the problematic nature of the term itself.[2] That he was fixated on decadent aspects of Hellenistic and Roman Alexandria as opposed to the celebrated glorious achievements of classical Greece is now axiomatic for any critical analysis of his poems. Yet the more substantial connections between Cavafy and decadence have remained rather underexplored and even negated, effectively cutting off the poet from his inspirational creative font. This is due in part to the efforts of certain critics, notably the Alexan-drian novelist and critic Stratis Tsirkas, who, in the late 1950s, somewhat overzealously defended Cavafy from the scurrilous charges of depravity made by Timos Malanos in his study *The Poet C. P. Cavafy* (1933). Mala-nos, although unfairly critical of Cavafy as a scheming, selfish promoter of "depraved" and "derivative" verse—a mere "parasite" and theatrical "prompter" as he put it (1957, 207, 77)—was nevertheless more in tune with Cavafy's decadent pulse than were many critics who have since re-fashioned the poet into a post-symbolist realist. As Dimitris Daskalopou-los (1988) aptly notes, certain Greek scholars were determined to sanitize Cavafian decadence in their efforts to recuperate the poet and enshrine him in the national literary canon.[3] What resulted was a gradual dimin-ishing of Cavafy's decadent aesthetic. A mere glance at the topics of his late *Unfinished Poems* (1918–32—which include subjects ranging from the demonic apparition of the Emperor Justinian ("From The Secret His-tory") to the miraculous slumber of the Seven Sleepers of Ephesus ("The Holy Seven Children") and telepathic exchanges between Saint Athana-sius and his monks ("Athanasius")—disproves the misleading conclusion that Cavafy's decadence was a mere passing fad. This book seeks to coun-ter this problematic revisionism and recontextualize Cavafy in terms of lit-erary decadence in order to show how the poet remained unapologetically committed to the tenets of this artistic movement from the time of its as-cendancy in the late nineteenth century (the period of Cavafy's early poetic awakening) up until the composition of his final unfinished poems prior to his death in 1933. Cavafy's daring expression of his "aesthetic individual-ism," to borrow Matei Calinescu's apt categorization of decadence, would lead him to employ the central tropes of decadence with idiosyncratic ex-uberance throughout his poetic career. To be sure, the late Victorian pe-riod out of which decadence emerged remains a neglected dimension of Cavafy's work, one that yields illuminating critical perspectives on assess-ing his current global popularity, as I hope to show in the pages of this book. Much of this mass appeal is directly related to Cavafy's deft appro-priation of grand Victorian lore, such as the British obsession with impe-rial Rome, the burgeoning fascination with the pictorial arts, an excessive preoccupation with death and the cult of mourning, and the renewed in-terest in Greek eros that was spearheaded by Oxford Hellenists, whose revolutionary writings sought to legitimate homosexuality. These seem-ingly retrograde facets of nineteenth-century culture animate many of Cavafy's thematic and aesthetic interests, and it is from the threshold of decadence that we are best positioned to assess the poet's imaginative re-working of these fin de siècle tropes into extraordinary twentieth-century poetic expressions.

Before we consider the specific delineation of Cavafian decadence, a brief overview of the concept itself is in order. As a widespread cultural phenomenon, decadence offered paradigms that were at once cosmopolitan, transnational, and global (Hall and Murray 2013, 18). The fluctuating contours of the movement defined as decadent have been redrawn in more recent studies by David Weir, Ellis Hanson, Linda Dowling, Matei Calinescu, Asti Hustvedt, Brian Stableford, Kirsten MacLeod, Richard Dellamora, and Matthew Potolsky (among others), the collective result of which has been the rehabilitation of a once-shunned term. David Weir, who views decadence as a major cultural mode of transition from romanticism to modernism —a movement in a dynamic relationship with other literary periods—offers the following encompassing account of the word's notorious ambiguity: "A number of literary movements and tendencies developed through decadence, either by reacting against its characteristic styles and themes, or by extending them in some way"; decadence, Weir argues, developed as an "independent movement at the same time that other, better known movements were developing through it. . . . In one sense, decadence is like the mystical sphere whose circumference is everywhere but whose center is nowhere: naturalism, Parnassianism, aestheticism, and the rest are all arrayed 'around' decadence, but they do not point toward a common center. In another sense, the center and the circumference are the same: decadence as an independent movement is a sphere closed and contracted upon itself" (1996, xix). Despite this paradoxical lack of a center, the term "decadence" was championed (and in turn repudiated) by a number of significant literary figures, many of whom ventured some very precise definitions. One such apologia was offered by Théophile Gautier, who, in his 1868 preface to Baudelaire's *Les Fleurs du mal*, articulated a highly influential exposition of the term: "The style of decadence . . . is the last effort of the Word, called upon to express everything, and pushed to the utmost extremity." In a similar vein, the French critics Désiré Nisard and Paul Bourget identified the decadent style as one in which language decomposes into a multitude of overwrought fragments. Jean Moréas wrote a manifesto in 1886 on the "new school" of decadence (although he preferred to use the term "symbolism") in which he denounced didactic pursuits, declamation, false sensitivity and objective description. For Friedrich Nietzsche, decadence was the inescapable hallmark of the modern age and of Western history in general—the essential condition of humanity. Walter Pater famously offered his own classical definition by connecting decadent aesthetics to "the sense of death and the desire of beauty: the desire of beauty quickened by the sense of death." Arthur Symons, in his essay "The Decadent Movement in Literature" (1893), later expanded and renamed *The Symbolist Movement in Literature* (1899), categorized the movement as one marked by "an intense self-consciousness, a restless curiosity in research, an over-subtilizing refinement upon refinement, a spiritual and moral perversity."[4] And Cavafy's contemporary Oswald Spengler, the grand design historian who gave voice to a tragic sense of historical life in *The Decline of the West* (1917), echoes the poet's pessimistic but delicate appreciation for the beauty and splendor inherent in the irreversible process of cultural disintegration.

Notwithstanding the movement's lack of an ideological center, there are several common themes that collectively define its theoretical essence. Decadent writers insist on the absolute autonomy of art (art for art's sake); revile bourgeois philistinism and utilitarianism; seek rare sensations and intense experiences in their struggle to dispel ennui (Macleod 2006, 1); value artificiality above nature; are haunted by the cruelty of time and the imminence of death (Balakian 1977, 69); cultivate a lyrical sense of doom, metaphysical restlessness, and despair; favor the dissolution of classical ideas and a late anticlassical style (North 1999, 88); prefer eroticism to real sexual pleasure (Pierrot 1981, 135); revolt against the romantic cult of nature and ideal love (Carter 1958, 150); are fascinated with the objet d'art and the fragment (Hanson 1997, 184); are intrigued by the irrational and antipositivist phenomena of magic, mysticism, and the occult; and ultimately question modernity's choice of comparisons. They prefer not classical Greece or the Renaissance but Alexandria, Rome, or Byzantium, thereby undermining "modernity's sense of superiority" by playing on its "deep-seated fear that the past has not in fact been overcome, that the triumph over superstition and autocracy has been incomplete, or that, having overcome previous societies, the process of history will continue and it will be overcome and replaced in its turn" (Morley 2005, 580).

This compilation of categories gleaned from the discourse of decadence applies quite fittingly to Cavafy's own aesthetic sensibility, which could be more precisely defined as follows: Cavafy's poetry is antiromantic and anticlassical; displays a rather morbid fascination with death; manifests a bittersweet melancholy and metaphysical restlessness; exhibits a sense of doom conveyed through highly theatrical tableaux; employs a vivid pictorialist palette; shows an interest in mysticism, church ritual, magic, and

Byzantinism; delights in an excess of learning and artifice; privileges and celebrates homosexuality; and is perversely compelled by disaster. These unmistakable aspects of decadence are all inscribed in varying degrees in Cavafy's verse, as will be seen in more detail throughout the following chapters. Coming of age during the fin de siècle and experiencing the rapid economic dwindling of his family's fortune, as the last male issue of his family line, Cavafy was acutely aware of how decline affected his life and world. This sense of marginalization informed his style as well. He was, as Edward Said notes, the last of the poets writing in the learned "late style" of the Greek Phanariots:[5] "The language, a learned Greek idiom of which Cavafy was self-consciously the last modern representative, adds to the parsimony, the essentialized and rarefied quality of the poetry. His poems enact a form of minimal survival between the past and the present, and his aesthetic of nonproduction, expressed in a nonmetaphorical, almost prosaic unrhymed verse, enforces the sense of enduring exile that is at the core of his work" (2006, 145). Not only in this sense of historic and stylistic belatedness is Cavafy thoroughly decadent (he would cultivate the neurotic mannerisms of an effete aristocrat throughout his life), but he was also deeply influenced by political events that led him to a certain despair, namely the catastrophic failure of Greece's irredentist policy, the Great Idea (Μεγάλη Ιδέα), which resulted in the wholesale destruction of Hellenism in Asia Minor and Anatolia.[6] By situating Cavafy within this complex array of aesthetic ideas and concepts, I aim to show how decadence—a "pioneering, profound aesthetic" paradoxically generated by a "languorous and rebellious state of mind" (Weir 1996, 10)—rather than undermining his originality as a poet, enabled him to emerge as one of the most dynamic and original poets of the twentieth century. By extracting the more striking images and conceits of the period and transposing them into highly personal poetic expressions, Cavafy remains one of the most important interpreters of literary decadence as well as one of its most devoted acolytes.

This book is partly an intellectual history of Cavafy's evolution as an artist through the literary movements of his time and partly a biocritical study of his relationship to literary decadence. As such, it is arranged both chronologically and thematically, beginning with Cavafy's early adolescent years in England, proceeding to his brief flirtation with prose and journalism, then moving on to his early compositions (published, unpublished, and rejected) before analyzing his mature and late poetry. Intermingled throughout this progression are readings of his canonical poems that are meant to illustrate important connections with decadent subjects. This critical methodology deliberately resists certain lines of demarcation—in regard to either the canonicity of the poems and essays or the date of their composition—classifications that are often less than helpful when treating a poet who continually revised and recycled material throughout his life. (The year 1911 is commonly seen as the date when Cavafy found his signature poetic voice, the dividing line between his early and mature poems.) Similarly, I have intentionally eschewed a doctrinal definition of decadence since the term is too polymorphous to be delineated as such, and the word and movement tend to fall apart under diachronic scrutiny. A more useful model for the concept is offered by Matthew Potolsky, who argues that "works are 'decadent' not because they realize a doctrine or make use of certain styles and themes but because they move within a recognizable network of canonical books, pervasive influences, recycled stories, erudite commentaries, and shared tastes" (2013, 5). It is this very notion of a decadent network—a community of taste, as it were—that best defines Cavafy's relationship to literary decadence and underlies the organizational approach of this book. The standard aesthetic trajectory commencing from Poe on through Baudelaire, Swinburne, Huysmans, and Pater serves as the basic axis of the book, one that intersects with numerous other figures. The book begins with a critical appraisal of the lingering impact of Victorian aestheticism on the young Cavafy and explores his exposure to various artistic circles while he was living in England. His direct filial connection to the Ionides family and their patronage of important Pre-Raphaelite painters and poets proved foundational to Cavafy's aesthetic sensibility. I consider the poetic influence of Swinburne, who, along with Gautier, first defined decadence as a project. Swinburne's subversive Hellenism is positioned within the broader framework of painterly influences, especially the palettes of Edward Burne-Jones and James McNeill Whistler, whose paintings, I argue, will later directly inspire various poems. This established the aesthetic pictorialism—a pervasive overlap between painting and poetry—that subsequently serves as one of the major decadent hallmarks that defines Cavafy's oeuvre.

Cavafy's exposure to the currents and canvases of British aestheticism prepares him for his initiation and immersion into French decadence. Chapter 2 takes up the profound impact of Charles Baudelaire on Cavafy's early poetic compositions and surveys the poet's relevant prose writings—both expository and fictional—that function as an important index of decadent subjects and interests he would later explore and rework in his mature poetry. The influence of Poe is significant here—refracted through Baudelaire—as is the concept of the flâneur and the prominence of the prose poem. Cavafy's brief journalistic apprenticeship and ill-fated experimentation with purist Greek prose offer clues as to why he abandoned a career as a journalist critic and translator, retreating instead to the more secluded haven of poetry. The chapter concludes with a reading of Cavafy's gothic short story "In Broad Daylight" in light of his struggle and anxiety vis-à-vis the vexed language issue, the Victorian cult of prose, and the ubiquitous presence of Greek folklore, all of which played a role in his decision to curtail his public performance in prose.

The book then proceeds to explore the poet's prevailing pictorialist strategy (one largely overlooked by critics bent on fashioning a modernist Cavafy) and traces his debt to both Parnassian and decadent writers and the *transposition d'art* tradition that he gleaned from the salon critiques of Gautier, Baudelaire, and Huysmans. The syncretic mode of interreferencing paintings, sculptures, and poetry derives from this genre, and its influence on Cavafy is fully evident in the early poems he wrote and published prior to the 1911 date that marks his poetic maturity. The ekphrastic tradition and the cross-pollination of ideas, motifs, and aesthetics between the "sister arts" is an imaginative strategy he refines and adapts in his mature phase in many of his canonical poems as well. Chapter 3 undertakes intertextual readings of poems and paintings that are meant to highlight Cavafy's affinity with the plastic arts, one that consequently explains his lasting appeal to visual artists. It concludes with a consideration of select twentieth-century artists who uncovered pictorial dimensions in Cavafy's poems that in turn inspired new pictorial variations of them.

Chapter 4 presents a parallel reading of Cavafy and Walter Pater and proffers a sustained argument for the weighty influence of the Victorian aesthete on the poet in terms of both a shared aesthetic historicism and an emerging homoerotic sensibility. Pater set an example not only with his singular distillation of art criticism into his "euphuistic" writings but also by inflecting his Hellenism with a sensuality that boldly celebrated the homosexual subject. Traces of Pater's influence are found in Cavafy's prose essay on Shakespeare, and he borrowed heavily from Pater when fashioning his own version of Pater's conversion narratives, which featured comradeship, mourning, and an abiding fascination with the early church. Cavafy's favoring of Rome as a setting for so many of his poems derives in large part from the Victorian obsession with *Romanitas*; Pater's short fiction, and *Marius the Epicurean* in particular, offered the poet the well-wrought exemplum of the imaginary portrait of the aesthetic youth corrupted by Hellenism that we encounter in so many of his poems. Moreover, Cavafy's debt to Victorian classicism with its immense popular appeal yields insights into understanding his present fame, especially as he reprises so many of the same motifs that enticed an audience obsessed with imperial decline and the waning of cultural hegemony.

Chapter 5 focuses on Cavafy's complex relation to Byzantium and addresses the conflicting schools of interpretation that read his Byzantine poems as either overtly ironic or nostalgically patriotic. After overviewing the historic association between Byzantium and decadence, I assess Cavafy's unique redaction of Byzantine history and revisionist approach whereby he counters the age-old post-Enlightenment bias against the Eastern Roman Empire as hopelessly corrupt with the countervailing view of Byzantine culture as sophisticated, dynamic, and paradoxically modern. Cavafy's poems channel both approaches and effectively transcend them by offering a contrapuntal decadent reification of both the exuberance of decline and the celebration of Byzantine culture as the precious repository of Roman polity and Hellenic culture. His treatment of defiant royal figures foregrounds the dramatic element he valued in Byzantine historiography while appreciating the dignified abjection inherent in the narrative of failed coups, overthrown dynasties, and thwarted ambitions. Byzantium thus serves as a central facet of Cavafy's ongoing engagement with decadence and remains his most significant contribution to the transhistorical and transnational network of writers who define decadent discourse.

The book concludes with a reflection on how the gay legacy of decadence effectively shaped Cavafy's poetic expression of homosexuality and continues to influence the ongoing attraction of queer artists and critics to his work. By focusing on the erotic poems, we see how, in the deviant manner of Huysmans, Cavafy often sublimates raw sexuality in favor of a more elevated passion transfigured by memory and aestheticized by art. Yet just as often he presents a genuine physicality in poems that worship male beauty and recount specific sexual encounters. In both instances,

Cavafy largely avoids the feelings of abject shame common to many pre-Stonewall poets and writers; yet there is certain hint of sentimentality in these erotic poems that, as W. H. Auden felt, lend themselves somewhat to kitsch, an aesthetic category that remains paradoxically useful in explaining the poet's mass appeal. Indeed, the roots of this lingering sentimental strain may be traced back to the influence of Victorian aesthetic painting and the highly emotive pictorialism that left a pronounced mark on his erotic verse. Thus the ongoing popularization of his work and his "kitschification" as a gay icon may be seen as yet another manifestation of his unique relationship to the decadent tradition.

Although Cavafy never left any direct statements on the subject of decadence either as a concept or as a literary movement, he apparently discussed the topic at length with E. M. Forster when the two first met in Alexandria. In his letter to Cavafy dated July 1, 1917, Forster writes, "[George] Valassopoulo was over this afternoon and told me that since I saw you something occurred that has made you very unhappy; that you believed the artist must be depraved; and that you were willing he should tell the above to your friends."[7] What Cavafy meant by this notion of depravity (by which he clearly implies decadence) has always intrigued me, and this book is in many ways an attempt to supply this missing narrative and expound Cavafian decadence based on his life's work and the only real testimony he left to the movement—what was really precious: his poetic form (to paraphrase a line from "The Tomb of Evrion"). This book aims to fill a long-standing void and encourage new critical interpretations of Cavafy's poems centered on a fuller appreciation of his decadent poetics.

1

"Aesthetic to the Point of Affliction"

Cavafy and British Aestheticism

In his ambivalent review of the 1887 opening of the Grosvenor Gallery, Henry James praised the aestheticism of this "Temple of Art"[1] with a precious rhetoric reflective of the British public's unease with the emerging decadent trends in British art: "It is the art of culture, of reflection, of intellectual luxury, of aesthetic refinement, of people who look at the world and at life not directly, as it were, and in all its accidental reality but in the reflection and ornamental portrait of it furnished by art itself in other manifestations; furnished by literature, by poetry, by history, by erudition" (1989, 144). Although these comments refer specifically to the Pre-Raphaelite canvases of Edward Burne-Jones,[2] they serve as an equally apt appraisal of the poetry of Constantine Cavafy, as may be seen in his poem "I've Brought to Art" (1921), in which we find a similar distillation of English aestheticism:

I sit in a mood of reverie.
I brought to Art desires and sensations:

things half-glimpsed,
faces or lines, certain indistinct memories
of unfulfilled love affairs. Let me submit to Art:
Art knows how to shape forms of Beauty,
almost imperceptibly completing life,
blending impressions, blending day with day.

(1992, 116)

By triangulating Cavafy via Henry James and Pre-Raphaelite art, I wish to draw attention to the undeniable influence of British painting on Cavafy's aesthetics and the pictorial dimension of his lifelong engagement with literary decadence. To date, Cavafy's relation to the aesthetic movement has not been adequately explored. Indeed, the London artistic milieu cast its spell on the precocious youth during the 1870s, the decade when he began acquiring the effete airs of an English dandy that he would retain throughout his life. It should be noted that he lived in England during the greater part of this decade,[3] a period usually passed over as the uneventful adolescent prelude to the early poetic blossoming of the 1880s and 1890s. To be sure, the 1870s mark the seedtime that would shape Cavafy's social, cultural, and literary tastes, a process greatly abetted by his direct exposure to the resplendent canvases and notorious personalities of numerous painters—Watts, Rossetti, Burne-Jones, and Whistler, to name a few—artists of the first rank who were effecting a revolution in British painting. It is perhaps a cruel irony that the poet's family was slipping into an irreversible economic decline during the very years when aesthetic decadence began emerging as an artistic movement in England and France.

The British Aesthetic movement of the 1870s, which would give birth in turn to the Arts and Crafts movement, Art Nouveau, and the decadent sensibility of the 1890s, decisively influenced Victorian cultural tastes.[4] Coincidentally, Cavafy was uniquely privileged to encounter and experience many aesthetic artists directly through his wealthy London relations, who were at once patrons, collectors, models, and even artists of avant-garde aestheticism. The presence of these important painters in Cavafy's extended family history invites speculation regarding their unmistakable mark on the impressionable young poet and on the formation of his pictorial aesthetic. In order to chart the nature of these artistic influences, a brief

digression into the family's business connections and patronage practices
is necessary, a subject that reveals the important role played by diaspora
Greeks in promoting art in England.[5]

In his carefully documented genealogy, Cavafy dutifully preserves his
family's preeminent status among the Greek mercantile families of Constantinople, Alexandria, and London.[6] He perhaps never fully adjusted to
his family's drastic economic tailspin in the late 1870s, a decline that he
must have felt acutely, especially as his cousins in England went on to ex-
pand their businesses and acquire even greater wealth and social prestige.
His meticulous family genealogy was an attempt to preserve the record for
posterity and especially for those who had forgotten the grand lifestyle that
once marked Cavafy's family as among the wealthiest in the Levant. The
family business—Cavafy & Co., an import-export firm dealing primarily in Egyptian cotton and Manchester textiles—evolved from a company
founded by the poet's grandfather John Cavafy, who emigrated from Constantinople to Manchester with a Phanariot friend, Constantine (Ionides)
Ipliktzis.[7] The two entered into a business partnership that soon opened
offices in Alexandria, Constantinople, London, Liverpool, and Manchester. The sons of these two Levantine entrepreneurs (among whom may
be counted Cavafy's father, Peter, his uncle George, and Alexander Constantine Ionides) soon became prosperous merchants, solidifying their business investments by marrying into their own and other mercantile families,
most notably the Cassavetti and Ralli clans. In addition to being business
partners with the Ionides family, the Cavafy family was doubly related, as
it were, as both in-laws (συμπέθεροι) and through baptismal sponsorships
(κουμπάροι). Cavafy's uncle George, whom he greatly admired as an intellectual and prose stylist, married Maria Thoma(s), whose mother (a Cassavetti) was the sister-in-law of Constantine (Ipliktzis) Ionides, the family
patriarch. George's son John Cavafy was baptized by Alexander Constantine Ionides, and John's daughter Kitty in turn married an Ionides cousin,
thus joining together three generations of Cavafy and Ionides descendants.
These diaspora families quickly assimilated themselves into the English
upper middle class and sought to flaunt their wealth by purchasing costly
works of art and building opulent estates in which to showcase them.[8]

The interaction between these ambitious Greek patrons and the artists they favored was socially complex, as numerous painters regularly

frequented the Ionides and Cavafy homes. Remarkably, the business savvy of these aesthetic patrons was matched by a discerning eye for good art and an almost bohemian relish for high aestheticism. As far back as the late 1830s, George Cavafy and Alexander Ionides had begun to commission portraits from the then-unknown but unmistakably talented George Frederick Watts. Cavafy knew of these paintings and mentions Watts's portrait of his uncle in his genealogical notes.[9] Similar patronage was extended to the American expatriate James McNeill Whistler, who early in his career received commissions to paint "river pictures for the Greeks" (Dorment and Macdonald 1994, 100). Whistler would retain his advantageous relations with the Ionides-Cavafy family; in the 1860s, George Cavafy made significant purchases from Whistler that included four well-known canvases: *The Last of Old Westminster*, *Battersea Reach*, *Harmony in Blue and Silver: Trouville,* and *Variations in Flesh Colour and Green: The Balcony*, which was exhibited at the Grosvenor Gallery in May 1878 and later at the Westminster Palace Hotel in November 1878 during the peak of the Whistler-Ruskin trial (Whistler sued Ruskin for libel over his critique of the painting *Nocturne in Black and Gold: The Falling Rocket*).[10] Alexander Constantine Ionides also owned many Whistler canvases, but more significant, his niece Helen Ionides married the painter's brother William in 1877. Soon the magisterial Ionides house at 1 Holland Park—itself a statement of high aestheticism—became a meeting place of artists, musicians, and diplomats, decorated as it was by William Morris, Philip Webb, and Walter Crane.[11] This flamboyant estate, a baroque hybrid of Japanese, Persian, and neoclassical styles, showcased the burgeoning Ionides art collection, which included Pre-Raphaelite works, Barbizon paintings, Hellenistic terra cotta "Tanagra" figurines, and engraved gemstones. Some 1,156 of these items would be donated to the Victoria and Albert Museum in 1901. In 2003, the 90 paintings of this collection were splendidly rehung in the museum's refurbished Ionides Gallery.[12]

In addition to the wealth and patronage of the Ionides-Cavafy clan, there is the equally significant participation of female relatives who modeled for some of the most famous and even infamous paintings of the nineteenth century. The cousins Maria Zambaco (née Cassavetti) and Aglaia Coronio (née Ionides) together with their friend Marie Spartali were collectively known in the Pre-Raphaelite circle as the Three Graces. Along with Marie's sister Christina Spartali, all had modeled at one time or another for

Figure 1. Edward Burne-Jones, *The Mill* (1870–82). Oil on canvas, Victoria and Albert Museum, London.

Watts, Whistler, Rossetti, and Burne-Jones, setting an aesthetic standard for Pre-Raphaelite feminine beauty.[13] Among the most famous of numerous renowned canvases to emerge from these sittings (paintings, it should be noted, that were variously exhibited at the Royal Academy, the Paris Salon, and the Grosvenor Gallery) were Burne-Jones's *The Mill*, which portrays all three graces (figure 1), his *Beguiling of Merlin*[14] (Maria Zambaco), and Whistler's *Rose and Silver: The Princess from the Land of Porcelain* (Christina Spartali), which became the centerpiece of the famous Peacock Room,[15] an interior similar to the Orientalist rooms of the Ionides Palace of Art at Holland Park.

These affluent women, in addition to studying painting and sculpture, had very unconventional and often intimate relations with the artists who painted them. The most scandalous of these was that between Burne-Jones and Maria Zambaco, a femme fatale with "glorious red hair and almost phosphorescent white skin," in the words of her cousin Luke Ionides (Mancoff 1998, 50). A Pre-Raphaelite icon and the "Fata Morgana" of Burne-Jones's imagination (Maliaras 1992, 129), she was openly known to be the painter's mistress, who, during one of his attempts to break with her, staged a melodramatically botched suicide in Regent's Canal. (That this debacle occurred outside the home of Robert Browning adds yet another layer of infamy to the act!)[16] The prominence of such flamboyant personalities in the Cavafy family history enhanced the family's already bona fide status as patrons of the arts and arbiters of avant-garde taste—a status much publicized during the Grosvenor Gallery exhibitions and the Whistler-Ruskin trial. The high profile of aestheticism in the poet's own lineage aligns him with the second-generation Pre-Raphaelites and their circle; more important, it inscribes Cavafy within the Victorian discourse on art and the debate about aesthetics that raged around him during his years of residency in England.

Ut Pictura Poesis: Erudite Painting and Pictorial Writing

The characteristic intertextuality exhibited by many aesthetic poems and paintings was deliberately cultivated by painter and poet alike; indeed, many artists had a penchant for writing poems to accompany their canvases and, conversely, for illustrating favored poems through their paintings—what Henry James referred to disparagingly as "erudite painting" and "pictorial writing."[17] The poet who perhaps best exemplifies this particular symbiosis is Algernon Charles Swinburne, whose poem "Before the Mirror" (1864) was inspired by Whistler's *Symphony in White No. II: The Little White Girl* (stanzas of the poem were printed on gold paper and fastened to the picture frame).[18] In a similar gesture of artistic tribute, Swinburne dedicated his scandalous *Poems and Ballads* (1866) to Burne-Jones, causing an uproar not only by the book's profane content but also by the speculation it aroused over the dissolute lifestyle of this circle of painters, poets, and patrons. The ripple effect was far-reaching, as the following comments by a friend of Whistler indicate: "Here's something funny which will amuse you, the way these Spartali girls have stepped in all this muck. . . . The day that this book came out they went round everywhere announcing they'd just read this Evangelist, that he was magnificent, nothing greater, so delicate, you know, such daft words—six days later the storm broke . . . so it was clear to everyone either these girls had approved of infamy, or they'd not read the book, or else hadn't understood what they'd read."[19] In particular it was the lesbian subject matter of certain poems and their association with the canvases of Whistler that led people to cast such malicious aspersions.

The succès de scandale of Swinburne's poems illustrates the social stigma attached to avant-garde aestheticism. In Swinburne's case, the list of outrages included masochism, hermaphroditism, necrophilia, and bisexuality.[20] The precocious Cavafy must certainly have been aware of the implications of his relatives' fellowship with and patronage of these artists. This daring goes some way toward explaining his own courageous homo-erotic verse decades later; for in a sense, his cousins had already paved the road to hedonism upon which he would tread so resolutely the rest of his life. Harriet Cavafy and her sons thus found themselves embedded within a bohemian camp of aesthetes, whether they wished to be or not. Cavafy and his brother and fellow poet John were uniquely exposed to the per-sonalities and artistry of Whistler, Burne-Jones, and Swinburne, as well as greatly influenced by the effusive Hellenism that, as Richard Jenkyns writes, was "in the bloodstream of later Victorian art" and would remain the "guiding star of decadence and aestheticism" (1991, 291).

Both John and Constantine were well versed in Swinburne, as is con-veyed in a letter dated 1883.[21] It should be remembered that prior to his demotion in the literary canon by T. S. Eliot, Swinburne—the "fever in the blood of the Pre-Raphaelites" (Williamson 1976, 161)—was "the most sedu-lously imitated of poets for twenty years after the appearance of *Atalanta in Calydon*" (Pittock 1993, 123). Despite the censure aroused by his risqué verse, he was even favored by many to succeed Tennyson as poet laureate.[22] Only since 2000 has Swinburne's aesthetic program, "a great, neglected cultural and scholarly obligation" in the words of Jerome McGann (2004, xvi), begun to be reevaluated, and thus it is not surprising that Cavafy's debt to him has been largely ignored. Swinburne's intimate social and artistic connection to the London Greek community and the aesthetic movement brought him more closely than any other Victorian poet into Cavafy's orbit. The impulse to imitate him therefore must have been great, as may be seen by the Cavafy brothers' early derivative compositions. Take, for instance, the following verses from Cavafy's long poem "Voice from the Sea" (1893/1898), in which the sea is foregrounded in a manner clearly Swinburnean:[23]

And if you are young, the longing for the sea
will run through your veins; out of its love
the wave will say a word to you; it will water
    your love with a secret fragrance.

The sea gives out a secret voice—
    a voice that enters
our heart, and moves it,
    and delights it.

Is it a song or a plaint of the drowned?—
the tragic plaint of the dead
who have the cold foam as their shroud,
and they weep for their wives, for their children,
for their parents, for their desolate nest,
   as the bitter sea lashes them.

                  (1989, 207–208)

A brief comparison with a stanza from Swinburne's "The Triumph of Time" that features the recurring apostrophe to the sea illustrates Cavafy's artistic debt:

O fair green-girdled mother of mine,
   Sea, that art clothed with the sun and the rain,
Thy sweet hard kisses are strong like wine,
   Thy large embraces are keen like pain.
Save me and hide me with all thy waves,
Find me one grave of thy thousand graves,
Those pure cold populous graves of thine
   Wrought without hand in a world without stain.
             (Swinburne 2004, 88–89)

In addition to the sea metaphor, there are numerous other instances of Swinburne's influence on Cavafy. The "algolagnic" sensibility exhibited by Swinburne's *Poems and Ballads* was to take root in Cavafy's imagination: the words "ἄλγος" (pain),[24] "λαγνεία" (lust), and "ηδονή" (pleasure) appear repeatedly in his poetry. It is quite telling that Cavafy would supply the title "Ἔρως Ἀλγοφόρος: A Dithyrambic" ("Eros the Pain-Bearer," 1893) to one of John's English poems, the saccharine opening lines of which again betray the mark of Swinburne:

I love thee, deep-voiced language of the Sea,
Thine accents are the epics of the free:
   Thine endless solitude,
The splendour of thy face, the impetuous sweep
Of mighty winds from deep to echoing deep:—
   On these I love to sit and brood
From these the wildest, sweetest visions rise.
           (Cited in L. Savidis 1983, 145)

It should be remembered that well before Constantine made his mark as a poet, it was John who was actually known as the family poet.[25] The two brothers would exchange poetic intimacies throughout their lives, and Constantine's early poems are often barely distinguishable from those of his brother.[26]

Included in Swinburne's *Poems and Ballads* was "Hermaphroditus," a response to the Hellenistic sculpture of the sleeping Hermaphrodite in the Louvre. Cavafy composed a poem "Salmacian Beauty" in 1892 (later expunged from the canon), the subject of which certainly owes something to Swinburne, who mentions the spurned nymph Salmacis in the final lines of his poem.[27] The prominence of Julian the Apostate in Cavafy's oeuvre also derives from Swinburne's preoccupation with the emperor, although, as Robert Liddell notes, "Cavafy had no Swinburnian sentimentality about the Apostate" ([1974] 2000, 197). The prevalence of the elegiac note in Cavafy is also rooted in Swinburne, who composed more elegies than any other English poet (McGann 1972, 293). In sum, the hedonistic and amoral Hellenism that Cavafy encountered in Swinburne, along with the deft use of the interior monologue, proved to have as great an influence on him as did the verse of Robert Browning.[28]

Swinburne, an enthusiast for French literature, was an early proponent of the aesthetic principle of art for art's sake and an ardent admirer of Baudelaire. As Robin Spencer writes, "The association of Baudelaire with Swinburne's *Poems and Ballads* of 1866 created a literary sensation which immediately crossed the Channel and lasted well into the following decade. Claiming his authority from, and quoting, Baudelaire's 'heresy of didacticism,' which Baudelaire derived from Poe, Swinburne pioneered the aesthetic morality of 'art for art's sake,' principally in his study of the painter-poet William Blake" (1999, 59).[29] Swinburne shared Baudelaire's distrust of overt morality, which tainted and falsified experience; moreover, he was greatly influenced by Baudelaire's melancholy awareness of ennui as a decadent facet of aestheticism. Both of these concepts would eventually become central to Cavafy's aesthetic ideology. In terms of specific themes, Swinburne's preoccupation with the quest for love—as both eros and agape—and the ensuing sadness of its loss would become a similar obsession in Cavafy's erotic poems. Swinburne articulated this lovesickness without Victorian prudishness or sentimentality; his choice of Greek subjects to express this could not but have appealed to Cavafy.

Indeed, Sappho's erotic dilemma in the opening lines of "Anactoria" will be echoed by many of Cavafy's lovelorn speakers:

> My life is bitter with thy love; thine eyes
> Blind me, thy tresses burn me, thy sharp sighs
> Divide my flesh and spirit with soft sound,
> And my blood strengthens, and my veins abound.
> [. . .]
> Yea, all sweet words of thine and all thy ways,
> And all the fruit of nights and flower of days,
> And stinging lips wherein the hot sweet brine
> That Love was born of burns and foams like wine,
> And eyes insatiable of amorous hours,
> Fervent as fire and delicate as flowers,
> Coloured like night at heart, but cloven through
> Like night with flame, dyed round like night with blue,
> Clothed with deep eyelids under and above—
> Yea, all thy beauty sickens me with love.
> (Swinburne 2004, 93–95)

Swinburne's radically erotic reveries with their open articulation of homosexual desire offered Cavafy a poetic point of departure conceptually aligned with a most seductive Hellenism. Thus one may justifiably conclude that Swinburne mapped out a creative course for Cavafy that pointed him in the direction of French decadence and encouraged an open celebration of Greek homoerotic love.

The extent to which Swinburne's sensual Hellenism continued to inform Cavafy's work is evident in his mature poem "Of the Jews (A.D. 50)" (1912/1919), a composition that dramatically collapses Matthew Arnold's humanistic binaries of Hebraism and Hellenism by privileging Swinburnian decadence:

> Painter and poet, runner and discus-thrower,
> beautiful as Endymion: Ianthis, son of Antony.
> From a family on friendly terms with the Synagogue.
>
> "My most valuable days are those
> when I give up the pursuit of sensuous beauty,
> when I desert the elegant and severe cult of Hellenism,

with its over-riding devotion
to perfectly shaped, corruptible white limbs,
and become the man I would want to remain forever:
son of the Jews, the holy Jews."

A most fervent declaration on his part: ". . . to remain
    forever
a son of the Jews, the holy Jews."

But he did not remain anything of the kind.
The Hedonism and Art of Alexandria
kept him as their dedicated son.

(1992, 98)

Swinburne effectively subverted the Victorian Hellenic revival, as Lionel Stevenson notes: "Arnold's 'Hellenism,' representing dignity, restraint, and 'sweetness,' was utterly unlike Swinburne's celebration of ancient Greece's fleshly indulgence, sexual deviances, and primitive fertility rites" (1972, 219). With its dedication to sensuous beauty and corruptible white limbs, Cavafy's poem is rooted in the "new counterdiscourse of homosexual legitimacy" (L. Dowling 1994, 26) that emerged from Pre-Raphaelite Hellenism, famously labeled the "Fleshly School" by Robert Buchanan. Several major Cavafian themes are manifested in this poem: Ianthis, notably both a painter[30] and a poet who is as beautiful as Endymion, is given to an aesthetic sensuality demanded by Hellenism. Greek homoerotic beauty conflicts with the Judaic beauty of holiness; in the end, Hellenism undermines Judaism and, despite his intention to reform, Ianthis remains locked in a decadent cycle of fleshly indulgence. The poem presents a repeated Cavafian formula: the portrait of a beautiful individual caught up in a spiritual crisis exacerbated by historically determined cultural conflicts.

Another example of the great allure of Hellenically tinged aestheticism on the Cavafy brothers may be found in John's English poem "Pygmalion Meditateth" (1890), which features the precious lines "Like a sun-flower grown in a dark cave / Writhing in pain to turn towards the place / Where shines the sun unseen" (quoted in L. Savidis 1983, 122). The poem, with its quaint archaisms, serves as an index of the decadent Hellenism that had been deeply absorbed by the Cavafy brothers. In addition to the presence of the sunflower here—that recherché emblem of aestheticism[31]—the poem alludes to a chapter of history from Cavafy's extended family; for it

Figure 2. Edward Burne-Jones, *Pygmalion and the Image 2: The Hand Refrains* (1875–78).
Oil on canvas, Birmingham Museums and Art Gallery.

should be noted that Maria Zambaco had posed for Burne-Jones's series of
paintings *Pygmalion and the Image* (figure 2), four canvases that powerfully
foreground the erotics of artistic inspiration.[32] Indeed, Pygmalion, a libertine artist who creates an ideal woman to fulfill his peculiar creative and

sexual desires, epitomizes "the very quintessence of decadent deviation" (Potolsky 2013, 109). One may conjecture that the brothers were drawn to the subject of a sculptor's relation to his statue because of an added impetus from the Zambaco–Burne-Jones paradigm. As Richard Jenkyns notes,

> Burne-Jones's [Pygmalion] cycle is related, it seems, to a crisis in his own emotional life; but ambiguously. . . . Burne-Jones's timidity in handling his theme seems to be not wholly due to reticence or decorum or fear of giving offence; in part it is a vehicle for expressing sexual emotion but in part it is also, one suspects, a means of damping it down. In real life it appears that Mary Zambaco's passionate temperament was rather too much for her admirer, and in the end he may have been glad enough to sink back into married respectability. On canvas, though, and through the myth of Pygmalion, he could make a Mary whom he could both worship and control; and at the same time he could paint over indiscretion with the gloss of high culture and soulful aspiration. (1991, 138–140)

This remarkable transformation of a social scandal into painting set a beguiling example of sublimating desire through art, an alchemical dodge that Cavafy would master later in life when expressing his own illicit passions through the narrative voices of his poetic personae.

Cavafy's Pre-Raphaelite Aesthetic

Cavafy would focus many poems on sculptors and statues, but one that comes closest to capturing the gorgeous palette of Burne-Jones with its quasi-classical style and semimystic mood is his "Before the Statue of Endymion" (1895/1916).

> I have come from Miletos to Latmos
> on a white chariot drawn by four snow-white mules,
> all their trappings silver.
> I sailed from Alexandria in a purple trireme
> to perform sacred rites—
> sacrifices and libations—in honor of Endymion.
> And here is the statue. I now gaze in ecstasy
> at Endymion's famous beauty.

My slaves empty baskets of jasmine
and auspicious tributes revive the pleasure of ancient days.

(1992, 68)

Interestingly enough, the centerpiece of the poem—Endymion's statue—
is not described: Cavafy expects his erudite reader to draw on an erstwhile
knowledge of the subject's iconography in order to visualize the scene
(Petros Vlastos's words quoted by Seferis come to mind here: "Cavafy's
poems are like pedestals without the statues" [1983, 77]). An example of
Cavafy's mastery of pictorialist poetics (a topic that is explored more fully in
chapter 3), the poem foregrounds the ecstatic male gaze of the votary who
engages in three separate but abbreviated acts: a land voyage in a majestic
chariot, a sea voyage on a sumptuous galley, and a beatific encounter with
the statue. The colorful touches of white chariots and mules contrasted
with purple sails and baskets of green and white jasmine—almost painterly details[33]—create striking visual images in the reader's mind. This technique of thinking through color is a hallmark of Pre-Raphaelite painting
and poetry, as Elizabeth Helsinger notes: "Color is used in a lyrical way to
increase sensory and emotional awareness in a moment of time" (2008, 83).
Endymion's statue—like that of Galatea—was an erotically charged symbol, a passively supine sleeping beauty posed in an inviting position. An example of male effeminacy and languorous masculinity (Endymion's eternal
sleep and perpetual youth made him a decadent icon of male beauty), this
luminous dream boy was usually represented in ancient art as a recumbent nude with one arm crooked behind his head.[34] The ecstatic attitude
of the speaker problematizes the erotics of the poem even further: the romantic topos of a poet distracted by beauty from pursuing ideal perfection
(à la Keats) is overturned in this overtly sensual inversion of the Pygmalion
theme. The Burne-Jones aesthetic is fully at play here, as Cavafy gives uninhibited poetic expression to the ideology of the so-called Fleshly School of
painting and poetry with its androgynous male beauties.[35]

The rather cryptic inner meaning of this poem, however, is explicitly
stated in "Desires" (1904), where sleep becomes a metaphor for the smol-
dering unfulfilled desires commonly associated with the sublimely erotic
canvases of the second-generation Pre-Raphaelites:

Like beautiful bodies of the dead who did not grow old,
and were shut away with tears in a splendid monument,

with roses at the head and jasmine at the feet—
that is what the desires are like, which have passed
without fulfillment; without any one of them granted
a pleasure's night, or a pleasure's radiant morn.

(2003a, 67)

The poem calls to mind Burne-Jones's somnolent tableaux *The Briar Rose: The Rose Bower* (1885) and *The Sleep of Arthur in Avalon* (1881). The controlling idea here is effectively articulated by Walter Pater in his essay "Aesthetic Poetry" (1883), where he notes the contrast of "the grace of Hellenism relieved against the sorrow of the Middle Ages": "One characteristic of the pagan spirit the aesthetic poetry has, which is on its surface—the continual suggestion, pensive or passionate, of the shortness of life. This is contrasted with the bloom of the world, and gives new seduction to it— the sense of death and the desire of beauty: the desire of beauty quickened by the sense of death" (1986, 528). These critical remarks ring as true for Cavafy as they do for the Pre-Raphaelite painter-poets and illustrate the profound overlap between aesthetic painting and poetry during this period.[36] (Pater's significant influence on Cavafy will be explored in chapter 4.)

Cavafy undoubtedly internalized many examples of the sensual Hellenism he would later distill into his poetry from the seductive art he encountered in London. A most extreme version of this Hellenism may be found in the figure of Maria Zambaco's brooding Venus in Burne-Jones's extraordinary canvas *Laus Veneris*, a work exhibited at the Grosvenor in 1878. The subject derives from the German folk tale of Tannhäuser at the Venusberg, a late medieval legend according to which a Christian knight is enticed to the mountain of Venus but after years of debauchery grows weary of her charms. It is essentially a story about a person who repents for his depraved years but whose soul in the end is damned (he is denied absolution by the pope and must suffer perpetually from unfulfilled desire). As Matthew Potolsky aptly notes, Venus is a prototype of the decadent femme fatale, and Tannhäuser foreshadows the sensual indulgence of the decadent hero (2013, 154). Burne-Jones's canvas emphasizes the rejected Venus who listens listlessly to her maidens playing music. The painting owes much to Swinburne's poem on the subject in *Poems and Ballads*, verses that were considered his most shocking in terms of their pent-up eroticism and emphasis on love through suffering (Powell 1992, 224). The tragically rejected Venus is depicted in a languorous state of ennui, at once the thwarted goddess of classical myth and the notoriously spurned mistress Maria Zambaco.[37] The theme of depravity through overindulgence perversely enshrined in the *Laus Veneris* poem and painting becomes common in Cavafy's erotic poetry, as may be seen in "Days of 1896" (1925/1927), where the dissolute subject (a nineteenth-century Tannhaüser, as it were) is presented from a decadent slant—a paradoxical beauty at once tainted and pure:

> He became completely degraded. His erotic tendency,
> condemned and strictly forbidden
> (but innate for all that), was the cause of it:
> society was totally prudish.
> He gradually lost what little money he had,
> then his social standing, then his reputation.
> Nearly thirty, he had never worked a full year—
> at least not at a legitimate job.
> Sometimes he earned enough to get by
> acting the go-between in deals he considered shameful.
> He ended up the type likely to compromise you thoroughly
> if you were seen around with him often.
>
> But this isn't the whole story—that would not be fair.
> The memory of his beauty deserves better.
> There is another angle; seen from that
> he appears attractive, appears
> a simple, genuine child of love,
> without hesitation putting,
> above his honor and reputation,
> the pure sensuality of his pure flesh.
>
> Above his reputation? But society,
> prudish and stupid, had it wrong.
>
> (1992, 146)

The unnamed protagonist in the poem—one of Cavafy's mature imaginary portraits set in fin de siècle Alexandria—calls to mind the plight of Oscar Wilde, who was serving the first full year of his prison sentence in 1896 (Ekdawi 1993a, 301). As Sarah Ekdawi notes, "'Days of 1896,' if not actually about Oscar Wilde, would at least appear to contain veiled allusions to his fate" (302), a decadent detail that further contextualizes the poem within Victorian aestheticism. The defiant refrain of "the memory of his beauty" that counters the poem's abject tone not only foregrounds the aesthetic fixation of Greek eros on the boy as the beloved (*eromenos*)— the proper subject of Greek poetry (Davidson 2007, 37)—but also inflects the poem with the "art for art's sake" credo, whose unapologetic obsession with the untainted purity of beauty is made explicit by the Greek words "της καθαρής σαρκός του/την καθαρή ηδονή" ("the pure sensuality of his pure flesh").

The repeated emphasis in Cavafy's poetry on pure sensuality conveyed through the fetishization of beautiful lips, eyes, hair, and facial features clearly owes much to the poet's adolescent exposure to the sumptuous and enticing canvases of Rossetti and Burne-Jones that he encountered in the grand homes of his Ionides relations. This is illustrated by the following selection of his verse, lines quintessentially Cavafian but clearly indebted to the Pre-Raphaelites in their visual aesthetic.[38] In "Kaisarion" (1914/1918), Cavafy imbues the doomed Alexandrian king with a decadent melancholia and almost metaphysical sadness:

> My art gives your face
> a dreamy, an appealing beauty.
> [. . .]
> pale and weary, ideal in your grief.
> (1992, 82–83)

In "Days of 1903" (1909/1917), the speaker pines for the idealized aesthetic face:

> I never found them again—all lost so quickly . . .
> the poetic eyes, the pale face, [. . .]
> those lips—I never found them again.
> (1992, 80)

The famed gray eyes of Rossetti's model Elizabeth Siddal are recalled in "Gray" (1917):

> When looking at a half-gray opal
> I remembered two lovely gray eyes—
> (1992, 75)

Lips are the sole object of desire in "One Night" (1907/1915):

> And there on that common, humble bed
> I had love's body, had those intoxicating lips,
> red and sensual,
> red lips of such intoxication
> that now as I write, after so many years,
> in my lonely house, I'm drunk with passion again.
>
> (1992, 57)

In "Long Ago" (1914) the poet lingers intensely on blue eyes and jasmine-white skin:

> I'd like to speak of this memory . . .
> but it's so faded now . . . as though nothing is left—
> because it was so long ago, in my early adolescent years.
>
> A skin as though of jasmine . . .
> that August evening—was it August?—
> I can still just recall the eyes; blue, I think they were . . .
> Ah yes, blue: a sapphire blue.
>
> (1992, 52)

And in "I've Looked so Much" (1911/1917), we are presented with an entire facial portrait:

> I've looked on beauty so much
> that my vision overflows with it.
>
> The body's lines. Red lips. Sensual limbs.
> Hair as though stolen from Greek statues,
> always lovely, even uncombed,
> and falling slightly over pale foreheads.
> Figures of love, as my poetry desired them
> . . . in the nights when I was young,
> encountered secretly in those nights.
>
> (1992, 78)

To these unmistakably aesthetic lines of verse may be added the peculiar Pre-Raphaelite scope of Cavafy's prose writings—another significant dimension of his debt to the English aesthetic movement (a topic explored in more detail in chapter 2). In fact, the subject matter of many of Cavafy's essays seems less haphazard and random when measured against the precious subjects favored by the Pre-Raphaelites with which they are virtually identical. He wrote essays on Keats ("Λάμια" ["Lamia"]); Shakespeare ("Ελληνικά ίχνη εν τω Σακεσπήρω" ["Traces of Greek Thought in Shakespeare"]); Troy ("Μία σελίς της Τρωικής ιστορίας" ["A Page of Trojan History"]); Dante and Tennyson ("Το τέλος του Οδυσσέως" ["The End of Odysseus"]); the Elgin Marbles ("Give Back the Elgin Marbles"); an untitled piece on Browning; and marginal comments on Ruskin, all of which comprise the shared topics of the aesthetic painters and poets.[39] Supplementing these prose compositions are his poetic translations into Greek of passages from Shakespeare's *Measure for Measure* and *Much Ado About Nothing*, a section from Dante's *Inferno*, the Scottish ballad "Auld Robin Gray" by Lady Anne Barnard Lindsay,[40] lines from Keats's *Lamia* and "Sonnet to the Nile," and verses from Tennyson's "Ulysses."[41] Cavafy also composed finished poems on the Grail legend ("Suspicion"), Lohengrin,[42] crusader knights ("Before Jerusalem"), and *Hamlet*'s King Claudius, all of which further suggest a lingering Pre-Raphaelite fixation.

Early in his career, Cavafy composed several poems directly related to important canvases; more significant, he would continue to feature artistic models as the very subject of his poetry, a penchant that he certainly imbibed during the heady days of aestheticism. His "Oedipus" (1896) was a direct poetic meditation on Gustave Moreau's canvas *Oedipus and the Sphinx*. Coincidentally, Moreau exhibited his watercolor version of Salome, *L'Apparition,* at the Grosvenor opening of 1877 alongside Burne-Jones and Whistler; this would likely have been Cavafy's first direct exposure to the French painter, who was frequently paired with Burne-Jones after this showing.[43]

Cavafy's "Salome" (1896*) also owes its inspiration to Moreau, and his reliance on themes taken up by the aesthetes becomes more apparent when viewed along a painterly trajectory. "Oedipus" and "Salome" were not the first poems to be indebted to painting; Cavafy's "Dünya Güzeli" (1884*) is clearly a meditation on an Orientalist odalisque that features a harem girl gazing narcissistically at herself in a mirror, a favored topos of Whistler, Rossetti, and J. F. Lewis, among others.[44] These poems were written well after Cavafy's sojourn in England, but their genesis owes much to the influence of the painters associated with the Grosvenor Gallery.

A curious poem on which Cavafy left written comments regarding the diction of his brother John's translation is his overtly allegorical and unmistakably Pre-Raphaelite "In the Soul's House" (1894*):

In the Soul's House the Passions circulate—
beautiful women in silk raiment dressed,
with sapphires glimmering darkly in their hair.
They rule the whole abode: from outer gate
to rooms the innermost and secretest;
and when the night's incontinences rouse
the riot in their blood, they congregate
tumultuously in the hall, and there,
flushed and disheveled and with bosoms bare,
    dance wildly and carouse.

Outside the House, pale-visaged, oddly dressed
in dress disused, the Virtues live through days
embittered by the sounds behind the wall;
and ever and anon, as the unrest
of the hetairae in inebrious craze
affrights their pensive silence, they advance
up to the windows, and with foreheads pressed
against the panes, survey the fevered hall,—
the lights, the flowers, the glittering gems, and all,
    the wonder of the dance.

                     (2003b, 47)

Cavafy's remarks on this unpublished poem (comments recorded in Greek but punctuated with English words and expressions) draw attention to the modest dress of his allegorical Virtues, whom he envisioned as "old-fashioned" and "provincial ladies" wearing dated clothing "from 1880 or 1875" (1963, 247). Cavafy is concerned that John's choice of the word "disused" (line 12) might not adequately convey this sense, as his explicit aim in the poem is to achieve a descriptive "picturesqueness" (248). This painterly poem, which functions as two contrasting visual stanza-panels, calls to mind Burne-Jones's *The Mill* (figure 1), a rather symbolist composition that features his cousins dancing before the walls of an industrial building while behind them nude male figures bathe and frolic in a mill pond.[45] (Perhaps Cavafy's depiction of the "Passions" here was meant to be a thinly veiled parody of the libertine lifestyle and ostentatious wealth of his London female relations.) The poem's iconography, with its descriptive detail and allegorical representation of the soul, unmistakably aligns it with the overtly emblematic compositions and symbolic portraits of the Pre-Raphaelite poet-painters of the period.[46]

Although Burne-Jones's artistic presence was prominent in the Ionides-Cavafy circle, his dreamy eloquence was not the only style poised to cast an aesthetic spell on the young Cavafy. As was already noted, Cavafy's cousin John owned four Whistler paintings, one of which—*Harmony in Blue and Silver: Trouville*—depicts a lone figure standing before a blue sea on an amber impressionist shore. The man in the foreground has been identified as Gustave Courbet, under whose influence Whistler had been painting before he fully embraced aestheticism. This canvas marks Whistler's break from realism and charts an important stage in his artistic development (Spalding 1979, 60). Although not a poet, Whistler was very connected with the literary developments of his day and, like Swinburne, he served as a disseminator of French decadent aesthetics in England. From Baudelaire Whistler surely gleaned his theory of the "correspondence" between the art of music and painting (Dorment and Macdonald 1994, 17). Moreover, he remained a notorious aesthetic persona with a talent for sensationally promoting both himself and his art, so much so that Arthur Symons could use him as a criterion to describe the complex decadent symbolist poetry of the late nineteenth century as exemplified by Verlaine: "It is the poetry of sensation, of evocation; poetry which paints as well as sings, and which paints as Whistler paints, seeming to *think* the colors and outlines upon the canvas, *to think them only, and they are there*" (cited in Siewert 2004, 71—emphasis added).

Impressions of Whistler's painting were discernibly in Cavafy's mind when he composed the poem " Sea of the Morning" (1915), which I cite in his brother John's translation:

Here let me stand, that, for a while, I too
may gaze on nature. Marvelous blue tints
of a morning sea and an unclouded sky
contrasting with an amber-coloured shore,—
all luminously beautiful and grand.

Here let me stand and think I see these things
(I really did see them for a moment,
soon after I had stopped)—and not, here also,
my fantasies, my reminiscences,
the incomparable idols of delight.

(2003b, 54)

In Whistleresque fashion, the poem paints with thought as it were and playfully blurs the line between imagination and reality. The speaker "thinks" he sees the blue and amber seascape described in the first stanza, but we know not whether he is recalling an actual moment at the seashore or the haunted memory or vision of such a scene. Similarly, the transcendent sea image in the poem could just as well be an artistic rendering of the morning sea, since the Greek reads "τα ινδάλματα της ηδονής," which also translates as "visions of sensual bliss" (2003a, 140) or "images of sensual pleasure" (1992, 58). Much like Whistler's painting with its dreamlike unfinished quality and dematerialized rendering of water and light, the poem's sea image ambiguously opens out into a fantasy-based reminiscence of a recollected impression. The reader is left with a highly artificial image of a man looking at the morning sea, which becomes equated with "incomparable idols of delight" rather than an actual seascape. The poem thus functions aesthetically as the memory of the sea recalled through impressions based on the painterly categories of pure color and luminosity. The intersection of poetic and pictorial elements could not be more pronounced.[47]

In addition to writing verses that either conveyed aesthetic principles or were direct responses to painted works of art, Cavafy composed poems that actually feature paintings or drawings of his own subjects. In the following lines from "Pictured" (1914/1915), we encounter a fatigued poet who looks to a bucolic painting for inspiration and rejuvenation:[48]

I am more minded now to see things than to write. I gaze
upon the picture of a boy lying down beside a spring:
in those green woods beyond he must have tired himself at play.
How beautiful the boy! What glorious noon is silencing
the atmosphere and lowering his eyelids drowsily? . . .
I sit and gaze a long time . . . And it is art again that stays
my weariness of the toil in my own art of rendering.

(2003b, 55)

The poem foregrounds the act of sitting and gazing at a picture—"submitting to art," as in the poem "I've Brought to Art" previously discussed; we have here the pose of the poet as art connoisseur who is roused to imitate the pictorial aesthetic in his endeavor to render artfully in words. Similarly, in "Of the Ship" (1919), we are presented with the sketch of a youth who is aesthetic to the point of affliction" ("μέχρι παθήσεως ήταν αισθητικός"):

> It does bear him resemblance,
> this small pencil sketch of him.
>
> Done in a hurry, on the ship's deck,
> one enchanted afternoon.
> All around us was the Ionian Sea.
>
> It's much like him. Yet I remember him as more handsome.
> He was aesthetic to the point of affliction,[49]
> and that illumined his expression.
> He appears to me more handsome,
> now that my soul recalls him, out of Time.
>
> Out of Time. These things are all so very old—
> the sketch, and the ship, and the afternoon.
>
> (2003a, 221)

The poem presents us with a version of the competition between the sister arts of painting and poetry to capture the pictorial image, with the written word mediated through memory emerging triumphant. Likewise, in "Picture of a 23-Year-Old Painted by His Friend of the Same Age, an Amateur" (1928), we encounter the portrait of a young dandy:

> He finished the picture yesterday noon.
> Now he looks at it detail by detail. He's painted him
> wearing an unbuttoned gray jacket,
> no vest, tieless, with a rose-colored
> shirt, open, allowing a glimpse
> of his beautiful chest and neck.
> The right side of his forehead is almost covered
> by his hair, his lovely hair
> (done in the style he's recently adopted).

He's managed to capture perfectly the sensual note
he wanted when he did the eyes,
when he did the lips . . .
That mouth of his, those lips
so ready to satisfy a special kind of erotic pleasure.

                                        (1992, 154)

Once again, Cavafy transports the reader into the realm of the painted image, but in this case there is no ambiguity about either the absolute aesthetic achievement of the image or for that matter the sensual arousal of the speaker/viewer.

"In an Old Book" (1892/1922), we uncover an old hidden watercolor with the Pre-Raphaelite-sounding title "Presentation of Love"[50] which vividly evokes the androgynous, enervated male figures who proved so troubling to Victorian art critics:

In an old book—about a hundred years old—
I discovered, forgotten between the pages,
an unsigned watercolor painting.
It must have been the work of quite a powerful artist.
It bore the title, "Presentation of Love."

Though more befitting would be "Love of the extreme aesthetes."

Because it was obvious, when looking at the work
(one could readily perceive the artist's conception),
that the ephebe in the painting was not intended
for the likes of those who engage in healthful love
by remaining, somehow, within sanctioned bounds—
with his chestnut, deep-colored eyes;
with the exquisite beauty of his face,
a beauty of deviant appeal;
with his ideal lips that bring about
sensual bliss to the beloved body;
with his ideal limbs, created for beds
that ordinary morality labels "shameless."

                                        (2003a, 265)

Here we are presented with a curious moment when the speaker discovers an unsigned watercolor by a powerful artist—the closest Cavafy comes to prodding his readers in the direction of aesthetic painting as a possible hermeneutical intertext for his poems. The beauty of the model's deviant appeal leaves no question as to the Pre-Raphaelite aesthetic at play. The poem's final jab at "ordinary morality" brings to mind the scurrilous criticism hurled against the British aesthetes by philistine critics—"society prudish and stupid" ("Days of 1896"). The pictorial essence of the poem surely aligns Cavafy with his Victorian artistic forebears—the Pre-Raphaelites and their circle of "extreme aesthetes"; his London relations who were their patrons, models, and lovers; and the avant-garde aesthetes who comprise a genealogy equally as important to our understanding of Cavafy as that of his own family, if not even more significant. The impact of his early brush with the great aesthetic artists associated with the Grosvenor Gallery was indeed profound, as is strikingly evident in both his poems and prose essays—even, one could say, in his personal demeanor. Whistler's dandyism, which set the standard for a generation, left an indelible mark on Cavafy (as it did on Wilde)[51], who retained his effete Victorian mannerisms throughout his life.

British aestheticism undoubtedly prepared the ground for Cavafy's immersion in the full-blown decadence of the late 1880s and 1890s. In particular, it was the emphasis on the lavish pictorial sensuality of the Victorian painters considered in this chapter to which he—like so many decadent writers—responded in kind. What Arthur Symons would identify as literary decadence's "over-subtilizing refinement upon refinement" owes much to this painterly tradition. As Desmarais and Baldick have noted, "Symons's preoccupation with the plastic qualities of language and the ability of Decadent writers in particular to use language so subtly that their words may be said to paint pictures, prefigures the debates among the Formalist critics in the early twentieth century, such as the Bloomsbury writers Roger Fry and Clive Bell" (2012, 9). These very plastic qualities will be taken up in the next two chapters, which explore Cavafy's indebtedness to French decadent writers and his subtle adaptation of the "transposition d'art" tradition to his own pictorialist poetics.

2

Translating Baudelaire

L'esprit Décadent *and the Early Writings*

The influence of the Pre-Raphaelites on Cavafy was decisive in terms of the poet's initial exposure to the debates on art for art's sake that played out during the latter part of the nineteenth century. Cavafy's familiarity with the work of Swinburne and Whistler, two of the primary conduits of Baudelairean aesthetic theory in England, would soon develop into a more direct engagement with Baudelaire and French decadent trends as they continued to evolve on both sides of the Channel. Indeed, it was Swinburne who may be credited with making Baudelaire's *Les Fleurs du mal*, *L'Art Romantique*, and *Curiosités Esthétiques* "part of the essential bibliography of Modernism."[1] Thus it is hardly a matter of chance that all three of these books were part of Cavafy's library. Their presence confirms him as an astute reader of Baudelaire and substantiates his ongoing poetic dialogue with the *poète maudit*. This chapter focuses on Cavafy's earliest writings (essays, fictional narratives, and prose poems) with a view to assessing the unmistakable influence of Baudelaire. By positioning Cavafy within the context of Baudelairean decadence, we may better appreciate his particular treatment of fin de siècle decadent tropes. For in keeping with Baudelaire's example, Cavafy will gradually become a professional decipherer of his city and a belated flâneur with an urban epistemology all his own.[2]

Days of 1891: Baudelaire and "Pleasures Even Stranger"

Although Cavafy never wrote a poem about the "Days of 1891," critics are well advised to approach the year 1891 as though he had. The reasons for this have more to do with philological pursuits than with the erotic trajectories usually associated with this titular formula. In fact, the year 1891 holds a twofold significance for Cavafy: it is the year when he would begin publishing prose in earnest,[3] and it also inaugurates his direct artistic engagement with Charles Baudelaire. (That year, as Eve Sedgwick [1990, 49] writes, also marks an epoch for readers fond of the male body with the appearance of Wilde's *Dorian Gray* and Melville's *Billy Budd*.) Cavafy's development as a poet coincided with his early preoccupation with journalism and his rather vexed attempt to craft a credible yet artistic prose style. Equally important is Cavafy's personal dialogue with Baudelaire, which has particular relevance for his prose compositions, especially the prose poems he penned between 1894 and 1897. A full understanding and appreciation of his artistic evolution must take into account both his early journalistic pursuits and his creative experimentation with prose, endeavors that resulted in his ultimate abandonment of prose as a viable mode of expression. To date, critics have tended to overlook Cavafy's brief stint as a journalist and his active engagement with the intellectual debates of the late nineteenth century, which he effected through his prose articles, book reviews, and translations. His largely ignored prose compositions— published and unpublished alike—remain an important repository of ideas and serve as a means of exploring artistic modalities that would later become foundational for his mature poetry. His prose poems in particular illustrate how eager he was to emulate Baudelaire's hybrid prose poems, avant-garde compositions that presage Cavafy's mature poems and influenced the development of his notoriously prosaic poetics.[4]

Perhaps the most revealing statement about Baudelaire's influence on Cavafy comes from the poet himself. In a curious note written in 1907, he

offers an intriguing comment on his conscious competitive engagement
with the French poet:

> This evening I was reading about Baudelaire. And the author of the book I
> was reading was like a shocked *épatè* with the *Fleurs du mal*. It's been some
> time since I re-read the *Fleurs du mal*. From what I remember, it isn't that
> shocking. And it seems to me that Baudelaire was enclosed within a very
> limited range of sensuality. Suddenly last night; or on the previous Wednes-
> day; and on many other occasions, I lived and acted and fantasized, and si-
> lently devised pleasures even stranger. (2010, 136)

Some sixteen years prior to penning this note, Cavafy had undertaken his
most direct response to Baudelaire; in 1891 he composed the poem "Correspondence according to Baudelaire," a variation on the sonnet "Correspondences," in which he frames his own translation of the original text with
verses that transpose it into a somewhat personal lyric. In his translation,
Cavafy prefaces Baudelaire's sonnet with lines that express his own eluci-
dation of the Baudelairean synthesis:

> Aromas inspire me the way music,
> rhythm and beautiful words do,
> and I am delighted whenever Baudelaire
> interprets in harmonious verses
> what the soul in its wonder feels
> vaguely in sterile emotions.
>   (1989, 217)

The "sterile emotions" alluded to here correspond to the pervading sense
of ennui, or "spleen," that dominates *Les Fleurs du mal*. The antidote
to this state of boredom is the contemplation of beauty, that particular
and strange beauty apostrophized in the "Hymne à la Beauté": "What
difference, then, from heaven or from hell, / O Beauty, monstrous in
simplicity? / If eye, smile, step can open me the way / To find unknown,
sublime infinity?" (Baudelaire 1998, 45). This "monstrous" beauty alone
alleviates the world-weariness that suffuses Baudelaire's poetic universe,
and only the urban poet initiated into the mysteries of decadence and experienced in the inspired meanderings of the flâneur is able to distill it
into poetry.

In this signature poem, sounds, colors, and decadent fragrances all combine to create the fundamental Baudelairean correspondence between the material and the spiritual, establishing the dialectic between spleen and ideal that generates the poetic tension of *Les Fleurs du mal*.[5] This peculiar modern beauty defines Baudelaire's decadent aesthetic, as Michel Brix aptly notes:

> We see that beauty according to Baudelaire is not Platonist; the beautiful forms are not those arousing the intuition of eternal realities, but really those bearing moral significance—sadness, melancholy, bitter disappointment, joy, passion for living, etc. . . . [T]he Baudelairean conception of horizontal correspondences (or synaesthesia) . . . does not tie the Beautiful to the qualities of proportion, harmony, or symmetry of things, but with the inner self of the observer. . . . The artist's task is to restore these moral impressions . . . and to recall the words which Baudelaire applies to Gautier, "to define the mysterious attitude which the objects of creation hold in the face of human observation."[6]

Cavafy evokes this complex emotion and mysterious attitude in his poem with the words "απορούσα" (wonder) and "αγόνοις" (sterile) and shows an impressive understanding of Baudelaire's admittedly "ασαφώς" (vague) yet complex aesthetic. This paradoxical tension between the observant interiority of the poet and the urban extroversion of the flâneur will gradually shape Cavafy's own poetic point of view, culminating in poems such as "The City," "The Next Table," "At the Theater," and "On the Stairs," compositions in which the urban gaze takes on a heightened urgency and partakes of an unmistakably splenetic beauty.[7]

Fittingly enough, Cavafy's introductory line about "rhythm and beautiful words" effectively paraphrases Edgar Allan Poe, whose aesthetics Baudelaire reinterpreted and promoted as his own proleptic version of art for art's sake. Poe's definition of poetry and simultaneous critique of progressive utilitarianism were expressed in his essay "The Poetic Principle," where he writes, "I would define, in brief, the Poetry of words as *The Rhythmical Creation of Beauty*. Its sole arbiter is Taste. With the Intellect or with the Conscience it has only collateral relations. Unless incidentally, it has no concern whatever either with Duty or with Truth" (Poe 1992, 1027).[8] Cavafy's framing of Baudelaire and emphasis on rhythm and beautiful words establish a trajectory of thought rooted in Poe that encompasses what Elizabeth Prettejohn terms "a transnational and transhistorical aesthetic brotherhood" (2007, 54).[9] During the days of 1891, Cavafy, it appears, was determined to enter into its ranks.

Following these initial lines is Cavafy's translation of the sonnet "Correspondences," not only the centerpiece of the decadent movement but also a foundational text of modernism.[10] Cavafy terminates the sonnet by adding his own poetic gloss:

> Do not believe only what you see.
> The eye of the poet is sharper.
> For them nature is a familiar garden.
>
> In dark paradise the other people
> grope on an arduous road.
> And the only brightness that sometimes lights
> their nightly march like an ephemeral spark
> is a brief impression of a chance
> magnetic neighborliness—
> a brief nostalgia, a momentary shudder,
> a dream of an hour of sunrise,
> a blameless joy suddenly flowing
> into the heart and suddenly fleeting.
>
> (1989, 217–218)

Cavafy's concluding lines juxtapose images of a groping crowd seemingly lost and damned but momentarily illuminated by an evanescent joy, the "mystic nourishment" of the flowers of the mind, the ideal beauty that strengthens both the crowd and the poet, who, as Walter Benjamin writes, "in the deserted streets, wrests poetic booty" (2006, 181).[11]

Baudelaire's considerable influence on his generation went well beyond his poetic compositions; his translations of Poe's tales and critical essays adumbrating Poe's poetics and grotesque, arabesque aesthetic would have a great impact on French letters. It bears noting that Baudelaire commissioned the artist Alphonse Legros to illustrate his edition of Poe's tales. Although these etchings never appeared with Baudelaire's published translations, they were highly prized by collectors. In fact, a set was acquired by Legros's patron, Constantine Ionides, and it is quite likely that Cavafy would have seen them and heard them discussed during his stay in England.[12] The curious proximity of Cavafy to Poe via Baudelaire and Legros suggests a direct line of influence linking Poe's aesthetic to Cavafy's evolving views on beauty and poetry. Surely Cavafy was well positioned to receive Baudelaire's almost maniacal rehabilitation of Poe, whom he famously termed "ill fated" because of his unappreciative American audience. A notable example of Baudelaire's apologia may be found in the opening paragraph of his essay "Further Notes on Edgar Poe," where he offers a wry defense of decadence:

> "Literature of the decadence!"–Empty words that we often hear dropping, with all the resonance of a flatulent yawn, from the lips of the sphinxes-without-a-riddle which stand guard before the holy portals of Classical Aesthetics. Each time that the dogmatic oracle echoes forth, you can be certain that you are in the presence of something more entertaining than the *Iliad*. It is undoubtedly a question of some poem or novel in which all the parts are skillfully interwoven to create surprise, a work superbly rich in style, in which all the resources of language and prosody have been employed by an unerring hand. . . . Civilized man has invented the doctrine of Progress to console himself for his surrender and decay; while primitive man, a feared and respected husband, a warrior obliged to personal valor, a poet in those melancholy moments when the declining sun bids him sing the past of his ancestors, comes closer to the fringes of the Ideal. (1995, 93, 99)

This attack on the dogmatic "doctrine of Progress" is carried even further in the essay "Exposition Universelle, 1855," where Baudelaire names progress as the preeminent heresy of his era:

> There is another error, very much in fashion, which I wish to avoid like the Devil himself. –I am referring to the idea of progress. . . . This grotesque idea, which has flowered on the rotten soil of modern folly, has released each man from his duty, freed each soul from its responsibility, and has liberated the will from all the bonds imposed on it by love of the beautiful. And if this deplorable madness continues for long, the decadent races will fall into the driveling sleep of decrepitude on the pillow of destiny. This infatuation is the symptom of a decadence that is already too obvious.[13] (1964, 82)

Here Baudelaire mischievously turns the tables on the critics of decadence by applying antidecadent invective to the very progressive ideology that habitually dismissed aesthetic writing as degenerate and effete.[14] Thus progress and its sister heresy "didacticism"[15] become the original sins that Baudelaire, taking his lead from Poe, successively excoriates throughout his writings.

Cavafy was only too aware of the highly problematic debate surrounding the term "decadence" and the opprobrium with which avant-garde artists viewed bourgeois notions of progress. This is most evident in his poem "Builders" (1891), where the heresy of progress is resoundingly debunked:

Progress is a tremendous edifice,—each carries
his stone; one carries words, others counsel, another
deeds—and day by day it raises its head
higher. Should a hurricane, a sudden swell

come, the good workers rush together
in a throng and defend their lost work.
Lost, because each one's life is expended
suffering abuse, pains, for a future generation,

that this generation may know honest happiness
and long life and riches and wisdom,
without base sweat or servile work.

But this fabled generation will never, never live.
This work will be wrecked by its very perfection
and all their vain toil will begin anew.

(1989, 176)

The cynicism evinced in this sonnet, which Cavafy published in the Athenian journal *Attic Museum* (1891) and later in the Alexandrian journal the *Twentieth Century* (1895), is more than hypothetical. Cavafy's family had witnessed its own financial progress crumble and experienced the toil and riches of one generation collapse upon the heads of another. The family's bankruptcy and the bombardment of Alexandria by the British in 1882 surely dispelled any illusions Cavafy might have had regarding stability, whether socioeconomic, cultural, civic, or other. The tremendous edifice of Greek diasporic progress informs this poem as much as any splenetic French influences. (That cosmopolitan Alexandria would all but vanish only two decades after Cavafy's death is a fitting footnote to this poem.)[16] Along with "Correspondence according to Baudelaire," "Builders" serves as an important ideological statement on fin de siècle notions of futility and pessimism, ideas that play out in Cavafy's early and mature writings. Cavafy's prose writings in particular offer an invaluable point of entry into the creative struggles and dilemmas that will remain central to his creative evolution, notably the problematics of crafting a prose style and the related challenge of navigating the perilous linguistic divide between the Greek purists and demoticists.

Performing in Prose

After three years in Constantinople, Cavafy returned to Alexandria in 1885 and began penning brief articles for various Greek diaspora newspapers, articles that necessarily required him to translate and transpose select texts that catered to the particular demands of his unique readership. The primary audience for which he composed his belle-lettrist journalistic pieces was the cosmopolitan Greek bourgeoisie residing in the great commercial cities of the Ottoman Levant—namely, Constantinople, Smyrna, Alexandria, and Cairo. Athens, the less cosmopolitan capital of the Greek kingdom, ranked lower on this list, although eventually it would become an important center for the dissemination and reception of Cavafy's work and, ultimately, for the establishment of his poetic reputation. He also published prose essays in Leipzig and had undoubtedly intended a British venue for his earliest English compositions, factors that betray the poet's highly ambitious but rather untenable internationalist posturing in the late nineteenth century. Cavafy's Greek readership expected a peculiar style of learned journalism that consisted of a formulaic blend of encyclopedic dilettantism interspersed with choice translations of foreign authors and foreign journalists.[17] The fact that the literary tastes of this late nineteenth-century fin de siècle readership differed drastically from those of the early twentieth century and post–World War I era—the period during which Cavafy found his mature poetic voice—surely induced him to view his early prose unfavorably in later years as unfashionably dated and even embarrassingly pretentious.

Much of the prose's philological appeal and linguistic complexity lies in the stylistic nuances generated by Cavafy's deft although not always elegant handling of puristic Greek (*katharevousa*). It should be noted that he was writing at a time when the raging debate between purists and de-moticists regarding the Greek language unduly complicated Greek writing of any kind.[18] As nearly all prose during this period was written in katharevousa, Cavafy had to display his journalistic mastery of the cumbersome purist idiom for the public while simultaneously satisfying his more private creative impulses, attempting in the process to craft a lucid, effective, and learned prose. His prose writings are at once a chronicle of this struggle and an index of his ultimate failure to achieve a satisfying aesthetic prose style marked equally by elegance, clarity, and erudition.[19]

The prominent place of translation in Cavafy's prose essays is more significant than many critics to date have realized. Like many poets, he used translation as a workshop of sorts for practicing and refining his own poetic craft.[20] Since Cavafy offered very little direct commentary on the translation process during his lifetime, the verses from his brother John's poem "Pygmalion Meditateth" that he appended to the end of his essay "Ολίγαι Λέξεις περί Στιχουργίας" ("A Few Words on Prosody,"1891) convey several important sentiments:

> Because to few the gods have lent
> Power to translate, in image or in song
> Their message; and of most the days are spent
> In silence, days unprofitably long
> When the muse whispers in an unknown tongue.
> (2003c, 46)

The reader of the essay is led to believe that these verses are Cavafy's own, since he somewhat disingenuously neglects to identify John as their creator. In fact, "Pygmalion Meditateth" could easily have been written by either Constantine or John, so closely were the brothers collaborating at the time and so similar were their poetic compositions.[21] Indeed, these lines serve as a fascinating testament to the intimate relationship between the brothers in matters of translation (it should be noted that John was Cavafy's first translator). Moreover, they highlight the rather romantic view the Cavafy brothers held about the artistic merits of translation ("Because to few the gods have lent / Power to translate"). Translating (here both the essential poetic act and the linguistic rendering of poetry in a language familiar) is a divine activity involving the inspired mediation of the poetic ear, which presumably understands the familiar language of the Muses. Precious though these sentiments may be, they go some way to explaining Cavafy's fussy and even obstructionist attitude toward translations of his own work, the complex history of which requires its own study.[22]

Evidently Cavafy viewed his early function as a translator and learned journalist in a most exalted light. There have been numerous attempts to assess the translation-laden expository prose of nineteenth-century Greek journalists; the term *"demosiologos"* (literary journalist or journalistic philologist) coined by K. Th. Dimaras—a position midway between a journalist and writer[23]—best conveys Greek print culture of the nineteenth century, which is essentially the main tradition out of which Cavafy's prose emerged. The erudite voice that comes through in Cavafy's essays is largely that of a keen appreciator of literature rather than that of a literary critic (a criticism T. S. Eliot once leveled at Algernon Swinburne). Complicating this hybrid role of learned journalist is the requisite task of translating, a demanding activity that necessarily sapped one's creative energies. Cavafy, as a fairly adept translator from English, French, and Italian into purist Greek, remained dutifully committed to satisfying the expectations of his readership while also attempting to fulfill the ideal Wildean function of the critic as artist. Striking this philological balance involved a constant struggle on the part of an aspiring intellectual like Cavafy, who, with a limited formal education, must have been acutely sensitive to any perceived deficiencies in his literary sophistication and linguistic abilities. To a large degree, his skills as a translator allowed him to drape himself in a romantic mantle while simultaneously concealing from the public any flagrant gaps in his knowledge or linguistic flaws in his proficiency with the Greek language.

Notwithstanding this romanticizing view of translation, Cavafy's professional capacity as a journalist must soon have come into conflict with his higher calling as an "eternalist" (to use the favored and somewhat precious Victorian terminology).[24] Cavafy would eventually abandon his professional journalistic aspirations after 1897 when he began to find writing prose and translating other poets and scholars less than gratifying. This waning enthusiasm clearly colored his views of his own essays. Two apocryphal statements have been passed down in this regard: Cavafy allegedly dismissed these writings as his "baggage in prose,"[25] and he delighted in a friend's claim that he famously refused three things: "Cavafy does not give lectures, he does not grant interviews, and he does not write prose."[26] The very fact that Cavafy never felt confident about his prose writings and effectively discouraged interest in them during his lifetime creates a dilemma for his readers: How should we approach this corpus of which Cavafy was neither particularly proud nor pleased? We would do well to apply George Seferis's comments on Cavafy's rejected poems to his spurned prose: "The poet has nothing to fear now from these . . . [and] the serious student cannot afford to ignore them."[27]

Cavafy's negative appraisals raise an even more intriguing question: Why did Cavafy, who clearly was a connoisseur of fine prose (historical narratives in particular), fail to make a mark as an accomplished prose stylist? Could he not have paralleled the achievement of his prosaic poetics with an equally stunning aesthetic prose—a euphuistic "poetic prosaics," as it were?[28] The fact remains that he effectively abandoned writing prose, and a careful scrutiny of his prose texts suggests a number of probable reasons for this retreat. These curiously dissatisfying but ultimately fascinating texts comprise a vexed corpus, to be sure. Contrary to Cavafy's qualifying comments, his prose remains fertile ground for furthering our critical understanding and evolving appreciation of the poet. Thematically, they serve as loci for many of his evolving literary, philological, and cultural interests; chronologically, they attest to the overall unity of his artistic output;[29] stylistically, they chart his movement away from a stiff katharevousa to a more relaxed *astiki demotike* (urban demotic), paralleling a similar movement in his poetry; and psychologically, they betray a profound authorial frustration: the failure to achieve a satisfying aesthetic prose style and voice comparable to the one he would later find in poetry. One would thus be justified in claiming that Cavafy felt increasingly stifled by the prose medium—boxed in, as it were, by the very prose texts he would in turn box up and store away for posterity.

Fortunately, Cavafy never acted on his animus against his prose; on the contrary, he carefully preserved a significant amount of this material for future readers. There are some sixty-four texts categorized as prose in the most recently published edition of his Πεζά (*Prose*) (2003c). Twenty-eight of these were actually published during Cavafy's lifetime in various newspapers and periodicals. Although these published writings roughly span the full period of his adult lifetime (1886 to 1931), the earliest pieces are unique in that they define the first public portrait we have of Cavafy: that of the journalist dilettante and aspiring man of letters. Thus they constitute a public performance of sorts—his performance in prose—and curiously anticipate his future international reputation and global performance on the world stage of poetry.

Supplementing the actual published texts are the remaining thirty-six unpublished prose pieces, many of which were undoubtedly composed with publication in mind. Preserved as well are diaries, notes on poetics and ethics, short reflections, and comments on poems and translations. Taken as a whole, this corpus gives us a fuller canvas of Cavafy's journalistic and cultural interests. The fact that he did not destroy these texts but preserved them in carefully arranged files is significant. He clearly meant them to be unpacked, edited, and studied. Indeed, Cavafy was fond of using container metaphors—boxes, chests, drawers—for conveying the storing up of valuable relics that document the examined life of the artist. His prose poem "Ενδύματα" ("Garments") offers a revealing meditation on safeguarding the relics of one's life, all of which are preserved in a bureau of precious ebony "with much reverence and much sorrow." If one reads this as an aesthetic fable à la Baudelaire allegorizing the "artistic quest,"[30] then Cavafy's prose narratives become much more than mere curiosities of literature; collectively they offer profound insights into his view of the creative process.

To date, Cavafy's archived prose writings have been referenced primarily by critics and scholars when they discuss his poems, serving the rather pedestrian function of helpful intertextual glosses. The well-known bias that poetry is to prose as dancing is to walking reflects a lingering critical view that has certainly influenced the reception of his essays. His prose writings have seldom been appreciated as a corpus on their own, since, rather than focusing on their content, readers tend to fixate on their challenging style—either quaint Victorian English, stiff puristic katharevousa, or formal urban demotic. On the most basic level, readers should certainly approach them as "garments" from the poet's life that provide valuable insights into his artistic mind and rare documentation of his literary and emotional interests.[31] On a more critical level, however, they would do well to engage directly with Cavafy's texts on their own terms—as independent autonomous texts, since in most instances they are highly finished pieces of writing that aspire to be both informative and persuasive, formal and personal.

Cavafy's rise to global fame and his undisputed place in the pantheon of world literature is a phenomenon not unrelated to his earliest cosmopolitan posturing and cultural aspirations as a journalist. We dwell perhaps too readily on E. M. Forster's image of the reclusive poet in a straw hat standing at a slight angle to the universe, on the self-absorbed artist who circulated limited editions of his personally bound broadsheets to select readers. Behind this retreating persona, however, was a man who craved fame but who calculated his moment cautiously, as is evidenced by his returning unsigned a publishing contract for an English translation of his poems to Virginia and Leonard Woolf's Hogarth Press in 1925. How peculiar in light of the recent publishing milestones of the *Oxford World Classics* bilingual edition of Cavafy's collected poems, the *Penguin Classics Selected Poems*, and the *Everyman Edition*. Timing, of course, is everything, and with the benefit of hindsight, we can now appreciate Cavafy's intuitive sense that the 1920s was not the right decade for him to be launched. Surely his years spent as a journalist taught him how to be print savvy, as did his early exposure to publicity in the press. The explosive period of the 1880s and 1890s, when publishing and journalism underwent a mass-market transformation analogous to today's Internet-based information revolution, provided Cavafy with a great deal of wisdom about the politics of publishing and fame. Thus his apprenticeship in prose and his brief sporadic media performances on an international stage would have significant ramifications for his future promotional strategies and his emerging reputation as a poet.[32]

One important fact to keep in mind is that many of Cavafy's early prose writings were in English, a detail that has been commented on but not fully appreciated. Stratis Tsirkas was of the opinion that the poet "thought" in English,[33] a notion borne out by these early texts, which attest to Cavafy's fluency in the language and lifelong interest in English literature. Certainly, given his family's extensive social and literary connections in England, he intended to publish his English essays in British periodicals; indeed, these essays show beyond a doubt that he could have charted a path for himself as an English prose stylist had he wished. Cavafy highly valued English prose and was conscious of the inspiring but equally intimidating emergence of the cult of Victorian prose. He was an avid reader of Ruskin, Macaulay, Pater, and Wilde, prose masters who surely could have served as examples for his own future aesthetic essays.[34] Edward Gibbon's magisterial *Decline and Fall of the Roman Empire* also remained one of Cavafy's favored texts, and he made numerous marginal notes in which he took stylistic issue with the historian.[35]

Cavafy's probable intention to publish in England was an ambitious but somewhat impractical goal, since his early essays are utterly awash in folkloric content. This was to be expected given the excessive omnipresence of the discourse of *laographia* (folklore) in Greek literary circles in the 1880s and '90s.[36] The problematic presence of folklore in Cavafy's early writing surely had a very significant impact on the course of his future essays. Although we do not normally associate laographia with Cavafy, it should be noted that the only teacher to be definitively linked with the poet is Constantine Papazis, with whom Cavafy studied in Alexandria in 1881–82. Papazis was a student of Nikolaos Politis, the "father" of Greek folklore,[37] and thus it comes as no surprise that Cavafy's earliest topics would include "The Romaic Folk-Lore of Enchanted Animals" (1884–86), "Coral from a Mythological Perspective" (1886), "Lycanthropy" (1882–84), "Beliefs Concerning the Soul" (1884), social customs in Burma, and African creation theories. While clearly informational in content, these essays document important interests in enchantment, the supernatural, and Orphic arcana, cultural preoccupations that will reappear in Cavafy's mature poetry, where Greek magic and the Hellenistic and Byzantine occult figure prominently.[38]

Although Cavafy would later reject the ethnocentric and nationalist literary conventions that were ushered in by folklorists when composing verse in his mature decadent mode, he does return rather curiously to the topic of folklore in 1914 and 1917 when reviewing Politis's *Εκλογαί από τα Τραγούδιᾀ του Ελληνικού Λαού* (*Selections of the Songs of the Greek People*) and M. G. Michailidis's *Καρπαθιακά Δημοτικά Άσματα* (*Carpathian Demotic Songs*). Additionally, in 1921 he worked on a student anthology of demotic folk songs for the Educational Association of Egypt, where, in a commentary, he advocated a healthy dose of this subject for students, implying that the folkloric excesses of his own days were indeed problematic and even stifling.[39] This interesting early and late presence of folklore in Cavafy's writings provides one clue perhaps to his eventual disengagement from journalism and consequently from prose writing itself. The excessive discourse of laographia ran counter to his own literary tastes, and he consciously withdrew from literary journalism largely because of the problematic ethnocentrism of laographia and its reification by prose writers and language theorists (Alexandros Papadiamatis, Kostis Palamas, and Jean Psycharis, among others). Cavafy chose to sidestep the intense public forum in which these philological culture wars were being waged, retreating instead to the more private realm of his poetic haven, where he could perform on his own terms and publish in a more controlled and strategic manner.

This is not to say that Cavafy did not engage directly with the issue of "Greekness," pronouncements on which from Greek journalists were expected by readers during this period. On the contrary, he rose to the occasion and chose topics that allowed him to appease the ethnocentric expectations and demands of his readership while simultaneously satisfying his own literary interests. The thematic focus on an unapologetic Hellenicity is another important hallmark of Cavafy's prose essays. Indeed, in many of his essays, the fine line between chauvinism and criticism does not always hold. The titles of the essays alone illustrate this Hellenocentric perspective well enough—"Ελληνικά Ίχνη εν τω Σακεσπήρω" ("Traces of Greek Thought in Shakespeare"), "Έλληνες Λόγιοι εν Ρωμαϊκαίς Οικίαις" ("Greek Scholars in Roman Houses"), "Οι Βυζαντινοί Ποιηταί" ("The Byzantine Poets")—essays that foreground the cultural supremacy of Hellenism. More often than not, Cavafy found himself promoting Hellenism in the high rhetoric of the day. An example of this bombast may be seen in the concluding sentence of the essay "Το Μουσείον Μας" ("Our Museum," 1892), which marks the opening of the Greco-Roman Museum of Alexandria: "[The museum] presents to us an image of that noble civilization that developed so robustly in Egypt, as in another Greece, which injected into the Orient the Greek spirit and bequeathed Greek refinement and grace to the Oriental ideas with which it came into contact."[40] A more sentimental view is expressed at the conclusion of his essay "The Byzantine Poets": "A beneficent fate has endowed the Greek race with the divine gift of poetry. The vast and garlanded realm of poetry is like our spiritual homeland. We Greeks are obliged to study our poetry attentively—the poetry of every period of our ethnic life. For in this poetry we will find the genius of our race in all its fineness along with the beating pulse of Hellenism's very heart."[41] Similar sentiments appear throughout these prose writings and illustrate how different Cavafy's approach to matters Hellenic remained without the mediation of poetic irony and literary decadence.

Offsetting and augmenting this preoccupation with Hellenism is the pronounced impact of British publications, whose influence on Cavafy cannot be overestimated, especially as regards his choice of topics and the shaping of his literary and cultural interests. We know that he was an avid reader of the *Gentleman's Magazine*, the *Nineteenth Century*, the *Temple Bar,* and the *Fortnightly Review.* He frequently confronts the featured topics of these publications, writing with the unmistakable poise and verve of a British subject, which, of course, he technically was, although he allegedly renounced his British citizenship in 1885. In 1891, Cavafy takes on the issue of the Elgin Marbles in what are perhaps his best-known essays. In 1893, he addresses the political plight of Cyprus in a review of George Chacalli's treatise *Cyprus and the Cypriot Question*, an English publication that he formulaically excerpts, translates, and critiques for his readers. His rather strident tone on both Cyprus and the Elgin Marbles reflects an uncharacteristic aggressiveness and political assertiveness, indicating that Cavafy was initially quite serious about following a journalistic career.[42] As Liddell points out, these topics, although atypically political for the poet Cavafy, were partly topical· "The Cyprus question was comparatively new in 1893, and one James Knowles had lately written a foolish article making fun of Frederic Harrison's suggestions that the Elgin marbles should be returned to Athens."[43] Cavafy's essays on the Elgin marbles fall squarely within the discourse of the period on Greece's national identity formation. On a secondary level, since the marbles are specimens of some of the most sensuous sculpture ever produced in the ancient world, one can assume that Cavafy's interest in their return is of a piece with his ongoing fixation on the representation of the male body and the Greek celebration of beauty. The essays, regrettably, refrain from any aesthetic discussion of the marbles' artistic merits, even though a precedent for this type of appreciation was readily at hand in Pater's essay on the German art historian Johann Winckelmann and his aesthetic views on Greek sculpture.

The weighty influence of British culture on Cavafy's writings during the 1890s is also apparent in the peculiar subject matter of his prose, which reflects aesthetic tastes he acquired during his stay in England between 1872 and 1877, as discussed in the previous chapter. The extent to which Cavafy was influenced by the Victorian press may be more fully appreciated by glancing at the table of contents of the periodicals he read and to which he responded in kind with essays and, in some instances, even poems.

The list of articles featured in the *Nineteenth Century* and the *Fortnightly Review* in the prolific year 1891 reveals a significant thematic overlap between Cavafy's reading and writing interests. The following list includes the relevant titles of articles from the two aforementioned periodicals:

The *Nineteenth Century*

"Give Back the Elgin Marbles" by Frederic Harrison
"The Joke about the Elgin Marbles" by James Knowles
"The 'Mimes' of Herodas" by C. Whibley
"French Authors on Each Other" by E. Delille
"The Poet of the Klephts: Aristoteles Valaoritis" by Rennell Rodd
"Shakespeare and Modern Greek" by John Stuart Blackie

The *Fortnightly Review*

"The Celt in English Art" [Burne-Jones] by Grant Allen
"The Poet Verlaine" by Edward Delille
"Baudelaire: the Man" by Edward Delille
"The Paris Salons of 1891" by Mabel Robinson
"Editorial Horseplay" [Elgin Marbles] by Frederic Harrison
"The Soul of Man under Socialism" by Oscar Wilde
"A Preface to *Dorian Gray*" by Oscar Wilde

Cavafy composed direct responses to many of these articles: he engaged with James Knowles and Frederick Harrison in the pieces he penned on the Elgin Marbles; he wrote a laudatory response to John Stuart Blackie's article on the modern Greek language; he composed a poem on the mimes of Herodas (1892*). In more general terms, the subject matter of French poetry, Baudelaire, Pre-Raphaelite painting and literary decadence discussed in these printed venues will resonate deeply in Cavafy's writings during the 1890s. In short, the contents of these two periodicals fully coincide with his journalistic and literary interests during this decade, constituting as they do a heady combination of Greek politics, archaeology, philology, and literary trends that dovetailed almost seamlessly with his own favored pursuits.

Perpetually lurking behind these sundry and wide-ranging topics is the problematic Greek language question, which garners a fair share of Cavafy's attention, specifically the philological viewpoints related to Greek grammar and prosody. Cavafy engages directly with the writings of three philologists: as previously noted, he reviewed and excerpted the theories of John Stuart Blackie, professor of Greek in Edinburgh, in an article published in 1891. In his essay on the Byzantine poets (1892) he pays homage to the philological views of Karl Krumbacher; and in unpublished essays we have Cavafy's reviews of Emmanuel Roidis's *Τα Είδωλα* (*The Idols,* 1893–97) and Hubert Pernot's book on modern Greek grammar (1918), all of which reveal Cavafy's interest in and anxiety over the language question. These texts shed much light on Cavafy's own gradual voyage from katharevousa to demotike; they also show how diligently he followed the Greek language debate and allow for speculation on the deleterious effect this debate had on the formation and evolution of his own prose style. In a revealing letter written in 1906, Cavafy makes the following comments on the problem of abandoning katharevousa:

> Some—myself included—hesitate to sacrifice katharevousa in its entirety, and do not agree to condemn all the linguistic work of an entire century (and more than a century). . . . We who are now returning to the demotic language are pilgrims, devoted and passionate pilgrims who are entering into a temple and will remove, of course, all of the gaudy decorations and the superfluous dressing that spoil it, but without violence and without prejudice, so that we do not risk overlooking and discarding in the heap—like fools—a certain golden oil-vase or a chest of bright mother of pearl.[44]

One cannot but notice in this decadent tableau of iconoclastic spoilage the favored metaphor of the precious container—the recherché motif of the treasure chest of language—and its immediate thematic proximity to matters of style and creativity.

From a stylistic point of view, Cavafy admired the learned elegance of Emmanuel Roidis, whose katharevousa he attempted to imitate, with rather mixed results. He pays tribute to numerous Greek prose stylists in his writings, both contemporary and ancient. Cavafy valued, in addition to Roidis, the prose writings of the historian Constantine Paparrigopoulos and the author Dimitrios Vikelas, as well as various Byzantine historians who he felt wrote history dramatically. The prose of Philostratus (AD 170–245) is celebrated in the essay "Λάμια" ("Lamia," 1892), as is that of the late-antique writer Lucian (AD 120) in the essay on Greek scholars in Roman houses (1896). Lucian's epideictic prose pieces were among

Cavafy's favorite; indeed, this early sophistic engagement with Lucian greatly influenced his own notion of Greek performativity—how being Greek was a cultural matter of performing in Greek[45]—something he would have experienced firsthand when displaying and proving his own acquired mastery of katharevousa in the public press.

The anxiety Cavafy felt over the dilemma of selecting a language that would optimize his literary performativity comes through in a comment he penned in December 1905:

> The wretched laws of society—neither the result of healthy or critical thinking—have diminished my work. They have inhibited my expressiveness; they have prevented me from imparting light and emotion to those who are made like me. The difficult circumstances of life have forced me to labor greatly in order to master the English language. What a shame. If I had labored equally in French—if circumstances had allowed it, and the French language was of equal use to me—then perhaps in French—owing to the ease that its pronouns provide, which both describe and hide—I would have been able to express myself more freely. In the end, what shall I do? I am, aesthetically speaking, wasting myself. And I shall remain an object of conjecture; and people will understand me more so by what I have denied. (2010, 134)

These thoughts, although clearly written in reference to Cavafy's problem of revealing and concealing his homosexuality in his poetry, speak equally to his stylistic predicament with prose. Here we have a clue as to why he never opted to pursue a Paterian path as an English prose stylist: the English language was less flexible and English literature too puritanical, as he states directly in comments written in October 1905:

> For me, that which makes English literature cold—besides some deficiencies of the English language—is—how shall I say it—the conservatism, the difficulty—or the unwillingness—to stray from the established, and the fear of offending morality, the pseudo-morality, since this is what we should call a morality that feigns naiveté.
>
> During these past ten years, how many French books—both good and bad—have been written that examine and bravely consider the new phase of eros. It is not new; it is just that for centuries it has been ignored, under the assumption that it was insanity (science says that it isn't) or a crime (logic

says that it isn't). No English book that I know of [mentions it.] Why? Because they are afraid of confronting prejudice. Nevertheless, this erotic tendency also exists among the English, as it exists—and existed—among all of the nations, to a limited extent, of course. (2010, 133)

Cavafy's sentiments betray his deep misgivings about the choices and limitations presented to him by his linguistic predicament; moreover, they reveal how deeply he agonized over his stylistic options. The notorious alternative example Cavafy has in the back of his mind here is that set by the Greek poet Jean Moréas, who chose a French path of letters for himself and effectively turned his back on the Greek language.

The Celebrated Dandyism of Jean Moréas

On February 3, 1891, a highly significant literary event took place in Paris: a banquet was held to celebrate the literary achievement of the Greek expatriate poet Jean Moréas (Ioannis Papadiamantopoulos) and the launching of his volume *Le Pèlerin passionné*. As John David Butler writes in his study of Moréas,

> A banquet [was] held on February 3 at the Hotel des Sociétés Savantes, on the rue Serpente, and presided over by none other than Stéphane Mallarmé. Given in honor of Jean Moréas' latest work, it was known as "le banquet du *Pèlerin passionné*," and signaled the apotheosis of the Symbolist movement and the apogee of public acclaim for Moréas. The list of names of those in attendance reads like a "Who's Who" in the world of letters and art of the time. . . . Suffice it to say that as a result of the publication of this volume and the acclaim given it at a banquet honoring the author and his work, Moréas's reputation as a leading poetic voice of the day was solidly established, and the extent of his acclamation by the public and his peers reached heights which were not to be surpassed even when he was later to publish his masterpiece, *Les Stances*. It seems that for a while, Moréas overshadowed even Mallarmé and Verlaine. (1967, 71, 73)[46]

Whereas Baudelaire stood at one end of the decadent-symbolist spectrum, the other end was occupied by Moréas. The fact that one of the chief apologists of *décadisme* (later renamed symbolism by Moréas)[47] in France was a

Greek poet would have been a matter of consequence for a budding poet like Cavafy, who from a young age sought to strike a cosmopolitan note in his writing and resist the trap of Greek provincialism. Indeed, the spectacular example of Moréas's rise to the pinnacle of French literary society set a formidable precedent for the young Cavafy, who could only fantasize about achieving such status.

Moréas was not only a master of the French language but also a notorious dandy and poseur who was sought out by aspiring poets and writers. Richard Ellmann relates the amusing details surrounding Oscar Wilde's desire to meet Moréas and their dining encounter in 1891 at the Côte d'Or:

> For once, Wilde had to yield the floor, as Moréas expounded the theories of the Ecole Romane. . . . At dessert . . . Wilde asked Moréas to recite some verses. "I never recite," replied Moréas. . . . [When others began reciting poetry about Moréas], Wilde grew visibly uneasy at the worship of Moréas. . . . Conquered, routed, he who had silence about him in the salons of London, asked for his hat and coat and fled into the night. He recovered later, and asked Moréas . . . and others to dinner. This time he ruled the table with his stories. Moréas commented as he left, "This Englishman is a shit." When Moréas was mentioned afterwards, Wilde would say, "Moréas, does he really exist?" Answered in the affirmative, he went on, "How strange! I've always thought Moréas was a myth." (Ellmann 1988, 347–348)

Although Cavafy never met Moréas, he left behind a few apocryphal comments on Moréas's career. In a remark recorded by Timos Malanos, Cavafy noted that Moréas had an easier path before him than he himself had:

> Cavafy supported the view that Moréas, by opting to compose in a malleable language like French, found himself as an artist of the poetic word in a much easier position than his Greek fellow poet of the same period who had, in addition, to wrestle with numerous obstacles in order to create an expressive medium. In addition, he maintained that had Moréas written his work in Greek, his position in a young literature like our own would have been much more significant than that which he secured in French letters. "I also found myself in the same dilemma"—he told me one day—"whether to write in our language or chose another." (Malanos 1957, 249–250)

From these comments and the previously cited note written in 1905, we may conclude that Cavafy certainly struggled with the temptation to follow Moréas's example. His reasons for rejecting this option likely have to do with his commitment to the Greek language as well as with apprehensions related to the problematic reception Moréas received from the mainstream bourgeoisie.

Cavafy was fully aware of the negative criticism heaped upon Moréas by the detractors of literary decadence. Moréas's rise to literary prominence in decadent-symbolist circles was written up in the pages of the *Nineteenth Century* and *Fortnightly Review* by Edward Delille, the literary critic who contributed regularly to these journals. His articles provide an important point of reference for the debate on decadence and were certainly read by Cavafy. In a comprehensive article titled "French Authors on Each Other" (1891), Delille overviews numerous polemical statements on the subject of decadence, focusing a significant amount of attention on Moréas. The critique of Moréas offered in this article is worth citing. Delille excerpts from Jules Huret's preface to *Enquette sur l'Evolution Litterairee*, a collection of interviews, pen portraits and revelations. Moréas's volume of poetry *Pèlerin passionne* is referenced numerous times in Huret's book. M. Lemaitre faults them for being a "mass of incomprehensible rubbish," while M. Naurice Barres writes, "As to the symbolists, I like Moréas, and I like his talent, but I, for my part, should hardly care to devote a lifetime to the task of chiselling phrases and reviving *obsolete terms*" (Delille 785—emphasis added). These stinging lines and the very mixed reception of Moréas's poetic oeuvre resonate in a note Cavafy wrote in English in 1902, "Obsolete Words":

> It is one of the talents of great stylists to make obsolete words cease from appearing obsolete through the way in which they introduce them in their writing. Obsolete words which under the pens of others would seem stilted or out of place, occur most naturally under theirs. This is owing to the tact & the judgment of the writers who know when—& when only—the disused term can be introduced, when it is artistically agreeable or linguistically necessary; & of course then the obsolete word becomes obsolete only in name. It is recalled into existence by the natural requirements of a powerful or subtle style. It is not a corpse disinterred (as with less skillful writers) but a beautiful body awaked from a long & refreshing sleep. (2010, 140)

In addition to being highly cognizant of Moréas as a great stylist, Cavafy also appears to have been influenced by his verse. The necromantic metaphor of a beautiful body lying in eternal slumber or awaking from a long sleep appears often in Cavafy's work, and it is quite likely that he appropriated it from Moréas's early poem "Chimaera" (from *Les Syrtes*),[48] in which Moréas creates a quintessentially decadent tableau:

> I lit the mortuary brightness of crystal lamps in the depths of the crypt where you lie, eyes rolled back; and my dream gathers swamp flowers to ennoble your pale mourning flesh. I spoke strange palatal sounds after the necromancer's rite for the dead, and on your lips of bloody foxglove red, sleeping potions suddenly fermented. Thus I created you from the ultimate essence, an unwitherable ghost haloed with stars, to purify myself of lust, to console my heart sunken into infamy. (Houston and Houston 1980, 121)

Several of Cavafy's funereal poems come to mind here—particularly "In the Month of Athyr" (1917)—as does his "Following the Recipe of Ancient Greco-Syrian Magicians" (1931). Cavafy's poem "Longings" (1904), however, presents the closest parallel:

> Like the beautiful bodies of those who died before they had aged,
> sadly shut away in a sumptuous mausoleum,
> roses by the head, jasmine at the feet—
> so appear the longings that have passed
> without being satisfied, not one of them granted
> a night of sensual pleasure, or one of its radiant mornings.
>
> (1992, 21)

Roses and jasmine conjure up the pungent odors of Baudelaire's "flowers of evil" in both Cavafy's and Moréas's poems. The overwhelming presence of such decadent tropes substantiates Timos Malanos's critical observation that during the turn of the century, Cavafy was writing under the full spell of French verse (1957, 221).

The Flâneur and the Prose Poem

The profound influence of Baudelaire is perhaps nowhere more apparent than in Cavafy's attempt to master the prose poem, undoubtedly the most satisfying of all his prose works. His prose compositions—"Το Σύνταγμα της Ηδονής" ("The Pleasure Brigade"), "Τα Πλοία" ("The Ships"), and "Ενδύματα" ("Garments")—may be read as "fables of the artistic quest" à la Baudelaire.[49] Moreover, they provide a glimpse of what Cavafy might have gone on to achieve in this hybrid genre had he not abandoned prose altogether. Along with his short story "Εις το Φως της Ημέρας" ("In Broad Daylight"), they constitute the apex of Cavafy's prose accomplishments, even though they all remained unpublished during the poet's lifetime.

Prior to composing these variations on the prose poem, Cavafy penned what is clearly his first flâneur narrative, "Μία Νυξ εις το Καλιντέρι" ("A Night on the Calinder," 1885–86). A recollection of his stay in Constantinople (the towns mentioned in the story—Kalinderi, Neochorion, Therapeia, and Büyükdere—are located on the shores of the Bosphorus, the area where Cavafy initially lived with his mother's relatives in 1882), this narrative attempts a rather ambitious synthesis of Poe's "Man of the Crowd" motif with elements of Greek folklore. Although opening with the unmistakable urban stroll of the flâneur, which includes sitting in a café and acutely observing people's faces and habits, the story soon veers in a sentimental direction owing to the overriding presence of a folk song about death overheard by the narrator:

Suddenly the silence was shattered. A large boat appeared sailing in the direction of Therapeia in which a group of people were singing. They sang beautifully. Not of course according to all standards of music—the simple peasants who were in the boat possessed no notion of the theories of the Conservatoires, nor did their ancestor the Thracian Orpheus who could enchant stones with his music. The song which interrupts—or should I say accompanies—the silence of the summer evening is one of the things I love best. This is natural music. It is the true music of the soul, I think, just as the frigid noise of the salon piano is the music of agitated nerves.

Don't take him so quickly to the grave,
let him enjoy the sun a little bit longer!
Don't take him so quickly, it's a shame—
he barely knew what it meant to live.

Laugh if you wish, or shed a tear,
all things in life are false,
all lies, all shadows.

If any single truth remains,
it is the cold, barren soil
to which all sorrows go, and all our joys.

I felt a tremendous emotional reaction. I was expecting a cheerful song about youthful exploits, full of happiness and life, one of those valiant songs which the fertile and vibrant shores of the Bosphorus produce. Instead of this I heard in these simple and unpolished verses—the invention of some rural poet's Muse—a bitter lament about the vanity of all things, that most ancient complaint of suffering man, "all lies, all shadows."

The flowers continued to exude their perfumed eloquence all around me; the waves continued to rush forward laughingly towards distant happy shores, the sky continued to present its resplendent peace-all things were harmoniously in sync with some mystical promise of complete bliss. Nevertheless, the voices of the singers did not desist but increased, melancholic and bold, as a protest against the enchanting but deceptive beauty of the world. (2010, 75)

Here we should note the Baudelairean venture into nature ("Man walks within these groves of symbols" ["Correspondences," Baudelaire 1993, 19]) and the synesthetic correspondence of sights, sounds, and smells that culminate in the splenetic message communicated to the poet. The folk song, however, introduces a maudlin note that lacks the macabre effect found in Poe's grotesque analogues. Moreover, the folkloric memento mori, which was clearly intended to satisfy Cavafy's prospective audience, proves less than effective since it causes a narrative digression from an urbane flânerie into folkloric sentimentality.

Curiously enough, Cavafy took a great interest in revising this piece. In a note to his friend Pericles Anastasiades, he wrote, "'A Night on the Calinder' is an old article which I have retouched. I am rather satisfied with its diction, over which I have taken many pains. I have tried to blend the spoken with the written language and have called to my help in the process of mixture all my experience and as much artistic insight, as I possess in the matter—trembling, so to speak, over every word" (2003b, 366). Despite its flaws, the narrative offers a fascinating autobiographical commentary on Cavafy's emerging artistic persona, specifically the complex synthesis of the dilettantish journalist, the aspiring flâneur poet, and the posing dandy, aspects of his personality that will develop in varying degrees during the 1890s.[50]

The Baudelairean decadent aesthetic is more clearly manifest in the prose poem "Το Σύνταγμα της Ηδονής" ("The Pleasure Brigade," 1894–97), which begins with the admonition "Do not speak of either guilt or responsibility. When the Pleasure Brigade passes by with music and banners, when the senses pulsate and tremble, those who keep their distance and refrain from taking up the good cause and its march toward the triumph of pleasure and passion are foolish and vulgar" (Cavafy 2010, 81). Moral laws and vague virtues are to be shunned in this aesthetic parable, which articulates the amoral hedonistic ethos of *Les Fleurs du mal*: "Be not deceived by the blasphemers who tell you that subservience to sensual pleasure is dangerous and painful. Subservience to pleasure brings perpetual joy. It exhausts you but exhausts with sublime intoxication. And when ultimately you collapse on the road, only then is your fate worthy of envy" (81).[51] The poem climaxes with a precious tableau of the poet's vindication after death: "When your funeral procession passes, the Forms which were shaped by your desires will throw lilies and white roses upon your casket, the young Olympian gods will lift you onto their shoulders and will bury you in the Cemetery of the Ideal where the mausoleums of poetry glisten in whiteness" (80). Cavafy's use of the term "ideal" here is clearly indebted to Baudelaire's quasi-platonic use of the word in his poetic dialectic between spleen and the ideal in *Les Fleurs du mal*, another example of how deeply he had imbibed the avant-garde thematics of the French poet.[52]

In a similar vein, the prose poem "Ενδύματα" ("Garments," 1894–97)—the only prose poem written purely in the demotic idiom—foresees a time when the poet will have experienced a full artistic life: "I shall place and safeguard the garments of my life inside a chest or in a bureau made of precious ebony. . . . I will look upon these clothes and will remember the great celebration—which by then will be completely finished" (Cavafy 2010, 80). Echoes of Baudelaire's poem "Spleen (II)" are evident here: "More memories than if I'd lived a thousand years! // A giant chest of drawers, stuffed to the full / [. . .] / I am a dusty boudoir where are heaped / Yesterday's fashions" (Baudelaire 1998, 147). Cavafy concludes with a piquant image of entombed somnolence: "Completely finished. The furniture scattered haphazardly throughout the halls. Plates and glasses broken on the floor. All the candles burned out. All the wine consumed. All the guests departed. A few weary people will be sitting all alone, like myself, inside dark houses—others who are even more weary will have gone to sleep" (2010, 80). The shortest of the prose poems, "Garments" offers a most succinct message regarding the precious value of an artist's archival memorabilia and the need to preserve and store away what one day might prove invaluable.

The most ambitious and impressive prose poem is "Τα Πλοία" ("The Ships," (1895–96), in which Cavafy's debt to Baudelaire is unmistakable. Originally titled "Το Ταξίδι" ("The Voyage"), the piece echoes Baudelaire's prose poems "Le Port" and "L'Invitation au voyage," as well as the poem "Le Beau Navire." It begins by evoking the whiteness of the blank page before the writer embarks on his imaginative journey and then proceeds to develop an elaborately extended metaphor of the voyage as an artistic experience: "From Imagination to Paper. It is a difficult crossing, a dangerous sea. At first sight the distance appears short, but in fact the journey is a long one, and very damaging for the ships that undertake it" (2010, 84).[53] The ships function allegorically as vehicles that carry precious thoughts and ideas, cargo that is alternately vulnerable to confiscation by customs agents (censors),[54] damage by mishandling (hostile philistines), or stagnation owing to the shallow harbors (the petty middle class):

> The first bit of damage occurs owing to the very delicate nature of the cargo being transported on the ships. In the markets of the Imagination, the majority of wares and the best items are fashioned out of delicate glass and diaphanous ceramic, and despite all worldly precaution, many break on the journey and many break when they are being unloaded on to land. Any damage of this sort is irreparable, since it is impossible for the boat to go back and procure similar wares. There is no chance of finding the same shop that sold the items. Although the markets of the Imagination have large and sumptuous stores, they are short-lived. They conduct brief transactions, they dispose of their wares quickly, and they dissolve immediately. It is very rare that, upon returning, a ship will find the same exporters with the very same goods. (2010, 84)

The overt focus on merchandise in the poem is in keeping with Baudelaire's own mercantilism in "L'Invitation au voyage," which, as Barbara Johnson notes, combines "metaphors of commerce with a panegyric to the priceless" (1980, 38).

The concluding paragraphs of the poem contain passages of great subtlety and evocative power and bear testimony to Cavafy's unrealized potential to master this hybrid genre:

There is one other thing that is lamentable, most lamentable. This is when certain great ships pass by, festooned with coral and masts of ebony, with great white and red flags unfurled, laden with treasures, which never even approach the harbor since either all of their cargo is banned or the harbor is not deep enough to receive them. And they continue on their way. A tail wind fills the sails of silk and the sun illumines the glory of their golden prows, and they sail off gently and majestically, distancing themselves from us and our shallow port forever.

Fortunately these ships are quite rare. At most we will see two or three during our lifetime. And we quickly forget them. However bright the vision might have been, its memory will fade just as quickly. And after a few years pass, if one day—while we sit indolently watching the light of day or listening to the silence—if by chance some inspired verses return to our mind's ear, reminding us that we have heard these melodies before—we do not recognize them at first, and we rack our brains to remember where we once heard them before. After much effort, our old memory awakens and we recall that these strophes were part of the song sung by the sailors—sailors as beautiful as the heroes of *The Iliad*—when the great ships were passing us by, those sublime ships that were heading—who knows where. (2010, 85)

The narrative imitatively evinces the "quasi-pictorial tonality"[55] found in Baudelaire's prose poems, which were, in many instances, attempts to transpose impressions of paintings into prose (the subject of Cavafy's pictorialist poetics will be taken up in the next chapter). "The Ships" climaxes in a striking vision that blends the visual and aural in a synesthetic combination that exemplifies the quintessential Baudelairean correspondence between the material and the spiritual, splenetic ennui supplanted by sublime beauty.

Cavafy's experiments in prose also extended to the short story; "Εις το Φως της Ημέρας" ("In Broad Daylight," 1895–96) remains his best-known prose composition, having been translated into English as early as 1983 by James Merrill for the literary magazine *Grand Street* and more recently by David Connolly and Nikolas Kostis.[56] The story is written in the gothic manner of Poe and involves a young man named Alexander A., who is visited by a ghost who instructs him to exhume treasure chests filled with gold and jewels that lie buried by Pompey's Pillar in Alexandria. The ghost requires only an iron box that is part of this bounty, the contents of which remain mysteriously ambiguous. The story's protagonist, whom most readers view as a thinly veiled portrait of Cavafy, panics after the third encounter with the ghost "in broad daylight" (the first two were in dreams) and flees in terror. The treasure is never excavated, the mysterious iron box never retrieved, and the story concludes with Alexander A. recovering from a nervous breakdown in the presence of his friend G. V., who happens to be steeped in magical lore. The narrative is written in an almost unbearably mannered purist style, which was undoubtedly a deliberate stylistic attempt to imitate Poe's arabesque, grotesque aesthetic.

For readers, critics, and translators of Cavafy, this prose narrative serves as a rather tantalizing parable that effectively dramatizes (albeit rather cryptically) a panic of some sort—quite possibly Cavafy's own philological panic[57] regarding his prose "baggage." The description of the specter in the story is curious: "I fell asleep again at around one-thirty, at which time it seemed to me that a man of medium height and around forty years of age entered my room. He was wearing fairly worn out black clothes and a straw hat. On his left hand he wore a ring set with a very large emerald. This struck me as being incongruous with the rest of his attire. . . . There was something strange about his eyes, a look at once sarcastic and sad" (2010, 87).[58] One cannot resist the temptation to view this ghost as Cavafy's doppelgänger—he has the straw hat that Forster famously attributes to him, as well as the shabby gentility and rings mockingly described by Timos Malanos.[59] (This reading should not be taken as a validation of Petros Vlastos's infamous categorization of Cavafy as a "Byzantine vampire," a demeaning affront that nevertheless serves as a valuable gothic gloss to the story.) The very quintessential Cavafian type of an older man sitting in a café, this ghost desires an iron box that contains something precious (here one is reminded of Cavafy's decadent vision of the stripping of the temple of katharevousa and the potential loss of a precious chest). Could this occult box be a displacement for Cavafy's prose writings that on some psychic level haunted and tormented him? Might this buried chest (so curiously reminiscent of the buried iron box containing the *Book of Thoth*)[60] express a repressed desire to acquire a hermetical euphuistic prose style that Cavafy so desperately sought but that evaded him his entire life? Certainly the story supports such an allegorical reading, fanciful though it might be. Ever controlling his reputation, it seems, from beyond the grave, here Cavafy haunts his only prose short story, seeking a mortal to give him an iron box that in effect constitutes some sort of posthumous interpretation, validation, or perhaps even translation of his ill-fated prose. The story thus dramatizes his doomed quest for a prose style appropriate to his art and high creative standards.

Reading the story as an allegorical tale of Cavafy's subliminal anxiety over his prose effectively synthesizes his many metaphoric references to his writings as hidden texts, abandoned baggage, and precious relics. Apropos of such metaphors of containment, it is curious to note that the first editor of Cavafy's prose, George Papoutsakis (1963) suggestively cites a passage from Arthur Ransome's study on Oscar Wilde, drawing a telling parallel to Cavafy by means of a metaphor of a locked casket. Ransome writes,

> An artist is unable to do everything for us. He gives us his work as a locked casket. Sometimes the words are very simple and all the world have keys to fit; sometimes they are intricate and subtle, and the casket is only to be opened by a few, though all may taste imperfectly the precious essences distilling through the hinges. Sometimes, when our knowledge of an artist and of the conditions under which he wrote have been entirely forgotten, there are no keys, and the work of art remains a closed casket, like much early poetry, of which we can only say that it is cunningly made and that it has a secret. (1913, 10–11)

Papoutsakis (1963, xi) opines that Cavafy's work (by which he means the poetry) belongs to the second category—writings hermetically obscure in the modernist symbolist mode. Implied in Papoutsakis's account is the hermeneutical hope that the prose texts he was presenting for the first time in 1963 would provide "keys for the few" critics able to appreciate them by applying them to critical interpretations of the poems. I suggest, however, that the third category—the closed casket for which there is no key—serves as an equally apt metaphor for Cavafy's prose—the paradox presented to the readers of a poet of world literature whose prose has remained undervalued, untranslated, and, relatively speaking, locked, boxed, and buried for decades. The mysterious box is to be "retrieved," as it were, by a mortal (a sympathetic reader, shrewd critic, or adept translator) and handed back to the poet's now famous specter.

The inauspicious fate of Cavafy's prose calls to mind Baudelaire's comment on Poe's tales, which he felt were ill received in America, prompting him to associate the term "ill fortune" with them. (The term also applies to Baudelaire's own poetry and illustrates the accursed predicament of the damned poet-painter of modern life.) Indeed, this concept informs the concluding lines of Baudelaire's sonnet "Le Guignon" ("Ill Fortune"), which offer a paradoxical semblance of solace to the poet whose writings are underappreciated: "But sleeping lies many a gem / In dark, unfathomed caves, Far from the probes of men; // And many a flower waves / And wastes its sweet perfumes / In desert solitudes" (1998, 31). Once again, the topos of entombed somnolence serves as an apt metaphor for the precious rarefied poem-story that, like a flower or precious gem, lies out of vulgar reach of the probing mob.

Cavafy's decadent prose poems are clearly attempts to imitate Baudelaire's prose pieces, hybrid compositions that subtly incorporate elements of art criticism into his creative writing in the tradition of *transposition d'art*. This decadent, Parisian, salon-based impressionism—an almost alchemical interchangeability between poem and picture—will find its way into many of Cavafy's poems and manifest itself as a full-fledged pictorial poetics, as will be seen in the following chapter.

3

PICTORIALIST POETICS

Transpositioning Word and Image

During the years 2003 and 2005, two noteworthy publications dealing with Cavafy and the fine arts appeared. In 2003, the Athens Concert Hall (Μέγαρο Μουσικής) published a catalog for an exhibit of Greek artists living in Egypt titled *C. P. Cavafy: His World and the Artists of His Era,* which brought together numerous canvases by artists who either knew or were known to Cavafy. Two years later, the Kastaniotis Publishing House issued a deluxe edition of Cavafy's poems accompanied by color illustrations of paintings by twelve contemporary Greek artists. Both publications emphasize a long-acknowledged but underappreciated fact: Cavafy's work enjoys a unique relationship with the visual arts, beyond the verity that so many of his poems (one-third according to Dimitris Daskalopoulos) deal with sculptors, painters, and models. That Cavafy actively sought out the company of artists is well known from his friendship with and interest in Greco-Egyptian artists (Pericles Anastasiades, Theodore Ralli, Thalia Flora-Karavia, Takis Kalmouchos, Konstantinos Maleas, Nikolaos Gogos, and Yiannis Kefalinos, among others) as well as from his desire to meet and view the work of the Athenian artist Yiorgios Roilos. Added to this are his documented visits to art venues in London, Athens, and Paris, all of which may be further contextualized within the framework of his extended family's patronage of artists and committed connoisseurship of their work, as was discussed in chapter 1. What has not received as much attention is the particular pictorial quality of Cavafy's poems themselves, one that not only drew inspiration and found an informing aesthetic in the fine arts but also proved in turn to be highly suggestive to painters who have illustrated Cavafy's poems, most notably Nikos Hadzikyriakos-Ghikas, Yiannis Tsarouchis, Alekos Fassianos, and David Hockney. The pictorial dimensions of Cavafy's aesthetic remain central to his work, a point well articulated by Efi Andreadi, the curator of the 2003 Athens art exhibit: "Beyond the emphasis on the decorative, Cavafy overlaps with the Orientalists but also to some extent with the English Pre-Raphaelites in his artifice, historicity, his insistence on describing with an impeccable 'mother of pearl' delicacy, along with the guise of aestheticism which often was a refuge and counterweight to Victorian puritanism" (2003, 36). Similar points are raised by Daskalopoulos in his introductory note to the 2005 edition of the poems: "Cavafy is pictorial. Such an assertion is based chiefly on elements contained in his poems: the manner, that is, by which they convey the forms of their personae, the skillful staging, the sense of spatial economy which encompasses both small and great human emotions, the chromatic vocabulary" (2005, 9–10). This chapter explores the rich connections between Cavafy and the fine arts by tracing the Parnassian proto-decadent lineage of his pictorial poetics back to its source in the "transposition d'art" salon critique, a genre that served as the inspiration and catalyst for the art-for-art's-sake movement, which both energized and transformed poetic writing during the second half of the nineteenth century. It concludes by considering some notable examples of pictorial art directly inspired by Cavafy's poems.

Art for Art's Sake: Parnassian Overtures

Cavafy's poetic evolution as an adherent of postromantic Parnassianism to full-blown decadence followed a rather predictable literary route and owed much to the lingering influence of the French poets collectively

associated with the Parnassian movement.[1] Highly influential for this
group of poets was the work of Théophile Gautier, whose pre-Parnassian
volume of poems *Emaux et camées* (1857–72) set a standard for the aesthetic quality most valued by the Parnassians, namely, the perfection of
form distinguished by an impersonal objectivity.[2] The characteristic Parnassian connection forged between poetry and the plastic arts of sculpture
and painting would become the defining aesthetic of this school of poetry;
indeed, the examples of Gautier and Baudelaire,[3] both of whom published
widely read salon critiques, reinvigorated the traditional rivalry between
the sister arts of painting and poetry, establishing a new synthesis that
would profoundly color Cavafy's poetics and enhance the Pre-Raphaelite
influence that he imbibed during the late 1870s and 1880s.

Cavafy's early poetry has been faulted for being derivatively Parnassian:
George Seferis famously objected to Cavafy's "cold Parnassian portraits,"
and the Greek critic Petros Vlastos dismissively characterized his poems as
"pedestals without statues." Doubtless there is a modicum of truth in these
critiques, but if we approach Cavafy from the broader framework of decadent aestheticism, we may perceive the seeds of his mature poetry in the
early work, compositions that possess more merit than many dismissive
critics have been willing to grant. This chapter ventures a critique of select
poems of the early period (1891–1908) with a view to delineating recurring
decadent themes. Cavafy's evolving "pictorialist poetics"[4] begin to emerge
during this period, ushering in a defining aesthetic whereby an intensely
visualized dramatic moment (one quite often framed by historical or historicizing events) is expressed pictorially through verbal strokes that convey image, color, and gesture. This quintessential Cavafian formula will
evolve and coalesce later in the canonical poetry in which Hellenistic and
late-antique Alexandria, Byzantium, and the homosexual underworld of
contemporary Alexandria become favored decadent settings.

Notwithstanding Cavafy's brief flirtation with romantic poets (namely,
Hugo, Byron, Keats, and Shelley),[5] during the last decade of the nineteenth
century Cavafy fell under the full spell of the Parnassians. Eleni Politou-
Marmarinou (1983, 341), in her influential article on Cavafy and French
Parnassianism, aptly concludes that a Parnassian breeze blows through
all of Cavafy's poems.[6] In a similar vein, George Savidis noted that "dur-
ing the 1890s Cavafy was both a Parnassian and a Symbolist" (quoted in
Ilinskaya 1983, 95). Cavafy's Parnassian pedigree may be assessed more

positively if we view the movement less reductively and more inclusively; as Aaron Schaffer wrote in his early foundational study, Parnassianism was "a poetic Colossus of Rhodes straddling the nineteenth century from its Romanticist beginnings to its Symbolist close" (1929, 210).

Pivotal in this straddling is Théophile Gautier, who is traditionally credited with coining the phrase "art for art's sake" and for introducing a heightened ekphrastic emphasis on painting and sculpture into poetry.[7] More specifically, it is Gautier's art criticism (which Baudelaire claimed "educated a whole generation" [Kearns 2007, 5]) that set the standard for conflating painting, sculpture, and poetry.[8] Gautier, it should be remembered, was the dedicatee of Baudelaire's *Les Fleurs du mal*—"the impeccable poet" and "perfect magician of French letters" (1993, 3)—as well as an important early interpreter of Baudelaire's work. His famous "Notice on Baudelaire" would become a defining document not only for the poet but for decadence itself and, as such, warrants being quoted at length:

> The author of *The Flowers of Evil* loved what is inaccurately called the decadent style, which is simply art that has reached the extreme point of maturity which marks the setting of ancient civilizations. It is an ingenious, complex, learned style, full of shades and refinements of meaning, ever extending the bounds of language, borrowing from every technical vocabulary, taking colours from every palette and notes from every keyboard; a style that endeavours to express the most inexpressible thoughts, the vaguest and most fleeting contours of form, that listens, with a view to rendering them, to the subtle confidences of neurosity, to the confessions of aging lust turning into depravity, and to the odd hallucinations of fixed ideas passing into mania. This decadent style is the final expression of the Word which is called upon to express everything, and which is worked for all it is worth. In connection with this style may be recalled the speech of the Lower Empire, that was already veined with the greenish streaking of decomposition, and the complex refinement of the Byzantine school, the ultimate form of decadent Greek art. . . . It is no easy matter to write in this style, despised though it be by pedants, for it expresses novel ideas in novel forms and uses words hitherto unheard. Contrary to the classic style, it admits of the introduction of shadows, in which move confusedly the larvae of superstition, the haggard phantasms of insomnia, the terrors of night, the monstrous dreams that impotence alone stays in their realisation, the gloomy fancies

at which day would stand aghast, and all that the soul has of darkest, most misshapen, and indefinably horrible in the depths of its uttermost recess. (Gautier 1909, 39–41)

With the exception of the emphasis on horror and the abyss, most of Gautier's critical assessment of Baudelaire could be applied equally to Cavafy: the complex learned style and refinement of the Byzantine school correspond to Cavafy's "Phanariot" elitist strain and cultural fascination with Byzantium; the occult superstition finds expression through various poetic personae (Apolonius, St. Athanasius, Justinian, and Greco-Syrian magicians, among others); gloomy fancies and dreams stayed by impotence are dramatized through the lives of Hellenistic monarchs, Byzantine emperors and empresses, and melancholy lovers. Such thematic illustrations of Gautier's definition abound in Cavafy's work, proving how significant this seminal decadent sensibility would remain for his oeuvre.

It is worth noting that Gautier's "Notice on Baudelaire" references numerous paintings; indeed, it has been observed that in the essay we meet not Baudelaire per se but rather various works of art.[9] The syncretic mode of interreferencing painting, sculpture, and poetry derives from the transposition d'art genre[10]—an ekphrastic description or evocation of a painting or sculpture in poetry or prose that, in the postromantic period, evolved in large part from the salon review. This poetic strategy pervaded many aspects of aesthetic writing in both France and England (the Pre-Raphaelite poets and painters were equally influenced by—and would in turn influence—French painting and poetry).[11] The "transpositional" approach to art—works sometimes directly identified in poems but just as often left unacknowledged—involves an almost alchemical translation from painting to poem. Although the ekphrastic mode of describing a work of art dates back to classical antiquity,[12] in nineteenth-century France this intertextual correspondence between painted and verbal images received heightened and renewed attention. Poets sought new sources of inspiration and a break from the classical ideal, perpetuating the romantic revolt in painting against the classical academism favored by the salons of the Académie des Beaux-Arts. Gautier writes of this phenomenon in his *L'Histoire du romantisme*: "This involvement of art in poetry has been and remains one of the characteristics of the new School. . . . The sphere of literature has expanded and now encompasses that of art in its immense orbit" (quoted in Snell 1982, 212).[13] This emerging focus on the visionary experience would eventually pave the way for symbolism, with its emphasis on "hermetic worlds, on dreams and the Ideal, on dazzling jewel-encrusted surfaces, on the precious and eternal as on the fatal and the macabre" (214).

Gautier and Baudelaire emerged as leading voices of French art criticism in the mid-nineteenth century; their widely read salon reviews and exemplary transpositional poems set a new literary standard by ushering in an innovative painterly aesthetic for aspiring poets.[14] As David Scott writes, "Painting's role, as Baudelaire saw it, was essentially to *fictionalize* reality, and he was therefore most drawn to those painterly genres— history painting (above all as exemplified in Delacroix), Orientalist painting (Decamps, Delacroix, Fromentin), erotic art (whether Ingre's *odalisques* or the 'sujets amoureux de M. Tassaert'), caricature and the macabre (Goya, Daumier, Cruikshank, etc.)—which heightened and transformed experience in new and often bizarre ways" (1988, 25). Many nineteenth-century poets attempted to imbue their compositions with painterly qualities and looked to painting for both inspiration and a new invigorating aesthetic—as was the case with the Pre-Raphaelite poets. Scott goes on to note that

> an important lesson transpositional poets learned from their study of painting was that the literary image or even images drawn directly from nature gained new autonomy when transposed into pictures; in other words, that the suggestive appeal of a literary subject was enhanced as it became transformed into a visual image. As a result, nineteenth-century poets were motivated to try to reinstate into the literary or poetic image some of the vivid impact, the visual appeal of the painted image. This, they discovered, was as much a function of the formal presentation of the image as of its subject. In a sense, then, the poem and the painting were seen to be striving towards a similar goal: that of the promotion of the sensual and suggestive qualities of the image. It followed that the role of the painter and poet (for Baudelaire, Delacroix was a "peintre-poète"), was fundamentally the same and that, therefore, an analysis of the formal structure of painting might have, by analogy, much to teach the poet. (1988, 25)[15]

Like Gautier before him, Baudelaire favored the romantic painter Eugène Delacroix, and many of his most important aesthetic views derive from his descriptive analyses and critical evaluations of Delacroix's paintings. The theoretical connections Baudelaire makes between romantic art, color and the splenetic melancholy of Delacroix's dramatic compositions[16] offer an important intertext for approaching Cavafy's early work. "No one," Baudelaire writes, "after Shakespeare, excels as Delacroix does in molding drama and reverie into a mysterious unity" (quoted in Lloyd 2002, 195). Baudelaire's commentary on Delacroix's painting *L'Entrée des Croisés à Constantinople* (*The Entry of the Crusaders into Constantinople*)[17] (Exposition Universelle of 1855) illustrates this new mode of impressionistic criticism and intense visualization of historical moments:

> What a sky and what a sea! Everything here is tumultuous and tranquil, like the aftermath of a great occasion. The city, rising up behind the crusaders who have just traversed it, spreads out with an impressive verisimilitude. Everywhere you look there are those glittering, undulating flags, unfolding and clacking their luminous folds in the transparent atmosphere! Everywhere you look the crowd surges, alarmed, there is the tumult of arms, the pomp of garments, the emphatic truthfulness of gestures made in the great moments of life! (194)[18]

Rosemary Lloyd, in her illuminating comments on this passage, offers an apt appraisal of Baudelaire's unique manner of translating the visual message to his reader: "The passage is remarkable for its ability to convey movement and color, sound and the play of light, and to set it within the heightened dramatic framework of a decisive historical turning point" (195).[19] This very pictorial formula—a unique molding of "drama and reverie into a mysterious unity"—is one that Cavafy will initially imitate and gradually adopt as his own. It is hardly surprising that a poet who was a historian manqué would have been inspired by the irresistible pictorialism of history painting when creating historical poems; there can be no doubt that he fully immersed himself in the study of painting in his poetic effort to transpose image into word. One has only to think of the highly staged signature poems "Alexandrian Kings" and "Waiting for the Barbarians" to appreciate this very combination gleaned from Delacroix and channeled through Baudelaire; in both poems we encounter a dramatic iconography—the histrionic grandiloquence of history painting—set against defining historical moments impressionistically evoked to convey a dire situation or crisis.

As was seen in chapter 2, Cavafy was extremely indebted to Baudelaire for much of his critical thinking in the 1890s. Baudelaire's transpositional poems in *Les Fleurs du mal* offered Cavafy concrete pictorial examples for imitation. Baudelaire wrote poems based on various works of art: on Delacroix ("On *Tasso in Prison*" and "Don Juan in Hell"); on Antoine Watteau ("A Voyage to Cythera"); and on Ernest Christophe ("The Mask" and "*Danse macabre*").[20] The Delacroix subjects in particular present some significant parallels in Cavafy. In "On *Tasso in Prison*," the final lines echo resoundingly in Cavafy's poem "Walls" (1896/1897): "This dreamer, sleepless from the horrors here, / Surely depicts the soaring Soul who falls / Into the Real, smothered within four walls!" (Baudelaire 1993, 313). In "Walls" Cavafy will depict his own smothered poetic persona similarly imprisoned: "Without reflection, without mercy, without shame / they built strong walls and high, and compassed me about. // And now I sit here and consider and despair. // My brain is worn with meditating on my fate: / I had outside so many things to terminate" (Cavafy 2003b, 28).[21] In his "Salon of 1859," Baudelaire comments extensively on Delacroix's *Ovid in Exile among the Scythians:*

> Look next upon the famous poet who taught the *Art of Love*; there he is, lying on the wild grass, with a soft sadness which is almost that of a woman. Will his noble friends in Rome be able to quell the emperor's spite? Will he one day know again the luxurious pleasures of that prodigious city? No: from this inglorious land the long and melancholy river of the *Tristia* will flow in vain; here he is to live and to die. (1965, 169)

The scenario functions as an informing mise-en-scène for three later poems in the Cavafy canon. In "The Satrapy" (1905/1910),[22] we find an analogous cultural displacement from the classical ideal: "You can't get any of these from Artaxerxes, / you'll never find any of these in the satrapy, / and without them, what kind of life will you live?" (1992, 29). Similarly, in "A Byzantine Nobleman, in Exile, Composing Verses" (1921), we discover a corresponding scenario, albeit one that elicits less sympathy from the reader, given the speaker's flippant demeanor as expressed in his opening line, "The frivolous can call me frivolous" (110) (his rather Parnassian hauteur may be read as Cavafy's campy attempt at self-parody). Likewise, in the canonical poem "Exiles" (1914*), we encounter yet another variation on this theme, in which Byzantine exiles await their return to Constantinople in an Arab-controlled Alexandria. Doubtless the intertextual aesthetic analogues and sources of signification for these poems derive from the salon critique that inspired many other poets during this period. (Delacroix would have loomed large for an emerging Greek poet such as Cavafy, especially given the painter's dedication to the Greek struggle of 1821, which he immortalized in some of his most famous canvases.)[23]

It bears repeating that Cavafy possessed and read Baudelaire's art criticism; although he left no marginal comments in these volumes as he did in his volumes on Ruskin (another instance in which Cavafy engages with the art criticism of his day), he did provide some interesting remarks on the art critics of antiquity—the Sophists of the Second Sophistic. In his unpublished essay "A Few Pages on the Sophists" (1893–97) penned during this very period, Cavafy writes:

> They greatly resembled today's artists in their love for the external beauty of works of art. The idea expressed might have been great; or it might not have made many demands. Its outward rhetorical expression however had to be perfect. They became intoxicated by the sculpting of phrases and the music of words. . . . The great variety of their topics allowed their art to encompass components of today's novels, poetry, criticism, and drama. They concerned themselves with the study of painting and sculpture. They composed descriptions of collections of paintings. They interpreted the ideas of the painter; they brought to light the meaning that lay hidden in the details—in the movement, in the folds of a garment, in the placement of a piece of furniture; and they identified the perfection of chromatic and linear execution. (2010, 112–113)

This curious resemblance between "today's artists" who love "external beauty of works of art" (Cavafy clearly had in mind the art-for-art's-sake movement here) and the Sophists of antiquity is of a piece with Cavafy's preference for a Greek cultural perspective, one that overlaps rather seamlessly with the Hellenic fixation of the Parnassians.[24] Cavafy's comments thus effectively apply to the genre of the salon review as much as they do to the antique writings of the Sophists, both of which exerted such a profound influence on his early work.

We may safely assume, then, that Cavafy had transposition d'art poems and salon commentaries in mind when he envisioned his own pictorial poem "Oedipus" (1895/1896) which, the subtitle informs us, was "written after reading the description of the painting *Oedipus and the Sphinx* by Gustave Moreau" (figure 3):[25]

> The Sphinx is fallen on him,
> with teeth and talons outspread
> and with all the furor of life.
> Oedipus succumbed to her first impulse;
> her first appearance terrified him—
> such a face, and such talk
> till then he had never imagined.
> But though the monster rests
> her two paws on Oedipus' breast
> he has recovered quickly—and now
> he no longer fears her for he has
> the solution ready and he will win.
> And yet he does not rejoice over this victory.
> His glance, full of melancholy,
> is not on the Sphinx; far off he sees
> the narrow path that leads to Thebes
> and will end at Colonus.
> And his soul clearly forebodes
> that there the Sphinx will accost him again
> with more difficult and more baffling
> enigmas that have no answer.
>
> (1989, 196)

Clearly Cavafy was following Baudelaire's precedent in his transposition, a manifold process involving numerous facets. As Emily Salines notes, Baudelaire's salon critiques and transpositional poems entail various steps, including a description of the painting which is, in many instances, purely metatextual, an interrogation, an interpretation, a rephrasing and finally a translation (2004, 218).[26] Cavafy's transposition from description to poem minimizes the descriptive aspect, focusing instead on the psychology of the scene, in particular the melancholy foreboding of Oedipus, which he felt dominates Moreau's canvas. He interrogates the painting in order to tease out the essence of the Greek tragedy it references, producing in the process a direct yet elegant meditation on Moreau's most famous work.

Figure 3. Gustave Moreau, *Oedipus and the Sphinx* (1864). Oil on canvas, Metropolitan Museum of Art, New York.

Critics have connected Cavafy's interest in Moreau's presentation of the brooding Oedipus to his own artistic conflicts—Michalis Pieris reads the poem as Cavafy's struggle to solve and anticipate artistic enigmas.[27] More broadly speaking, the canvas expresses the sexual anxieties that haunted fin de siècle artists, particularly the flagrant misogyny that infected so much of this period's writing.[28] It is quite likely that Cavafy was inspired by J.-K. Huysmans's ekphrasis of Moreau's *Salome* and *The Aparition* in *À Rebours*, perhaps the most notorious prose transposition of a painting ever penned.[29] The fact that Cavafy would compose his own Salome poem the same year he wrote "Oedipus" suggests such an artistic trajectory, although curiously he shifts his focus from Salome's perverse sensuality to the equally perverse aesthetic indifference of the young Sophist:

> Salome brings on a golden tray
>   the head of John the Baptist
>   to the new Greek sophist
> who bends indifferent to love.
>
> "Salome," answers the young man,
>   "I wanted them to bring me your head."
>   He said this jokingly.
> And the next day one of her servants comes running,
>
> carrying the blonde head of his beloved
>   on a golden tray.
>   But while studying, the sophist
> had forgotten his desire of yesterday.
>
> He sees the blood dripping and it disgusts him.
>   He orders this bloody thing to be removed
>   from before him, and he continues
> to read the dialogues of Plato.
>
>   (1989, 245)

It is interesting to note how deftly Cavafy deconstructs the supreme icon of decadence: by vividly staging two concise dramatic moments (the presentation of the heads of John the Baptist and Salome) with great visual intensity (the gold of the tray, the red blood, and the white toga presumably worn by the Sophist offer a striking palette), Cavafy inverts the traditional hierarchy of Salome's seduction. Instead, he paints a scene wherein the femme fatale falls victim to the indifferent Sophist aesthete.

When creating his imaginary Sophist, Cavafy may well have had in
mind the Sophist art critics Philostratus and Callistratus, the authors of
the ekphrastic texts *Imagines* and *Descriptions,* respectively, ancient Greek
sources that the poet had in his library.[30] His ironic poem implies that the
sophistic work of the art critic must retain a studied indifference to raw
sensuality in preference for the erotic idealized beauty of art; even the flesh
and blood of the archseductress fail when confronted with the preferred
idealization of the image. The poem may be read as a perverse transposition that pays tribute to the sophistic tradition of art criticism (the topos
of decadent connoisseurship, as it were) while ironically commenting on
the fin de siècle overkill of the Salome tradition. Much like Wilde before
him, Cavafy kills Salome off, thus dispensing with the problematic "un-
controlled and murderous female energy" of the phallic woman.[31]

Equally transpositional in nature are Cavafy's unpublished "image
poems"—"Indian Image" (1892*), "Pelasgian Image" (1892*), and "Chal-
daic Image" (1896*)—all of which are heavily indebted to an ekphrastic Parnassian Orientalism. Certainly "Indian Image" may be read as an
iconographic homage to Moreau's Orientalist canvases—the Greco-Indian
setting of the painting *Salome* comes to mind, as does the bejeweled excess
of *Jupiter and Semele*.[32] The poem is saturated with the lapidary details so
prevalent in Moreau's work:

> The universe has four gates
>   which four angels guard.
> One is the North; the South facing it;
>   and the others West and East.
>
> The Eastern gate is of glistening pearl;
>   in front of it a bright angel
> wearing a diamond crown and a belt of diamonds
>   stands on a ground of agates.
>
> The Southern gate is made of purple amethyst.
>   Its angel sentinel holds in his hands
> a magic sceptre made of dark sapphire.
>   A dense cloud of turquoise
> hides his feet.
>
>   On a bank covered
>   with red delicate shells

the angel of the West stands and guards
    the gate of precious coral.
He wears a wreath of artificial roses, and each rose
    is made of pure ruby.
The Northern gate is built of gold,
    and has a throne near the entrance.
. . . .

                        (1989, 221)

Cavafy's fanciful edifice expresses his decadent interest in lapidary lore, which he explored in his essay "Coral from a Mythological Perspective" (1886)[33] as well as in numerous poems featuring precious gems. The cosmological exoticism of "Pelasgian Image" involves a highly visual and detailed description of a sleeping giant who selfishly guard his treasure hoard: "His tremendous neck / supports thirty heads / and each has twenty sharpest eyes, / through which the day and the deepest gloom / of the deepest earth are bright" (1989, 222). The very same Parnassian ethos is evident in Cavafy's sonnet "Singer" (1892), which presents the movement's quintessential emphasis on the rarefied perfection of the poetic craft:

Far from the world, poetic magic intoxicates him;
    for him beautiful verses are the whole world.
Fantasy has built for her songster
    a strong house of the spirit that destiny cannot shake.

You may say, "Life is cold and futile. It is folly
    to think that life consists of the pleasant
sounds of a flute, and nothing else." Or, "Hard insensibility
    lashes the one who was never wracked by the pain

of the struggle of life." But your judgment
    is delusion and injustice. His Nature is divine.
Judge not in your logical, blind sickness.

The walls of his house are of magic emerald—
    and voices within them whisper, "Friend, be quiet;
meditate and sing. Be of good heart, mystic apostle!"
                        (1989, 186)

The poem foregrounds the precious permanence of art and its mystical immunity to life's natural processes in a manner reminiscent of the final poem of Gautier's "L'Art," from *Emaux et camées,* in which the eternal forms of art are celebrated: "Yes, the work emerges more beautiful / from a form that resists / working, / verse, marble, onyx, enamel. [. . .] Everything passes—Only vigorous art /is eternal; [. . .] The gods themselves die. / But sovereign lines of verse remain stronger than bronzes."[34] Baudelaire's comments on this volume bear witness to how influential Gautier's poems were during this period: "that series of little poems of a few stanzas each, those erotic or dreamy interludes, some of which resemble sculptures, others flowers, others again jewels, but all have a color finer and more brilliant than the colors of China or India, and all have a shape purer and more precise than objects in marble or crystal. Everyone who loves poetry knows them by heart" (quoted in Kopp and Poulet 1969, 103).

Whether or not Cavafy knew *Emaux et camées* by heart, he was clearly caught up in the Parnassian zeitgeist that Gautier's poems inaugurated. His "In the Soul's House" (1894*) features an impregnable house of art where the Passions, "beautiful women in silk raiment dressed / with sapphires glimmering darkly in their hair. / . . . flushed and disheveled and with bosoms bare, / dance wildly and carouse" (2003b, 47).[35] The poem was inspired by a verse from *La Jeunesse blanche* by the Belgian symbolist poet and novelist Georges Rodenbach, whose work focused on the city of Bruges, a "dead city" and place of fascination for decadent writers. As Will Stone notes, Bruges served as an "ideal landscape from which to evoke the sensations of drawn-out decline and aesthetic decay" (2005, 136).[36] In 1893, Cavafy composed and published his own Bruges poem— "Vulnerant Omnes, Ultima Necat" ("All wound, the last one slays")— a common inscription found on medieval sundials. It features a curious dialogue between a clock and a priest regarding boredom and the passing of time:

> The metropolis of Bruges, which a mighty
> Flemish duke once built and lavishly dowered,
> has a clock with silver portals
> that has been telling time for many ages.
>
> The Clock said, "My life is cold,
>   and colorless and cruel.
> For me each day on earth is the same.
> Friday and Saturday, Sunday, Monday,

are no different. I live—without hoping;
my only amusement, my only diversion
in my destined bitter monotony,
        is the world's destruction.
As I turn my hands sluggishly, languidly,
the delusion of everything earthly appears before me.
End and fall everywhere. Dins of unassailable strife,
groans buzz around me—and I conclude that
each of my hours wounds; the last one slays."

The Archpriest heard the audacious word
and said, "Clock, this language grates against
your ecclesiastical, your lofty rank.
How did such an evil thought creep
into your mind? O foolish, heretical idea!
        For a long boredom
has filled your mind with a dense mist.
        The chorus of hours
received another mission from the Lord.
Each one rekindles; the last one begets."

                                        (1989, 187)

Cavafy contextualizes the decadent splenetic preoccupation with ennui
in the form of a theological dialogue wherein a world-weary "heretical" clock languorously voices a suicidal despair and a priest counters
with an optimistic gloss on mortality. The poem concludes on a note
of salvation, a peculiar deviation that reflects the sustained flirtation of
many fin de siècle writers with Catholicism and church ritual. This very
religious obsession—the dialectic of shame and grace, as Ellis Hanson
terms it[37]—informs other of Cavafy's published and unpublished compositions of this period, namely, "Hereafter (1892*), "In the Cemetery"
(1893*), "Terror" (1894*), and "Confusion" (1896*). (Cavafy's complex
engagement with Christianity will be more fully explored in the next
two chapters.)

Rodenbach resonates in two other poems as well: "Rain" (1894*)—
likely inspired by the canals of Bruges[38]—and "La Jeunesse Blanche"
("Our Dearest White Youth") (1895*), which, with its painterly visionary
emphasis on the pale evanescence of youth, is highly reminiscent of Burne-
Jones's ethereal angels. The title and first line of the latter poem derive

from Rodenbach's sonnet "La Mort de la Jeunesse," which was also the source for Cavafy's "In the House of the Soul":

> Our dearest, our white youth,
>   ah, our white, our snow-white youth,
> that is infinite, and yet so brief,
> spreads over us like the wings of an archangel! . . .
>   It is forever exhausted, forever loving;
> and it melts and faints among white horizons.
> Ah, it goes there, is lost in white horizons,
>   goes forever.
>
>   Forever, no. It will return,
>   it will come back, it will return.
> With its white limbs, its white grace,
> our white youth will come and take us.
>   It will seize us with its white hands,
> and with a thin shroud drawn from its whiteness,
> a snow-white shroud drawn from its whiteness,
>   it will cover us.
>
> (1989, 199)

There are distinct echoes here of Cavafy's prose poem "The Pleasure Brigade," which concludes with a similar cenotaphic vision of sepulchral whiteness.[39] The poem foregrounds the cult of youth while contrasting a seemingly pure innocence with a more complex wistfulness, one that hints at a more dissolute lusting not only after youth but also after youths. It stands as an early example of Cavafy's sublimated obsession with young men and death, which he will take to a new level when composing his openly homoerotic poems.

The poem "'Nous N'osons Plus Chanter les Roses'" ("'We No Longer Dare Sing of the Roses,'" 1892*) borrows its title from Sully Prudhomme's Parnassian poem "Printemps Oublié":

> Fearing the commonplace
> I leave many words unuttered.
> Many poems are written in my
> heart; and those interred songs
> are the ones that I love.

O first, pure, only freedom
of youth for pleasure!
O sweet intoxication of the senses!
I fear lest some platitude
abuse your divine form.
. . . .
                    (1989, 220)

The poem brings together many of the decadent themes of the 1890s—hedonistic pleasures, intoxication, and the fear of vulgar platitudes of bourgeois society. Although the title cautions poets to eschew the clichéd topic of roses, Cavafy will nonetheless take up the cult of flowers in a set of his own flower poems. In "Elegy of Flowers" (1895) we encounter a maudlin meditation on youth, old age, and the cycles of nature—precisely the platitudinous poem Cavafy should be avoiding—concluding as it does with the lines

For us this year no fields will blossom anew.
The roses of forgotten August wreathe us,
our former years swiftly return,
beloved shadows sweetly beckon us,
and lull our poor heart to deep slumber.
                    (1989, 189)

Fortunately Cavafy found an antidote for such sentimentalizing verse in Baudelaire's *Les Fleurs du mal* and Huysmans's *À Rebours*, texts that offer an ironic variation on the mawkish thematics of flowers. It bears noting that the cult of flowers, which during the romantic period came to have "unprecedented importance both for serious writers and for wider culture" (Knight 1986, 60), underwent a Baudelairean transformation. As Philip Knight writes, Baudelaire's treatment of traditional flower rhetoric (the flower code, flowers of transience, or flowers of idealization) becomes "boldly and variously ironic": "floral sentimentality" is undermined by the "subversive beauty of a transient flower."[40]

Thus we detect a similar shift in Cavafy from a romantic sentimentality in "The Elegy of Flowers" to an ironic subversiveness in "Bouquets" (1897*), where he attempts to imitate the floral abominations of Huysmans's Jean des Esseintes:

Absinthe, datura and bean plant,
aconite, hellebore and hemlock—
all the bitters and the poisons—
will donate their leaves and horrible flowers
to make up the large bouquets
that will be placed upon the bright altar—
ah, the splendid altar of Malachite stone—
of the horrible and very lovely Passion.
                                    (1989, 248)

As glossed by M. Kopidakis, the poem's six preliminary words express Cavafy's lexicographical interest in ancient Greek (four of the words may be found in a passage from Plutarch).[11] The initial word, "absinthe," conjures up associations with the favored beverage of the French decadents (Cavafy's trip to Paris in 1897 is certainly reflected in this poem), and the horrible flowers are obvious references to Baudelaire as well as to des Esseintes's monstrously syphilitic flowers in *À Rebours* (real flowers bred to imitate artificial flowers).[42] The presence of a malachite altar here concludes the poem on a note at once sacred and profane, as does the curious expression "του Πάθους του φρικτού" ("the horrible Passion"), which a Greek reader would immediately recognize from the Byzantine hymns of Holy Week, where sublime variations on "Τα φρικτά/σεπτά πάθη") ("the awful and holy passion of Christ") may be readily found. Here the dialectic between religious suffering and erotic passion is superbly distilled into the poem, the overwhelming perversity of which led George Savidis to conclude that Cavafy's capitalization of the words "Malachite" and "Passion" indicates that they are code words for onanism.[43]

Likewise, in "Artificial Flowers" (1895/1903*) we encounter the predictable lapidary motifs of decadence (especially des Esseintes's jewel fetishism)[44] but with the intellectual rhetoric of poetry (contemplation, rhythm, and learning) worked into the equation:

I do not want the real narcissus—nor do lilies
        please me, nor real roses.
They adorn the trite, pedestrian gardens.
        Their flesh embitters, tires, and pains me—
        I am weary of their perishable beauties.

    Give me artificial flowers—glories of glass and metal—
with never-wilting, never-spoiling, never-aging forms.

Flowers of superb gardens of another land
   where Contemplations and Rhythms and Learning dwell.

I love flowers fashioned of glass or gold,
   genuine gifts of a genuine Art,
dyed in hues lovelier than natural colors,
    wrought with mother-of-pearl and enamel,
     with ideal leaves and stalks.

They draw their grace from wise and purest Taste;
they did not sprout unclean in dirt and mire.
   If they have no aroma, we will pour fragrance,
   we will burn myrrh of sentiment before them.

                            (1989, 210)

Here we should note the exalted role of "Taste" in conceiving and imag-
ining these hybrid flowers of art; indeed, the final touch infusing them
with the artificial "myrrh of sentiment" nearly pushes the composition
into the realm of kitsch. Related to this poem is the brief stanza "Forgetfulness" (1896*)—based on verses adapted from Arthur Symons's
decadent paean "London Nights"—in which we are presented with
a hothouse variation of the flower theme: "Shut up in a green house /
under the glass cases the flowers forget / what the sun's brightness is /
and how the dewy breezes blow when they pass" (1989, 244). All these
decadent floral tropes find their poetic culmination in "For the Shop"
(1912/1913), a canonical poem that powerfully illustrates the "trope of
the secret," the dualism that queer theorists have identified as the double bind of secrecy and disclosure that has shaped the modern gay identity (Sedgwick 1990, 70):

He wrapped them carefully, smartly
in green silk that was quite pricey.

Roses of rubies, lilies of pearl,
violets of amethyst. According to his rule,

his will, they seemed beautiful, still
not as in nature or books. In the till

he'll leave them, samples of his bold and able work.
Whenever some customer enters the shop

he brings out other fine items for sale—rich things—
bracelets, chains, necklaces and rings.

(2013, 79)

Thus with this series of Parnassian flower poems, Cavafy completes his imitative apprenticeship in the innovative French tradition of flower rhetoric, which, as Knight notes, effects a revolutionary transformation of sorts in the decadent poetics of the late nineteenth century[45]—the reason perhaps why he dared to sing about them after all.

The Painting in the Poem

The prevalent influence of French culture on Cavafy was further intensified when the poet traveled to Paris and London in 1897, a trip that included visits to the Paris Salon—where Theodore Ralli, the brother of his close friend Mikes, exhibited Orientalist paintings[46]—and to the Royal Academy in London (Liddell [1974] 2000, 95–96). Upon returning to Alexandria, Cavafy would complete and publish a series of poems that are highly pictorial in their formal structure and poetic idiom.[47] In "Horace in Athens" (1893/1897) he sets forth a most striking iconographic tableau:

In the room of Leah the hetaera
where elegance, wealth, a soft bed are found,
a young man with jasmine in his hands is talking.
Many stones adorn his fingers,

and he wears a himation of white silk
with red oriental embroidery.
His language is Attic and pure,
but a slight accent in his pronunciation

betrays his Tiber and Latium origin.
The young man confesses his love
and the Athenian girl hears him in silence,
listens to Horace, her eloquent lover.

And dazzled she sees new worlds of Beauty
in the passion of the great Italian.

(1989, 206)

A sonnet most befitting the begetter of the phrase *ut pictura poesis* (as is painting, so is poetry),[48] here Cavafy presents a scene that was popular with history painters, most notably Thomas Couture (*Horace and Lydia*, 1843)—the famed painter of the sensational canvas *The Romans of the Decadence* (1847)[49]—and the English Pre-Raphaelite artist John Collier (*Horace and Lydia*, 1924)[50] (figure 4). Although painted well after Cavafy's poem, Collier's canvas replicates the scene of Cavafy's poem in a remarkable manner—serving as the picture in the poem, as it were—and illustrates how akin the poem is to a painterly rendition of the same subject. This juxtaposition of poem and painting allows us to assess some of the traditional aesthetic challenges that emerged from the age-old rivalry between the sister arts. As Wendy Steiner writes, "Just as a poem gains the immediacy of an actual object by making us think of physical objects, painting gains the lifelike property of motion by making us see bodies in action. In both cases the arts approach each other by appropriating a

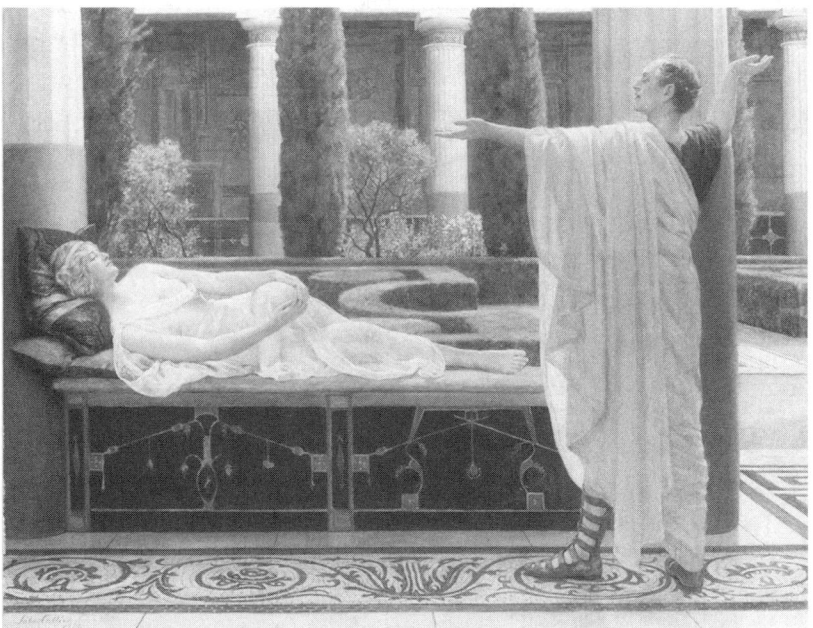

Figure 4. John Collier, *Horace and Lydia* (1924). Oil on canvas, private collection.

crucial feature from the other that it lacks—visuality in poetry, motion in painting" (1982, 12).

Cavafy is consciously manipulating the relative aesthetic qualities of poems as speaking pictures and paintings as mute poems in his own pictorial poem. The first two sentences paint a visual scene, achieving in their direct simplicity the quality of ενάργεια (*enargeia*) (vividness) so esteemed by the Greek Sophists in their art criticism.[51] The setting is a Greek room with a soft bed; Horace holds a sprig of white and green jasmine, is wearing colorful rings, and is dressed in a white toga with ornate red embroidery. The poem then shifts its visual focus to the aural subject of the beautiful rhetoric for which Horace was famous; it attempts to convey motion through its emphasis on grandiose gesture—Horace is speaking and moving with the traditional sophistic theatricality. Yet readers are left to supply the missing words for themselves, depending, that is, on their erudition and familiarity with the classical texts implied and signified by the poem. They are thus faced with the same hermeneutical challenges that they would encounter when viewing Collier's painting, which functions, in effect, as a mute iconographic rendition of Cavafy's poem.

Cavafy's speaking picture tells us that Horace's language is Attic Greek, which he pronounces with a slight accent; yet the poem refuses to supply its readers with a verbal sample of Horace's speech, allowing them instead to imagine it. (George Savidis made the apt observation that Cavafy identified with Horace on a number of levels: like Horace, Cavafy spoke Greek with a slight accent [British]; he lost his family fortunes at a young age; and he was forced to work as a public servant.)[52] The poem then shifts to the hetaera, who in her recumbent splendor is dazzled while she ponders over the future oratorical achievements of her lover. She too is silent, and we are left with juxtaposed visual images that signify a mute oration and a silent reverie. The poem could not be more pictorial in its overall aesthetic, and it exhibits the intersemiotic qualities of a transposition d'art text except that, in this case, the signified remains an unidentified or wholly imagined painting.[53]

A similar example of Cavafy's reliance on a visual image may be found in his poem "The Funeral of Sarpedon" (1892/1898 [revised 1908]),[54] which was certainly suggested by the engraving of Henri-Léopold Lévy's painting *Sarpedon* featured in the March 1892 volume of the *Attic Museum,* an Athenian journal that published Cavafy in the early 1890s (figure 5). Cavafy's poem is based on Homer's account in *The Iliad* (2.876, 5.471, 627, 6.198) but relies heavily on the baroque iconography of Lévy's painting:

> Heavy affliction has befallen Zeus:
> Sarpedon has expired, slain by Patroclus;
> and now the Achaeans with Patroclus rush
> to seize the body and to disfigure it.
>
> But Zeus will nowise suffer this to pass.
> The child well-loved of him, he has allowed
> to be destroyed,—(the Law had ruled it so),—
> but he will honour after death at least.
> And lo, he charges Phoebus to descend,
> instructed in the ways to save the body.
>
> The hero's corpse—with reverence and sorrow
> Phoebus takes up and carries to the river.
> He washes out the stains of dust and blood;
> stanches the lamentable wounds, nor leaves
> least trace thereof; then purifies the body
> with fragrances ambrosial and attires it
> in robes magnificent, Olympian.
> He smooths the face, and with a comb of pearl
> combs the luxuriance of sable hair.
> The beauteous limbs he settles and lays at peace.
>
> The lifeless warrior has the aspect now
> of a king-charioteer in lusty youth—
> aged five and twenty, say, or twenty-six —
> taking his rest when he has won the prize,
> with golden chariot and with fleetest horses,
> on some occasion of illustrious games.—
>
> Whereupon, having in such wise fulfilled
> his mission, Phoebus summoned the two brothers
> Sleep and Death, bidding them remove the body
> to Lycia, the land of affluence.

And thither, to the land of affluence,
to Lycia these journeyed—the two brothers
Sleep and Death; and when they were come, at last,
to the high gate of the king's dwelling-house,
they handed over the perfected body,
and to their other cares and works returned.

And as it was received there, at the house,
the doleful obsequies—with long processions,
with full libations out of sacred vessels,
with threnodies and all things meet—began.
And, afterward, skilled workmen from the city,
and artisans renowned for work in stone,
fashioned the funeral mound and built the stela.

(2003b, 20–21)[55]

Much like a Greek vase that depicts a narrative event in a sequenced frieze,[56] Cavafy's poem may be divided into four scenes: Phoebus snatching Sarpedon's dead body from the Achaeans; Phoebus washing and lavishly preparing the dead body; Sleep and Death transporting the body and presenting it to the king of Lycia (the engraving conflates the king of Lycia with Zeus, who receives the dead body of Sarpedon in heaven); and finally the building of a monument to the dead youth. The poem, while purely classical in content, evinces a decadent preoccupation with the death of a beautiful youth and the eternizing of his memory through a fitting monument of art, motifs that will remain prominent in Cavafy's canonical poems. More subversively, it subtly conflates the traditional apotheosis motif with the iconography of the Pietà, which it inflects with an unmistakable homoeroticism, injecting as it does an element of the profane into a heroic and sacred subject.

Other poems from this period invite similar pictorial readings that explore the dialectical tension between a mute descriptive visuality (motion or gesture) and a narrative speaking voice. "The Horses of Achilles" (1896/1897), a companion poem to "The Funeral of Sarpedon," involves a double scenario: a description of Achilles's horses Xanthos and Balios, who stomp and mourn the dead Patroklos, and then a shift to the

Figure 5. Henri-Léopold Lévy, *Sarpedon* (1892). *Attic Museum* engraved illustration.

speaking voice of Zeus, who comments on the significance of the horses'
actions:

> When they saw Patroklos dead
> —so brave and strong, so young—

the horses of Achilles began to weep;
their immortal nature was upset deeply
by this work of death they had to look at.
They reared their heads, tossed their long manes,
beat the ground with their hooves, and mourned
Patroklos, seeing him lifeless, destroyed,
now mere flesh only, his spirit gone,
defenseless, without breath,
turned back from life to the great Nothingness.

Zeus saw the tears of those immortal horses and felt sorry.
"At the wedding of Peleus," he said,
"I should not have acted so thoughtlessly.
Better if we hadn't given you as a gift,
my unhappy horses. What business did you have down there,
among pathetic human beings, the toys of fate.
You are free of death, you will not get old,
yet ephemeral disasters torment you.
Men have caught you up in their misery."
But it was for the eternal disaster of death
that those two gallant horses shed their tears.

                                        (1992, 5)

This visual majesty of the horses summoned in the first stanza evokes similar portrayals of the subject by painters both ancient and modern (Henri
Regnault's famous canvas *Automedon with the Horses of Achilles* [1868]
comes readily to mind). The poem, which paraphrases the text of *The Iliad*
(book 17), is set at the dramatic moment just prior to Zeus's "breathing
fresh fire" into the horses so that they might regain their composure and
return Achilles's chariot driver Automedon to safety. The dramatic inci-
dent captured by the poem is the raging and thrashing of the mournful
horses. The horses know that Patroklos's death presages the dire fate of
their master, but their behavior is explained by Zeus as having to do with
the misery of humanity and ephemeral disasters. The speaker of the poem,
however, qualifies both the visual and the aural content of the poem with
the closing lines, which offer a somewhat more weighty interpretation:
they are lamenting not the strife of war but, more profoundly, the disaster
of death itself (this anticipates a scene later in the epic when Balios, given
the ability to speak by Hera, alerts Achilles about his impending death).

Cavafy masterfully channels the grandiose aesthetic of history painting when composing his own "problem picture,"[57] the enigmatic "Waiting for the Barbarians" (1898/1904):

What are we waiting for, assembled in the forum?

    The barbarians are due here today.

Why isn't anything happening in the senate?
Why do the senators sit there without legislating?

    Because the barbarians are coming today.
    What laws can the senators make now?
    Once the barbarians are here, they'll do the legislating.

Why did our emperor get up so early,
and why is he sitting at the city's main gate
on his throne, in state, wearing the crown?

    Because the barbarians are coming today
    And the emperor is waiting to receive their leader.
    He has even prepared a scroll to give him,
    replete with titles, with imposing names.

Why have our two consuls and praetors come out today
wearing their embroidered, their scarlet togas?
Why have they put on bracelets with so many amethysts,
and rings sparkling with magnificent emeralds?
Why are they carrying elegant canes
beautifully worked in silver and gold?

    Because the barbarians are coming today
    and things like that dazzle the barbarians.

Why don't our distinguished orators come forward as usual
to make their speeches, say what they have to say?

    Because the barbarians are coming today
    and they're bored by rhetoric and public speaking.

Why this sudden restlessness, this confusion?
(How serious people's faces have become.)
Why are the streets and squares emptying so rapidly,
everyone going home so lost in thought?

    Because night has fallen and the barbarians have not come.
    And some who have just returned from the border say
    there are no barbarians any longer.

And now, what's going to happen to us without barbarians?
They were, those people, a kind of solution.

(1992, 18–19)

The chief poetic analogue for this poem is Paul Verlaine's sonnet "Langueur,"[58] which, since its appearance in *Le Chat Noir* in 1883, has been regarded as "the departure point of the decadent movement in poetry" (Stephan 1974, 42). Conceptually, the implied image and anticipated but perpetually delayed event of the poem is the onslaught of the barbarians, a scenario that evokes the iconography of the so-called great-invasions paintings, a subgenre of nineteenth-century history painting.[59] The invasion is the implied visual signified of the poem, the matching pictorial diptych to the scene actually depicted. Thus the dramatic tension and acute urgency of the deferred invasion become more striking since the interruption prevents us from proceeding toward the inexorable historical progression demanded by the dramatic premise of the poem: Attila's impending advance on Rome (figure 6). The daunting pause invites

Figure 6. Eugène Delacroix, *Attila and His Barbarians Overrunning Italy and the Arts,* (1847). Hemicycle of the Library, Palais Bourbon, Paris.

us to pose numerous questions about the nature of civilization and barbarism as we linger in the imaginative hiatus of the poem's suspended moment.

Cavafy's poem functions as a vast canvas on which various clusters of events are dramatically depicted—much like the *grandes machines* of the French salons with which Cavafy is, visually speaking, in creative dialogue.[60] The poem's monumental canvas includes a large number of figures engaged in a complex narrative; in this sense, the rhetorical questions asked by the two voices of the poem function as a hermeneutical interrogation of sorts, their questions analogous to those which viewers would pose before a painting as they attempted to scrutinize its meaning. Cavafy sets the stage with civilized people shown waiting in the forum; he then proceeds to a depiction of the emperor sitting at the city's gate; next he shows us consuls and praetors elaborately dressed. The curious absence of orators is noted, a silence that calls attention to the theme of muted rhetoric. Here once again Cavafy is conflating the aesthetic qualities of paintings as mute poems and poems as speaking pictures—in effect imbuing his highly pictorial poem with the intrinsic silence of painting. The rest of the poetic canvas is filled in by the restlessness and confusion of the crowds as they empty the streets and squares. The final verses add the only noniconic element to the poem—the arrival of night, which poses the problematic question of what will happen without the barbarians.

Cavafy's poem has been scrutinized from many angles and remains one of his most acclaimed compositions.[61] The received decadent interpretation of the poem summons fantasies of cultural annihilation—the only possible solution to the decadent dilemma.[62] When read in light of more recent historical theories regarding the reciprocal osmosis that existed between Rome and its barbarian conquerors, the poem problematizes Europe's suppressed barbarian heritage and critiques the received cultural elitism that rejected the necessary paradox of the barbarian contribution to the renewal and reinvigoration of the European identity. (Equally suppressed is the tableau of the barbarian invasion, which would balance out the poem's lopsided canvas.) Indeed, Romanitas—the dream of Rome—haunted the barbarian imagination, an ironic fact that led to the inverse perpetuation of the Greco-Roman legacy through the Romanization (and subsequent Christianization) of the Germanic conquerors of Europe.[63] Such a reading of the poem necessitates a barbarian imaginary—the accompanying iconography of the barbarian invasion that completes the poem's iconic incompleteness—and teases the reader into a visual dialogue and cultural dilemma that can be resolved only with the arrival of the barbarians. In short, the poem both suppresses and conjures up the pictorial tradition of the great invasion by reminding the reader of the perverse realization that the arrival of the barbarians assured Europe of its cultural perpetuity. This was an indisputable fact that Cavafy's acute historical sensibility could not deny, aligning him more with recent theories of late antiquity's "transformation" than with notions of decline and fall.[64]

The final poem from this period that invites an overtly transpositional pictorial reading is "Prayer" (1896/1898) which, as George Savidis opined, was likely inspired by one of Theodore Ralli's many Orientalist paintings that featured women in various devout poses of supplication (figure 7).[65]

> The sea took a sailor down to her depths.—
> His mother, unaware, goes and lights
>
> a tall candle before the Virgin Mother
> for his quick return and for good weather—
>
> and ever towards the wind she cocks her ear.
> But while she pleads and says her prayer,
>
> the icon listens, sad and solemn,
> knows the son she awaits will never come.
> (2013, 35)

The oracular silence of the icon that knows that the youth has died evinces occult and theurgic properties that reflect Cavafy's acknowledgment of the mystical traditions of Byzantine Orthodoxy.[66] In his essay "The Poetry of Mr. Stratigis" (1893), Cavafy comments favorably on a poem titled "At the Iconostasis," in which he notes the "meditative and mystical devotion which the Greek people harbor for the Mother of Christ—an emotion that causes them to approach her sacred icon as a great symbol of consolation."[67] Cavafy's poem expresses this same reverence and documents the centrality of the painted image in the everyday life of the Greek people; it also foregrounds the sublime intersection between icon and prayer, image and word, and painting and poetry—a central facet of modern Hellenism to which he pays humble tribute in a manner at once religious and personal. Indeed, the worshipful stance of the viewer before the painted

Figure 7. Theodore Ralli, *The Supplication.* Used with permission of the
Theodoros Rallis Bequest, National Gallery—Alexandros Soutzos Museum inv. 486,
Athens. Photograph by Stavros Psiroukis.

image serves as a paradigm of the interpretative position of the reader before the poem; this aesthetic stance—or rather this transpositional posi-
tionality from which Cavafy wrote so many of his early poems—invites a
similar hermeneutical entreaty on the part of the reader.

Cavafy will continue to employ this pictorial mode selectively throughout the rest of his career, never fully renouncing his Parnassian predilection for the fine arts and the transposition d'art tradition. This is surely one
of the reasons why so many painters have been drawn to his work. Three
renowned Greek painters from the second half of the twentieth century
whose popular works have become visually synonymous with modern
Hellenism—Nikos Hadzikyriakos-Ghikas (1906–94), Yannis Tsarouchis
(1910–89), and Alekos Fassianos (1930–)—have created what are among
the most striking painterly interpretations of Cavafy poems. Ghikas's
sketches illustrate a 1966 Ikaros edition of the Cavafy canon. His interpretation of "Waiting for the Barbarians" emphasizes the staged theatricality
of the poem and the visual centrality of Rome as its iconic setting. Tsarouchis's interpretation of "Lovely White Flowers" (1929) (figure 8) presents
the sad narrative of a young love affair cut short: "He laid flowers on his
cheap coffin, / lovely white flowers, very much in keeping / with his beauty,
his twenty-two years" (Cavafy 1992, 166). The surviving lover is presented
as a winged eros, and the funereal moment is charged with the erotic sadness that distinguishes Cavafy's poems about bereft young lovers.[68]

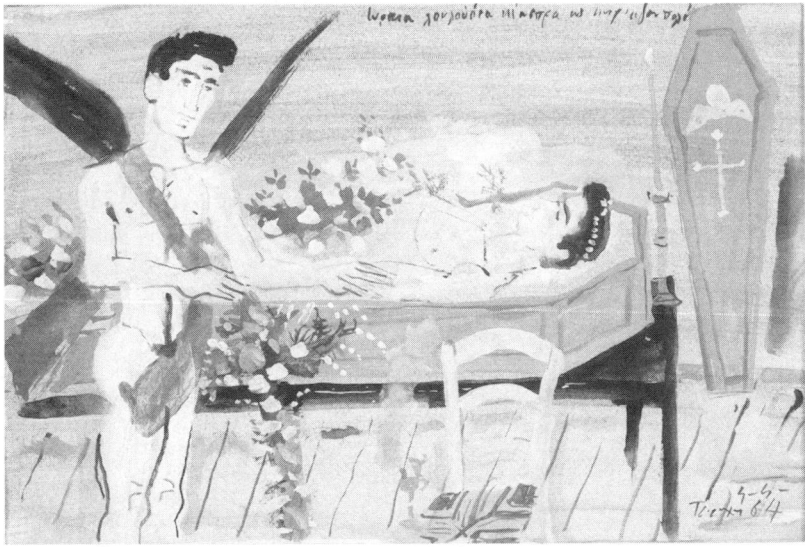

Figure 8. Yannis Tsarouchis, *Lovely White Flowers, So Very Becoming* (1964).
Gouache on paper. © Yannis Tsarouchis Foundation.

Alekos Fassianos's rendition of "The City" (figure 9) portrays a youth in profile looking out a window at the city that will follow him. The view of the city is interestingly framed and appears more like a painting within a painting than a view from a window, drawing attention to the

Figure 9. Alekos Fassianos, *The City*. Acrylic on paper. Used with permission from the artist.

Figure 10. David Hockney, *Kaisarion with All His Beauty* (1961). Etching in two colors (22 ¼ × 15 ¾″). © David Hockney, Inc. Photo Credit: Richard Schmidt.

claustrophobic predicament of the dissolute youth: "As you've wasted your life here, in this small corner, / you've destroyed it everywhere else in the world" (Cavafy1992, 28). Fassianos's bold visualization of "The City" adds a self-reflexive touch by foregrounding the decadent sense of entrapment— an inverse flânerie as it were, whereby the city stalks the person—thus calling attention to the inability of the urban persona to break free from artifice and urbanity.

A similar aesthetic informs David Hockney's abstract interpretation of "Alexandrian Kings," *Kaisarion with All His Beauty* (figure 10), which features the doomed prince in a highly staged moment of artificial glory.[69] Hockney pays ironic tribute to the poem's pictorial spectacle by including the processing crowds (albeit in highly stylized form) in the lower left of the etching. The ambiguous figure of Kaisarion stands on what appears to be the head of either a soldier or a slave and is flanked by the unmistakable face of his mother, Cleopatra.[70] When the etching is viewed in tandem with the poem, the overall aesthetic effect is one of deliberate dissonance, a postmodern anticlassicism replete with Hockney's graffiti-like text, which functions ironically as a Greek epigram identifying the subject of the work. Hockney's interpretation of one of Cavafy's most visually stunning painterly poems offers an apt illustration of how his readers are continually invited to discover the picture within the poem. It bears witness to the extraordinary pictorial quality of so many of Cavafy's compositions and to his profound indebtedness to the post-Parnassian legacy of transposition d'art poetics.

4

Paterian Decadence

Hellenism, Hedonism, and the Matter of Rome

Cavafy's poetical fixation on periods of decline has been commented on rather routinely, and it remains a commonplace of Cavafy criticism to note the poet's interest in the waning power of the Hellenistic monarchies and their political eclipse by an increasingly powerful and corrupt Rome.[1] Most critics concur that Cavafy found this historical period rich in terms of dramatic possibilities as well as highly suggestive for the ironic commentaries these scenarios allowed him to make on both the past and present. The nexus of decadent themes that runs through Cavafy's historicizing poetry calls for a more systematic analysis beyond the established and predictable textual connections made between the poems and the primary and secondary historical sources that chronicle decadent phases of history. While Cavafy's meticulous use of historical sources is certainly central to appreciating his poetic project, his literary debt to the nineteenth-century decadent writer who effectively "elevated historiography to an art form"—Walter Pater—has been largely overlooked.[2] That Pater exerted a quickening influence on Cavafy should come as no surprise; Pater remained the

Victorian aesthete par excellence who generated some of the most significant critical writing not only on Hellenism and Roman decadence but also
on the interartistic dependency of painting and poetry. Augmenting these
topics is Pater's pioneering formulation of a distinct homoerotic aesthetic
that, as I hope to show, paved the way for Cavafy and invited the poet to
draw heavily on many Paterian motifs and conceits when fashioning his
own historicizing imaginary portraits.

Pater has recently undergone a gradual critical reappraisal following
his virtual demotion by modernists bent on distancing themselves from
his controversial but indisputable position as one of the great aesthetic critics and prose writers of the late nineteenth century.[3] Gerald Monsman,
who has done much to rehabilitate Pater's reputation, reminds us that
"by 1894, Pater stood pre-eminent among the living English critics of the
day—Matthew Arnold, the great critical voice of the century, had died
in 1888 and John Ruskin had long since sunk into despair and insanity"
(1977, 157). Harold Bloom furthers this appraisal of Pater's distinct Victorian achievement, which was "to empty [in conjunction with Swinburne
and the Pre-Raphaelites] Ruskin's aestheticism of its moral bias and so to
purify a critical stance appropriate for the apprehension of Romantic art"
(1985, 21).[4] Patricia Clements extends this trajectory by arguing that "Pater
is an essential base for modernism in English literature: he was, as Yeats
wrote, of 'revolutionary importance'" (1985, 138). And Richard Dellamora
has elucidated Pater's foundational role in the discourse of gay studies that
emerged from Oxford Hellenism and Victorian aestheticism. Thus it follows as a matter of course that Cavafy would have been drawn to Pater in
the nineties when he was seeking to discover his poetic voice, explore his
sexual identity, and launch his literary career.

Within the array of aesthetic influences on Cavafy that have been considered thus far, Pater occupies a unique position as an aesthetic theorist
who brought the tradition of pictorial poetics to his sui generis impressionist historicism.[5] Indeed, Pater's writings established the generic precedent
of the historicizing imaginary portrait[6] that Cavafy replicates in his mature
poems, a genre that features imaginary figures set in historical contexts
much like those found in the dramatic monologues of Robert Browning
and Dante Gabriel Rossetti (Brake 1994b, 26). Before analyzing Cavafy's
poems in light of Pater's writings, a brief excursus on Pater's oeuvre and its
relevance to the decadent movement is in order, followed by a reading of

select poems that exemplify Cavafy's use of Paterian motifs and decadent themes.[7]

Paterian Decadence: Burning with the Hard Gem-Like Flame

Pater's infamous concluding lines to *The Renaissance: Studies in Art and Poetry* (1873, 1877, 1888, 1893) created such a stir when they first appeared in 1873 that they had to be omitted from the book's second printing in 1877.[8] They still remain central to any discussion of decadence in the nineteenth century, possessing as they do an unmistakable allure and singular relevance:

> It is with this movement, with the passage and dissolution of impressions, images, sensations, that analysis leaves off—that continual vanishing away, that strange, perpetual weaving and unweaving of ourselves. . . . To burn always with this hard, gem-like flame, to maintain this ecstasy, is success in life. . . . Great passions may give us this quickened sense of life, ecstasy and sorrow of love, the various forms of enthusiastic activity, disinterested or otherwise, which come naturally to many of us. Only be sure it is passion—that it does yield you this fruit of a quickened, multiplied consciousness. Of such wisdom, the poetic passion, the desire of beauty, the love of art for its own sake, has most. For art comes to you proposing frankly to give nothing but the highest quality to your moments as they pass, and simply for those moments' sake. (Pater 1980, 188–190)

In an earlier version of the essay, in which Pater critiques the poetry of William Morris ("Aesthetic Poetry" [1868/1889]), he articulates what in hindsight we could readily term an equally Cavafian formula: "One characteristic of the pagan spirit the aesthetic poetry has, which is on its surface—the continual suggestion, pensive or passionate, of the shortness of life. This is contrasted with the bloom of the world, and gives new seduction to it—*the sense of death and the desire of beauty: the desire of beauty quickened by the sense of death*" (1986, 528, emphasis added).[9] Cavafy was no doubt familiar with these essays, which function rather proleptically as aesthetic glosses for much of his own poetry. One need look no further than Cavafy's "Ithaca" for a similar impressionist emphasis on experiencing pleasure for pleasure's sake, the promise of nothing other than the present experience of the journey with its precious and intense moments.[10] Similarly, the "desire of beauty quickened by the sense of death" is a formula that animates several Cavafy poems that prominently feature this distinctive "funereal eroticism," as Ellis Hanson (1997, 185) terms it; these include particularly the so-called tomb poems, in which we encounter this very dialectic between beauty and death. Take, for instance, "The Tomb of Iases" (1917):

> Here I, Iases, lie. All over this great city
> the youth most famous for his beauty.
> The very wise marveled at me, as did the ordinary
> common people. And I enjoyed both equally.
>
> But from the people's taking me for a Narcissus or a Hermes so much,
> the excesses beat me down, killed me. Passerby,
> if you're an Alexandrian, you will not scold. You know
> how fast and furious our life is, how hot it is, pleasure's fullest pitch.
>
> (2013, 108)

Although set in Alexandria, the poem replicates a quintessential Paterian motif: the handsome urbane youth literally exhausted by Hellenic sensuality after experiencing the greatest amount of pleasurable sensations as per Pater's aesthetic dictum.[11] This is even more apparent in "Passing Through" (1914/1917), although here the setting remains historically indeterminate:

> The things he timidly imagined as a schoolboy
> are openly revealed to him now. And he wanders around,
> stays out all night, gets involved. And as is right (for our kind of art)
> his blood—fresh and hot—
> is relished by sensual pleasure. His body is overcome
> by forbidden erotic ecstasy; and his young limbs
> give in to it completely.
>   In this way a simple boy
> becomes something worth our looking at, for a moment
> he too passes through the exalted World of Poetry,
> the young sensualist with blood fresh and hot.
>
> (1992, 70)

The phrase "our kind of art" and notion of an "exalted World of Poetry" signals a coterie of sensual artists, and the forbidden experience betrays a Paterian initiation into a quickened state of ecstasy. Similarly in the "Tomb of Evrion" (1912/1914), the combination of erudition, male beauty, and death creates the quintessential Paterian-Cavafian effect, which culminates in the homoerotic beatific vision:

> In this tomb—ornately designed,
> the whole of syenite stone,
> covered by so many violets, so many lilies—
> lies handsome Evrion,
> an Alexandrian, twenty-five years old.
> On his father's side, he was of old Macedonian stock,
> on his mother's side, descended from a line of magistrates.
> He studied philosophy with Aristokleitos,
> rhetoric with Paros, and at Thebes
> the sacred scriptures. He wrote a history
> of the province of Arsinoites. That at least will survive.
> But we've lost what was really precious: his form—
> like a vision of Apollo.
>
> (1992, 50)

All three poems clearly partake of Pater's decadent aesthetic, whereby the forces of Greek hedonism (Iasis), classical paideia (Evrion), and sensual sophistication ("Passing Through") exercise a seductive, fatal, and corrupting power over those who indulge in them. In *Marius the Epicurean* specifically, Pater dramatizes this piquant combination, at once presenting the historic allure of Hellenism and foregrounding the acute susceptibility of Roman Philhellenes to Greek culture both as vaunted *paideia* (Greek learning) and as sublimated sensuality.[12] But it is the short story "Emerald Uthwart" (1892) that supplied Cavafy with a direct source for inspiration when composing his tomb poems.

The story—one of Pater's imaginary portraits—involves two young English cadets who form a platonic but intense friendship ending in the death of both following a military mishap for which they are unfairly court-martialed. The protagonist, Uthwart, possesses an ideal Greek beauty, and the story commences with a nekrotaphic mise-en-scène in which the narrator reflects on the beguiling nature of epitaphs: "We smile at epitaphs—at those recent enough to be read easily. . . . Their very simplicity, of course, may set one's thoughts in motion to fill up the scanty tale, and those of the young at least are almost always worth while" (Pater 1986, 343). The narrator then proceeds to Uthwart's actual grave site in a British cemetery: "In a very different neighborhood, here at home, in a remote Sussex churchyard, you may read that Emerald Uthwart was born on such a day 'at Chase Lodge, in this parish; and died there,' on a day in the year 18—, aged twenty-six" (344).[13] We next learn the story of the young man's life, including his exceptional Greek paideia:[14]

> A rather sensuous boy! you may suppose, amid the wholesome, natural self-indulgence of a very English home. . . . In fact, by one of our wise English compromises, we still teach our so modern boys the Classics. . . . He felt it, felt the intellectual passion, like the pressure outward of wings within him—η πτερού δύναμις, says Plato, in the *Phaedrus*; but again, as some do with everyday love, withheld, restrained himself. . . . "Young Apollo!" people say—people who have pigeon-holes for their impressions, watching the slim, trim figure with the exercise books. His very dress seems touched with Hellenic fitness to the healthy youthful form. "Golden-haired, scholar Apollo!" they repeat, foolishly, ignorantly. He was better; was more like a real portrait of a real young Greek, like *Tryphon, Son of Eutychos*, for instance (as friends remembered him with regret, as you may see him still on his tombstone in the British Museum) alive among the paler physical and intellectual lights of modern England, under the old monastic stonework of the Middle Age. (345–357)

There can be no mistaking the duplication of the phrases "youthful form" and "scholar Apollo" in "The Tomb of Evrion." Indeed, Pater's term "sensuous boy" serves as a coded homoerotic point of departure for virtually all of Cavafy's tomb poems.

"Emerald Uthwart" concludes with the surgeon's postmortem description of the dead youth's immobile beauty, which offers a daring contemplation of male beauty that effectively transforms Uthwart into a work of Greek sculpture:[15] "Deceased was in his twenty-seventh year, but looked many years younger; had indeed scarcely yet reached the full condition of manhood. The extreme purity of the outlines, both of the face and limbs, was such as is usually found only in quite early youth. . . . The flowers were then hastily replaced, the hands and the peak of the handsome nose remaining visible among them; the wind ruffled the fair hair a little; the lips were still red. I shall not forget it" (371–372). Nor, would it seem, did Cavafy, who introduced this very elegiac eroticism into his tomb poems. We encounter a reprisal of the much beloved dead youth and grave visit and epitaph-reading motif of Lefkios in "In the Month of Athyr" (1917):

> With difficulty I read   this ancient stone.
> "L[OR]D JESUS CHRIST."   I can decipher a "SO[U]L."
> "IN THE MON[TH] OF ATHYR"   "LEFKIO[S] FELL ASLEEP."
> At the mention of years,   "HE LI[VE]D TO THE AGE OF,"
> the Kappa Zeta reveals   he was young when he fell asleep,
> On a worn away part I can see   "HI[M] . . . ALEXANDRIAN."
> There follow three lines   that are extremely mutilated,
> but I can make out a few words— like "OUR T[EAR]S," "GRIEF,"
> then "TEARS" again,   and "MOURNED B[Y] HIS [F]RIENDS."
> It seems to me Lefkios   was deeply loved.
> In the month of Athyr   Lefkios fell asleep.
>
> (2013, 109)

This singular conflation of tomb, epitaph, and Christian mourning betrays the heavy influence of Pater. Thus we may presume that Cavafy would have been fully receptive to Pater's writings, which were revolutionary for their time and brought the aesthetic sensibility and art-for-art's-sake credo to new heights. As Matthew Beaumont notes, Pater's tome had an incendiary effect on its initial readers: "It was as if the book had on its publication instantaneously constituted a secret society of readers for whom 'the human body in its beauty,' specifically the male human body, 'as the highest potency of all the beauty of material objects,' enshrined the deepest spiritual truths" (2010, ix). As early as his 1864 lecture "Diaphaneitè," Pater sought to imbue art criticism with a homoerotic sensibility by defining the "diaphanous type" of aesthetic artist-critic:[16] "Over and over again the world has been surprised by the heroism, the insight, the passion, of this clear crystal nature. Poetry and poetical history have dreamed of a crisis, where it must needs be that some human victim be sent down into the grave" (Pater 2010, 139). It should be noted that the word *diaphaneitè* constituted a "homosexual code" of sorts (Donoghue 1995, 112), inaugurating a strain of thought in Pater's mature writing that critics today appreciate as expressing a "queer subjectivity." As Michael Davis aptly notes, "The primary goal of Pater's work was not just to represent the homosexual subject as he understood it but also to conceptualize the homosexual subject and, more importantly, to theorize the 'subject' of same-sex desire as a field and mode of inquiry" (2002, 262). One could certainly include Cavafy among those Paterian initiates who would have picked up on this coded use of Hellenism and art criticism, avid reader of nineteenth-century British periodicals that he was.[17]

In addition to the pronounced aesthetic influence of *The Renaissance* and the stories from *Imaginary Portraits* (1887/1890) on Cavafy's creative thinking, other Paterian texts resonate significantly in the poet's work as well, particularly the novel *Marius the Epicurean* (1885/1892) and the essays from *Appreciations* (1889/1890). As Pater was exceedingly interested in the fine arts, his writings are distinguished by an acute painterly sensibility, one that derived from the discourse of art criticism, which, in Pater's case, reached its fullest realization in the essays collected in *The Renaissance*. (In fact, *Marius* was criticized by David Cecil for being too static in this regard: "The impression left in the memory by Marius . . . is that of tableaux, in which in front of an elaborate and beautifully painted background are posed figures beautifully and elaborately clothed, but who are faceless, speechless and incapable of motion" [quoted in Iser 1987, 129].) As Elizabeth Prettejohn (1999) has convincingly shown, during the late nineteenth century, aesthetic writings and artwork overlapped in deliberate and significant ways. Pater's essays in particular, she notes, "are marked by innumerable intertextual links with paintings of the same period. . . . The practice of intertextual reference constitutes a defining feature of the Aesthetic work of art" (37). This was a new type of writing that "originated in an interplay of the sister arts, literature and painting, and so reflected a characteristic late nineteenth-century concern with artistic hybridization" (Bizzotto 2002, 214). Pater's contribution to this tradition augments the pictorial influences of other writers, art critics, and painters whose work shaped Cavafy's poetics, as has been explored in previous chapters. The impressionist lyricism that suffuses Pater's art criticism introduced an even more rhapsodizing dimension to the genre, one that famously led Yeats to identify Pater's passage on *La Giaconda* as the first modern poem and to include it printed as vers libre in his 1936 edition of the *Oxford Book of Modern Verse 1892–1935.*

In chapter 2 I suggested possible reasons why Cavafy opted out of pursuing a career as a prose writer, deliberately forgoing a Paterian path as an accomplished stylist and euphuist. From his ardent reading of British periodicals, Cavafy would not only have been fully conversant with Pater's work and reputation but would likely have found himself intimidated by the Victorian "prosateur's" stylistic achievement. This anxiety of influence might have led him to conceal his debt to Pater—much as Pater suppressed his debt to Baudelaire.[18] Pater's fetishization of Hellenism and bold celebration of the homoerotic element in Greek art alone would certainly have drawn Cavafy to his work. In addition, there was Pater's seductive style, in particular his erudite treatment of English as a classical dialect (Dowling 1986, xv)—as a dead language in fact—which would have provided Cavafy with a ready aesthetic prototype for emulation. Philologically (and psychologically), Pater's decadent approach to language as a system confronting its own linguistic decay would have resonated powerfully with Cavafy's particular linguistic predicament as an aesthetic writer bound to an artificial and erudite idiom—the Greek katharevousa. As Linda Dowling writes, decadence "emerged from a linguistic crisis, a crisis in Victorian attitudes brought about by the new comparative philology earlier imported from the Continent. For it was the new linguistic science . . . that raised a specter of autonomous language—language as a system blindly obeying impersonal phonological rules in isolation from any world of human values and experience—that was to eat corrosively away at the hidden foundations of a high Victorian ideal of civilization" (1986, xi-xii). Pater's almost Byzantine emphasis on extreme erudition—the "collapse from narrative into scholarly discourse" (Reed 1985, 65)— an element associated with decadence (Dowling 1986, 150), parallels a similar pedantic emphasis on learnedness featured by the Greek Phanariot writers of the nineteenth century, the Constantinopolitan Greek prose tradition out of which Cavafy was working.[19]

Pater also set an important example regarding the publishing and collection of his aesthetic essays; he published the essays that were later collected as *Greek Studies* in mainstream periodicals and thus moved the subject of Hellenism out of the academy and into the public sphere (Brake 2000, 138). Pater was featured in the pages of the *Fortnightly Review* in the late 1880s—his essay "Style" appeared in 1888, "Giordano Bruno" in 1889, and "Prosper Mérimée" in 1890. This journalistic precedent offered

Cavafy a ready prototype of the journalist as aesthete-scholar rather than the more common model of journalist as dilettante. But more important, Pater's book *Appreciations,* a collection of various essays including three on Shakespeare's plays, was published in November 1889, with a second edition appearing in May 1890.[20] The timing of this text's publication is significant and points to evidence of carefully concealed Paterian influences in Cavafy's essay "Shakespeare on Life" (1891), which is an "appreciation" (in the Paterian sense) of *Measure for Measure* that relies quite heavily on Pater's essay "Measure for Measure" (*Appreciations*). The opening line of Cavafy's essay immediately betrays its provenance:

> I esteem the observations of great men more than I do their conclusions. Minds possessed of genius observe with exactitude and assurance; indeed, when they outline the pros and cons of a matter for us, we are able to draw conclusions for ourselves. But why shouldn't they, you will ask me? Simply because I do not have much confidence in the absolute worth of a conclusion. From any given observations I formulate one judgment and someone else another; and it is possible for both to be at once mistaken and correct as regards each person because these observations have been determined by our unique circumstances and idiosyncrasies or happen to conform to them. (2010, 27)

Pater's essay, although much lengthier than Cavafy's, contains the seed of Cavafy's main motif: the notion of observation:

> [A]nd as the poetry of this play is full of the peculiarities of Shakespeare's poetry, so in its ethics it is an epitome of Shakespeare's moral judgments. They are the moral judgments of an observer, of one who sits as a spectator, and knows how the threads in the design before him hold together under the surface: they are the judgments of the humourist also, who follows with a half-amused but always pitiful sympathy, the various ways of human disposition, and sees less distance than ordinary men between what are called respectively great and little things. (Pater 1986, 505)

Here the resonance between ideas and words is unmistakable. Cavafy's concluding line criticizing excessive dogmatism is a curious addendum but one not unrelated to the legacy of decadent analogues: he is echoing Edgar Allan Poe's censure of the heresy of didacticism (and here we should note the curious line of quasi-plagiaristic borrowings that link Cavafy to Pater, Pater to Baudelaire, and Baudelaire to Poe).[21]

In addition to borrowing the theme of Shakespeare as a "keen observer," Cavafy follows Pater's cue in his choice of the passages that he analyzes and translates. Pater narrows his focus on the relationship between the brother and sister Claudio and Isabella, specifically act 3, scene 1, precisely the place where Cavafy begins his translation of and commentary on Shakespeare's text. Moreover, Pater frames his discussion on the consideration of Claudio's love of life, fear of death, and terror at the unknown, themes that Cavafy echoes almost verbatim.[22] Cavafy's focus on the topic of vanity as the play's overarching theme is indeed curious (there is only one line in *Measure for Measure* directly dealing with vanity, uttered by Duke Vincentio: "O heaven, the vanity of wretched fools!" [5.1. 164]).[23] After this thematic analysis of the theme of vanity, Cavafy concludes the essay with a passage from Lucian's "Dialogues of the Dead."[24] Although these references do not appear in Pater's Shakespeare essay per se, the inclusion of both the topic of vanity and the persona of Lucian here clearly derives from Paterian precedents. In *Marius the Epicurean* (book 2, chapter 12), Emperor Marcus Aurelius harangues the Roman Senate at length on the topic of vanity, offering a protracted philosophical oration on the subject.[25] And in the final pages of the novel, Marius writes down his thoughts on the subject in his concluding journal entry just prior to his untimely death.[26] Thus vanity functions as a pronounced leitmotif in the novel. Augmenting this thematic link to Pater is Cavafy's inclusion of a passage from Lucian that also betrays a distinct Paterian provenance. Indeed, Lucian actually figures as a character in *Marius*, and Pater presents two extensive excerpts from Lucian's writings in his narrative: a section from "The Halcyon" is read during the decadent banquet in chapter 20, and an extensive dialogue is exchanged between Lucian and the youth Hermotimus in chapter 24 (an abbreviated transposition of Lucian's dialogue "Hermotimus").[27] It appears, then, that Cavafy deftly conflated his Paterian sources when composing his Shakespeare essay, concealing them carefully, unlike his explicit acknowledgment of James Russell Lowell's critical work in his later essay "Traces of Greek Thought in Shakespeare" (1893).[28] One may assuredly conclude that Cavafy was reading Pater quite diligently during the early 1890s and was highly influenced both by the content of Pater's writings and by his aesthetic sensibility.

Victorian Aesthetic Historicism

While Pater's hedonistic notion of life experienced intensely for the "moments' sake" features prominently enough in Cavafy's work, it is undoubtedly Pater's aesthetic treatment of history to which Cavafy is exceedingly indebted. Pater practiced a unique brand of aesthetic historicism by treating history as a fine art, as is particularly evident in his historical novel *Marius the Epicurean*. As Carolyn Williams argues in her book-length study on the very subject of Pater's historicism, "both Marius and his second-century context are staged against the second-order background of the narrator in the late nineteenth century. The position of the narrator then, becomes that retrospective, metafigural place of recontainment, the position from which the historical figure against its background is transfigured, recontextualized, thrown into relief against another ground, to become the composite figure of aesthetic historicism" (1989, 171). Cavafy employs this same technique of aesthetic recontexualization in many of his poems, as will be seen in due course. Closely related to this is Pater's precedent of the historicizing imaginary portrait that Cavafy also replicates frequently. Like Pater, Cavafy often chooses a fictitious or unremembered character (Lefkios, Imenos, Aristovoulos, Ignatius, Myrtias, Temethos, Kleitos, Myris, Kaisarion, and Dimaratos, among others) who functions as a diaphanous vessel "transparent to his culture, the medium through which pass the voices of his age" (Williams 1989, 183). These aesthetic modalities are worked by both novelist and poet to create what are in effect historicizing reveries.

Pater's *Marius* was, from its very inception, considered something of a bible of decadence; by foregrounding the topos of the fatal "golden book,"[29] Pater self-consciously positioned his own text in this very tradition, even though he ostensibly intended *Marius* to function as a corrective of sorts to *The Renaissance* and its alleged corrupting influence on young male readers.[30] Set in second-century Rome under the reign of the Hellenophile philosopher emperor Marcus Aurelius and written in a highly mannered style characterized by an arabesque flow of euphuistic sentences (a deliberate imitation of Heraclitean flux), the novel chronicles the adventures of the Hellenized Roman Marius as he samples various philosophies—Epicureanism, Stoicism, and Christianity—adventures that include entering into highly emotional but ultimately chaste relationships with two men: the decadent and corrupt pagan Flavian and the noble and chivalric Christian Cornelius. With this elaborate plot, Pater deliberately sought to manipulate the Victorian genre of the historical conversion romance, inflecting it with a distinctive homoerotic dimension. Examples of such period pieces that featured the early church in transition include Charles Kingsley's *Hypatia*, Nicholas Wiserman's *Fabiola,* Cardinal Henry Newman's *Callista*, Edward George Bulwer-Lytton's *The Last Days of Pompeii*, and Lew Wallace's *Ben-Hur*, where an emerging Christianity is juxtaposed and contrasted with older and established schools of pagan thought and practice. Cavafy picks up the thread of this conversion romance tradition with his frequent foregrounding of the binary opposition between pagan and Christian culture; he dramatizes not only the internal struggles of young men dabbling with pagan and Christian religious creeds but also the doomed romance of sometime lovers caught between clashing cultural, political, and religious movements. It should be noted that there was an expanding ideological context for this sort of historicizing conversion writing that expressed Victorian crisis anxieties about the health of the empire and the decline of British culture. As Maureen Moran writes, "In the latter half of the nineteenth century, conversions along with other emotional religious experiences like mystical sensations are analyzed in terms of hysteria, and attributed to trauma, nervous illness, or sexual panic. . . . Homophobia and anti-Catholicism combine in popular and high culture representations of 'the other side' and those who convert to it" (2002, 172).[31] Cavafy, it appears, was working out of an established Victorian genre featuring dramatically staged historical tableaux to which Pater had significantly contributed by infusing an unmistakable homoeroticism.

Simon Goldhill (2011, 156) has noted that more than two hundred novels on Roman themes were published in English between 1820 and 1914.[32] Cavafy's relation to this tradition has been virtually overlooked; indeed, when comparing the overlap in their common thematic interests, one sees how highly influenced he was by the Victorians. What makes these novels so interesting, Goldhill writes, is their "heady combination of religious controversy, the power of nationalist narrative coupled with self-conscious debate about the reach and aim of Empire, the educational anxiety and idealism attached to classical antiquity, the heightened appreciation of history in the age of progress. . . . As such, these books played a fundamental role in the construction of the cultural imagination of the Victorian reading public, and with their often huge sales, these narrative fictions acted as an instrumental, mediating form between high-level intellectual, theological, university-led argument, and popular culture" (2011, 157). It would not be too much of a stretch to extend this mediating capacity between elitist and popular culture to Cavafy when assessing his present global popularity, which, with the addition of the pronounced homoerotic dimension, transects the very same cultural axes.[33]

One novel that invites immediate comparison to Cavafy's poetry is Bulwer-Lytton's *The Last Days of Pompeii* ([1834] 1979). Although it is set in Pompeii in AD 79, the city and culture Lytton re-creates possess much of the Hellenized sophistication that Cavafy creates and conjures in his antique Alexandrian settings.[34] Pompeii, with its mixture of Greeks, Romans, Egyptians, and Christians, is an amalgamation of Greco-Roman paganism, Egyptian magic, and Christian idealism, the strands of which are tightly interwoven in the novel and foregrounded in a highly dramatic manner. The cast of characters includes Glaucus, a beautiful Greek youth—"an Alcibiades without ambition" ([1834] 1979, 19)—who is both elegant and sophisticated and who, at the end of the novel, survives the volcanic eruption and converts to Christianity; Arbaces, an evil and decadent Egyptian magus;[35] Apaecides, a Greek who serves as a priest of Isis; and his sister Ione, the love interest of both Glaucus and Arbaces. The complex plot is interlaced with fastidious thick descriptions of Pompeii based on Lytton's visit to and study of the archaeological excavations of the buried city's Greco-Roman architecture and spectacular frescoes. Given that Cavafy appears to have been well read in Bulwer-Lytton and quoted him in an early unpublished essay,[36] we can safely conclude that the poet was conversant with this genre and would have been highly attuned to the intersection between the ancient and contemporary religious, historical, and educational issues especially as they related to the wider Victorian anxieties over the rise, decline, and fall of empire. Cavafy adapted much of the material from such historical novels to his own poetic and artistic purposes; the underlying tension between Alexandrian culture (decadence) and Roman imperial hegemony that becomes one of his favored themes is clearly related to the larger cultural preoccupations of the British empire during this period. This reshuffling of historical themes and literary motifs constitutes what may be readily defined as the Cavafy's Victorian legacy.

The corrupting allure of Hellenism in relation to Roman imperial decline may be further contextualized within the decadent framework of what in the latter part of the nineteenth century was rather derisively termed "Alexandrianism," a word of opprobrium explicitly used to designate moral decline and cultural dissolution, symptoms of which were noted in critiques of euphuistic eclecticism and excessive learnedness in writing.[37] In an article published anonymously in *Macmillan Magazine* in 1886 titled "An Alexandrian Age," the author (later identified as Mowbray Morris) makes the direct analogy between the waning glories of Hellenistic Alexandria and Victorian Britain, based largely on the symptomatic resurgence of the mannered literary affectations of the euphuists:

> To inquire into the causes which have brought our literature to its present pass, if haply they may be found to have any affinity to those which worked on the literature of Greece, would be interesting, but not to our purpose. Who was our Philip of Macedon? Who is our Alexander? When is the great division of Empire to be? Great questions!—but happily not ours to answer. Enough for us that the literary tendencies of the age (which Mr. Swinburne, who has, as every one knows, a neat hand at an epithet, has also marked as a "ghastly, thin-faced time") are distinctly Alexandrian. Literature has become an industry, more or less polite; mannerism and affectation have—one can hardly say, indeed, begun to invade it; the temptation is rather to say, have taken entire possession of it. (Morris 1886, 28–29)[38]

In addition to singling out the precious cult of style associated primarily with Pater, the article's alarmist use of the term "Alexandrian" may be extended beyond ostensible concerns with literary and political decline by playing directly on bourgeois fears of degeneracy and acute anxieties about cultural decadence and moral confusion (Bolus-Reichert 2009, 15).

Doubtless Cavafy would have been attuned to the ideological nuances of this term, and he deliberately adopts a Paterian pose in his poetry by stridently espousing the decadent notion of Alexandria's belated Hellenism and infusing it with an even more pronounced homoerotic dimension.[39] Several of his poems aptly illustrate this Victorian fascination with the historical conversion romance that Cavafy sets in a late-antique Alexandrian context. In "Dangerous Thoughts" (1911), we encounter Myrtias, a youth partly pagan and partly Christian who perfectly embodies this dialectical tension:

> Said Myrtias (a Syrian student
> at Alexandria; in the reign of Augustus
> Constans and Augustus Constantius;
> partly a pagan and partly Christianizing)
> "Fortified as I shall be by theory and study
> I shall not, like the timorous, stand in fear of my passions.
> I shall deliver my body to pleasures,
> to the joys of which one dreams,
> to the boldest erotic desires,
> to the lustful promptings of the flesh,
> without any fear, because whenever I wish—
> and I shall have the will fortified
> as I shall be by theory and study—
> whenever the crisis comes I shall regain
> a spirit ascetic as before.
>
>   (2009a, 135)

This nearly schizophrenic interplay and precarious amalgamation of pagan hedonism and Christian asceticism is wholly reminiscent of Pater; Cavafy fully co-opts the Victorian aesthete's "odd fusion of the delicious and the disciplined, of decadence and *ascesis*" (to quote David Weir [1996, 97]) and adapts it to his own ends.[40] The informing text for the allure of Christianity for a curious young pagan is, of course, *Marius,* where Pater establishes the prototype of a young scholar struggling not so much to reject the cultural and religious practices of the pagan world but rather to "remold them according to a higher pattern" (Monsman 1967, 67). This theme is readily emulated by Cavafy in "The Tomb of Ignatius" (1916/1917):

> Here no longer am I Cleon who was famous
> in Alexandria (where people are not prone to admire)
> for my rich houses, for my gardens,
> for my horses and for my chariots,
> for the jewels and for the silk robes that I wore.
> Begone; here no longer am I that Cleon;
> let his twenty-eight years be obliterated.

I am Ignatius the deacon
who came late, very late, to contrition; but even so
I lived ten happy months
in the peace and in the safe keeping of Christ.

(2009a, 173)

Cleon's late conversion to Christianity recalls the final days of Marius, who finds not only belated comfort in the new religious creed but also an unexpected sense of cultural fulfillment: "He [Marius] felt there, felt amid the stirring of some wonderful new hope within himself, the genius, the unique power of Christianity. . . . For what Christianity did centuries later in the way of informing an art, a poesy, of higher and graver beauty, as some may think, than even Greek art and poetry at their best, was in truth conformable to the original tendency of its genius" (Pater [1885] 2008, 230, 234–235).

Similarly, in Cavafy's "From the School of the Renowned Philosopher" (1921), we have yet another example of the strained tension between Greek paideia, male beauty, and sensuality that is set against the backdrop of a contemplated but ultimately rejected religious conversion:

For two years he studied with Ammonios Sakkas,
but he was bored by both philosophy and Sakkas.

Then he went into politics.
But he gave that up. That Prefect was an idiot,
and those around him, somber-faced officious nitwits:
their Greek—poor fools—absolutely barbaric.

After that he became
vaguely curious about the Church: to be baptized
and pass as a Christian. But he soon
changed his mind: it would certainly have caused a row
with his parents, ostentatious pagans,
and—horrible thought—
they would have cut off at once
their extremely generous allowance.

But he had to do something. He began to haunt
the corrupt houses of Alexandria,
every secret den of debauchery.

In this fortune favored him:
he'd been given an extremely handsome figure.
And he enjoyed the divine gift.

His looks would last
at least another ten years. And after that?
Maybe he'll go back to Sakkas.
Or if the old man has died meanwhile,
he'll go to another philosopher or sophist:
there's always someone suitable around.

Or in the end he might possibly return
even to politics—commendably remembering
the traditions of his family,
duty toward the country,
and other resonant banalities of that kind.

(1992, 117–118)

The Paterian prototype of the world-weary scholar evoked by the poem is Marius's friend and fellow student Flavian, who "embodies that as yet unresolved dialectic of beauty and corruption which runs throughout the novel" (Monsman 1967, 88). Cavafy will offer variations of Flavian—the distracted student who, suffering from ennui, grows bored studying with Sophists and prefers to explore unbridled pleasures in search of the ideal hard, gem-like flame and ecstasy, along with the unnamed youth in "Passing Through," as discussed. Indeed, Marius's relationship with Flavian constitutes a barely concealed male romance:

> As the intimacy grew, the genius, the intellectual power of Flavian, began its sway over him [Marius]. The brilliant youth who loved dress, and dainty food, and flowers, and seemed to have a natural alliance with, and claim upon, everything else which was physically select and bright, cultivated also that foppery of words, of choice diction, which was common among the *élite* spirits of that day; and Marius, early an expert and elegant penman, transcribed for him his verses (the euphuism of which, amid a genuinely original power, was then so irresistibly delightful to him) in beautiful ink; receiving from him in return the profit of his really great intellectual capacities. (Pater [1885] 2008, 36–37)

Although Flavian ostensibly dies of a plague-induced fever, in essence he succumbs to his hedonistic cultural pursuits, burnt out as it were by his literary passion and exquisite stylistic excesses. (Lene Ostermark-Johansen makes the interesting comment that Flavian's death was "perhaps as much a case of death by Euphuism as the death of Euphuism" [2002, 6].) A parallel scenario plays out in Cavafy's unfinished poem "And Above All Cynegirus" (1919*), the title of which is a direct quote from Lucian's satiric "Teacher of Orators." The poem features a student who travels to Smyrna to learn rhetoric but soon finds himself seduced by other pleasures; it concludes with the youth calculating how much money he will receive from the old man Fulvius to pay off his debts, while in the background the Sophist continues to orate, practically in tears, on the subject of Cynegirus. In this composition, Cavafy introduces an ironic dimension to the standard Paterian formula by showing how, for the Romans, Hellenism had become a cultural commodity, a corrupting influence and standard of decadent elitism that functioned largely as a pretentious acquisition for pseudosophisticates.[41] He explores these themes in depth in his essay "Greek Scholars in Roman Houses," an appreciation of Lucian's essay "On Salaried Posts in Great Houses," which is a satirical exposé of the precarious status of Greek intellectuals living in Rome.

Conversion, Comradeship, and Mourning

The paired components of male comradeship and the subsequent mourning for the inevitable death inherent in the Victorian male romance are central to Pater, as Ellis Hanson (1987) has effectively argued.[42] In Pater's novel, Marius is intrigued by the Christian approach to death, an impression that predisposes him to the circumstantial conversion he undergoes by the end of the narrative.[43] In leading up to this, Pater presents two extended scenes in which Marius experiences Christian practice and ritual:[44] he encounters Christian burial practices in the villa of Saint Cecilia in one, followed by the celebration of the Christian liturgy in the other. His reflections while walking in the cemetery grounds with Cornelius (the initial source of Marius's attraction to the new religion) are

striking in terms of the mood they set, and they express Pater's historical project of presenting Christianity not only as the aesthetic fulfillment
of the classical world but also as a revolutionary system of belief in its
own right:[45]

> Yet certainly it was unlike any cemetery Marius had ever yet seen. . . . All
> [catacombs] alike were carefully closed, and with all the delicate costliness at
> command; some with simple tiles of baked clay, many with slabs of marble,
> enriched by fair inscriptions—marble, in some cases, taken from an older
> pagan tomb—the inscription sometimes a *palimpsest*, the new epitaph being
> woven into the fading letters of an earlier one. . . . Penetrating the whole
> atmosphere, touching everything around with its particular sentiment, it
> seemed to make all this visible mortality, death itself, more beautiful than
> any fantastic dream of old mythology had ever hoped to make it. (Pater
> [1885] 2008, 223–224, 226)

(Here again we encounter the curious precedent of the palimpsest epitaph
inscription, which is recast "In the Month of Athyr.") Subsequent to this
visionary scene, Marius returns to the house to witness a liturgy celebrated
over the tomb of one of the family members:

> What profound unction and mysticity! The solemnity of the signing was
> at its height when he [the pontiff] opened his lips. It was as if, a new sort of
> *rhapsodos,* he alone possessed the words of the office, and they were flow-
> ing fresh from some source of inspiration within him. The table or altar at
> which he presided, below a canopy of spiral columns, and with the carved
> palm-branch, standing in the midst of a semicircle of seats for the priests,
> was in reality the tomb of a youthful "witness," of the family of the Caecilii,
> who had shed his blood not many years before, and whose relics were still in
> this place. (Pater [1885] 2008, 247)

Marius departs with a strange peace, wondering, "Was this what made the
way of Cornelius so pleasant through the world?" (250). The novel's climactic convergence of the elements of ritual lament, friendship, and prospective
conversion effectively emphasizes Pater's aesthetic celebration of the "marvelous liturgical spirit of the church" and its "wholly unparalleled genius
for worship" (239). (Cavafy's "In Church" evokes a similar aesthetic appreciation for ecclesiastical ritual and decor, as will be discussed in chapter 5.)

These very themes—ritual lament, friendship, and prospective conversion—will become significant points of departure and informing ideas for several of Cavafy's mature poems. Cavafy recasts Pater's staging of the scenario in which a pagan witnesses and reacts to Christian funereal rites in his longest poem, "Myris: Alexandria. A.D. 340" (1929), where comradeship, mourning, and conversion are presented in a negative and reactionary light. The name Myris—perhaps adapted from that of the Greek poet Thamyris[46]— is nearly homonymous with Marius (Ricks 2001, 25), a fact that invites a comparative reading; the length of the poem would indicate an attempt on Cavafy's part to achieve a more substantial narrative imaginary portrait. Here Cavafy problematizes the concepts of comradeship, mourning, and conversion by presenting an inverse redramatization of Pater's tableau in which the poem's pagan speaker reacts with panic to the religious rites he witnesses, repudiating in effect the proffered peace and salvific vision in preference for the preserved memory of his passionate attachment to his lover, Myris. The poem presents not only the Paterian narrative elements of a visit to the house but also the affluent decor of the family and the fervid tones and prayers witnessed by Marius. In similar fashion, Cavafy lavishes great attention on the meticulous details that combine to overwhelm Myris's lover.[47] The potent drama of the scene is such that the only possible response for the speaker (other than converting) is to flee and try to preserve the memory of his vanished passion.[48]

Two other poems feature a similar mise-en-scène of mourning, the problem of conversion anxiety, and the pull of paganism. In "Priest at the Serapeum" (1926), we encounter a Christian convert who is anxious about the salvation of his pagan father:

> The good old man my father,
> whose love for me never changed;
> the good old man my father I mourn
> who died day before yesterday, just before dawn.
>
> Jesus Christ, the commandments
> of your most holy church to keep
> in my every act, in my every word,
> in my every thought is my endeavor
> every day. And from all who deny you
> I turn away.— But now I mourn;

I grieve, Christ, for my father
though he was—horrible to say—
priest at the accursed Serapeum.
                    (2013, 173)

And in "Kleitos' Illness" (1926), we are presented with a servant—a convert to Christianity— who attempts to pray for the love-sick and fever-
stricken Kleitos, the dying Christian youth whose family she serves:

Kleitos, an appealing
young man, about twenty-three years old—
with a superb education, with uncommon Greek learning—
is seriously ill. He was stricken by the fever
that mowed down Alexandria this year.

The fever found him already morally beat,
agonizing over his partner, a young actor,
who ceased to love or want him.

He is seriously ill, and his parents are in distress.

An old woman servant who reared him
is also shaken up over Kleitos' life.
In her horrific anxiety
there comes to mind an idol she worshiped
as a child, before she arrived there as a servant,
at the home of prominent Christians, and became a Christian herself.
In secrecy she brings cakes, wine, and honey.
She brings them before the idol. She chants whichever parts
of prayers she can remember: random bits and pieces. The dimwit
doesn't get it that the miserable demon could care less
if a Christian recovers or not.
                    (2013, 171)

This character type of a highly Hellenized youth with a rare knowledge
of Greek burning with an erotic fever is yet another Cavafian variation on
Pater's Flavian, ironically framed here by a religious skepticism and somewhat irreverent censure of primitive superstitious practices.[49] Distilled into
these poems is the essence of Alexandrian decadence, a subject that Cavafy
paints with broader brushstrokes in his more historical poems that deal

directly with the decline of the Ptolemaic kingdoms and the ascent of a corrupt Rome.

Cavafy's literary grounding in Pater's culturo-religious paradigm and aesthetic historicism allowed him to refine his decadent sensibility while further exploring his own choice of poetic subject matter. He will compose a number of signature poems that flagrantly showcase late-Hellenistic decadence. In "Alexandrian Kings" (1912), he employs his pictorial poetics to paint a vibrant canvas that dramatizes a historical scene in striking detail:

> The Alexandrians turned out in force
> to see Cleopatra's children,
> Kaisarion and his little brothers,
> Alexander and Ptolemy, who for the first time
> had been taken out to the Gymnasium,
> to be proclaimed kings there
> before a brilliant array of soldiers.
>
> Alexander: they declared him
> king of Armenia, Media, and the Parthians.
> Ptolemy: they declared him
> king of Cilicia, Syria, and Phoenicia.
> Kaisarion was standing in front of the others,
> dressed in pink silk,
> on his chest a bunch of hyacinths,
> his belt a double row of amethysts and sapphires,
> his shoes tied with white ribbons
> prinked with rose-colored pearls.
> They declared him greater than his little brothers,
> they declared him King of Kings.
>
> The Alexandrians knew of course
> that this was all mere words, all theatre.
>
> But the day was warm and poetic,
> the sky a pale blue,
> the Alexandrian Gymnasium
> a complete artistic triumph,
> the courtiers wonderfully sumptuous,
> Kaisarion all grace and beauty
> (Cleopatra's son, blood of the Lagids);

and the Alexandrians thronged to the festival
full of enthusiasm, and shouted acclamations
in Greek, and Egyptian, and some in Hebrew,
charmed by the lovely spectacle—
though they knew of course what all this was worth,
what empty words they really were, these kingships.

(1992, 41–42)

Based largely on Plutarch's "Life of Antony," the poem ingeniously recon-
figures the little known persona of Kaisarion by presenting him from the
vantage point of a twentieth-century poet historian.[50] The speaker envi-
sions the staged scene of the "Donations of 34 B.C." with ironic hindsight
and in full possession of the young kings' tragic fate following the imped-
ing suicides of Antony and Cleopatra. The narrative focuses instead on the
deceptive spectacle and the diaphanous Kaisarion's exquisite raiment in
order to comment more fully on the decadent dimensions of the scene.[51]
Critics have noted the particularly lavish description of Kaisarion's regal
attire, specifically the precious detail of the pink silk, which was a deliberate touch on Cavafy's part (he allegedly remarked to Timos Malanos,
"I dressed him in pink silk because at that time, an ell of that sort of silk
cost the equivalent of so-and-so many thousand drachmas" [Liddell (1974)
2000, 123–124]). The bejeweled splendor of the costume—an almost fetishistic display[52]—was also meant to convey the absolute extravagance of Hellenism in Egypt. The only thing left to the dynasty prior to its inevitable
collapse (Cleopatra's shrewd political strategies vis-à-vis Rome notwithstanding) was a defiant outward show of opulence.[53] The ultimate effect of
Cavafy's Paterian recontextualization of the historic event is its transfigu-
ration into a purely aesthetic object—"a complete artistic triumph"—that
presents Kaisarion solely from the perspective of aesthetic history.

A similar restaging of Alexandrian history may be found in the unfinished poem "Ptolemy the Benefactor (or Malefactor)" (1922*):

The poem read by the poet concerns the
feelings which the campaign
of Agisilaos will have evoked in Greece.

The corpulent, indolent Ptolemy,
bloated and sluggish from over-eating,

observed, "Wise poet,
your verses exaggerate somewhat.—
As to the aforesaid on the Greeks,
it is historically inaccurate."
"Great Ptolemy, these matters are secondary."

"Secondary, How? You state that
'The pride of the Greeks . . . is aroused
their pure patriotism . . . the Greeks' irresistible
impulse for heroism was evident.'"

"Great Ptolemy, these Greeks
are Greeks of art, fictional compositions;
they are compelled to feel as I do."

Ptolemy was scandalized and declared,

"Alexandrians are incurably frivolous."

The poet: "Great Ptolemy,
of Alexandrians you are the foremost."

"To a certain degree," replied Ptolemy, "to a certain degree.
I am of Macedonian descent, entirely pure.—

Ah, the great Macedonian race, wise poet,
which is full of energy and temperance."

But from his great corpulence, heavy as a rock,
and drowsy from over-eating,
the most-pure Macedonian
could barely keep his eyes opened.
                    (1994a, 146-147, my translation)

The subject of this poem—Ptolemy, nicknamed "Physkon" (Corpulent) because of his great weight—exemplifies the slothful, debauched depravity of the late Hellenistic dynasties just prior to their annihilation by Rome. The debate is meant to be purely farcical: Ptolemy objects to the idealizing portrait of Agisilaos, the Spartan king who mounted a bold campaign against the Persians in 396 BC, one that provoked the Thebans, Corinthians, and Athenians to band against him. Clearly the indolent successor to Alexander resents the obvious contrast of his slothful inactivity and political ineptitude with the heroic and glorious past. Lavagnini suggests that Ptolemy is venting his displeasure at the factiousness of the Greeks, which resulted in the demise of the Greek world (Cavafy 1994a, 145). A similar fate awaits Ptolemy, whose future was decided in Rome (see "Envoys from Alexandria" [1915]). Indeed, the political subtext of the poem gives it a comically ironic tension. It is the poet's bold claim to exercise poetic license that brings the narrative to its climax; with consummate rhetorical skill, he shamelessly flatters his royal patron, creating in the process a proper Hellenistic farce.[34]

The Return of the Gods

In Cavafy's "One of Their Gods" (1899/1917), we have the reworking of a mythological motif that Pater made popular in two of his *Imaginary Portraits* as well as in his essay "A Study of Dionysus" (*Greek Studies*): the return of the exiled gods. In Pater's "Denys L'Auxerrois," we are presented with the story of the return of Dionysus, "a denizen of old Greece actually finding his way back again among men" (Pater 1986, 163); similarly, in "Apollo in Picardy," we encounter a version of the return of the exiled god Apollo;[55] and in "A Study of Dionysus," Pater analyzes the myth of the god of revelry in terms that resonate in both his own and Cavafy's imaginary portraits:

> To this stage of his town-life, that Dionysus of "enthusiasm" already belonged; it was to the Athenians of the town, to urbane young men, sitting together at the banquet, that those expressions of a sudden eloquence came, of the loosened utterance and finer speech, its colour and imagery. Dionysus, then, has entered Athens, to become urbane like them; to walk along the marble streets in frequent procession, in the persons of noble youths, like those who at the *Oschophoria* bore the branches of the vine from his temple. (Pater 1925, 39)

Cavafy borrows this motif of the return of the god ambling through urban streets and sets it in the decadent setting of Hellenistic Seleucia:

> When one of them used to pass by the market-place
> of Seleucia, about the time of nightfall,
> a tall young man of perfect beauty,
> with the joy of immortality in his eyes

and perfumed black hair,
the people used to watch him
and ask one another whether they knew him,
whether he was a Syrian Greek or a stranger. But some
who looked with greater attention
understood and made way;
and while he disappeared under the archways
among the evening lights and the shadows
on his way to the place that lives only at night
with orgies and drunkenness
and every kind of lust and debauchery,
they wondered which of Them it was
and for what unavowed pleasure
he had come down to the streets of Seleucia
from the Sacred and Hallowed Dwellings.

(2009a, 160)

The association with debauchery and orgies suggests that the implied god is Dionysus (a theme explored in "The Retinue of Dionysus" [1903/1907]). The heavy infusion of homoeroticism in "One of Their Gods" recalls Pater's imaginary portraits, where we encounter a dangerous commingling of the human and the divine. As though signaling to those few "who looked with greater attention," Cavafy invites his readers to make the intertextual connection and identify the poetic tradition out of which he is working.

Although there are numerous poems that further exemplify this decadent Paterian trajectory, the one that best encompasses Cavafy's unique distillation of the fine art of sculpture, Greek hedonism, and Roman patronage is the "Sculptor of Tyana" (1893/1903/1911):

As you'll have heard, I'm no beginner.
I've handled a lot of stone in my time,
and in my own country, Tyana, I'm pretty well known.
Actually, senators here have also commissioned
a number of statues from me.

       Let me show you
a few of them. Notice this Rhea:
reverential, all fortitude, very old.
Notice Pompey. And Marius here,

and Paulus Aemilius, and Scipio Africanus.
The likeness as close as I could make it.
And Patroklos (I still have to touch him up a bit).
Near those pieces of yellowish marble there
stands Kaisarion.

And for some time now I've been busy
working on a Poseidon. I'm studying
his horses in particular: how to shape them exactly.
They have to be made so light
that it's clear their bodies, their legs,
are not touching the earth but galloping over water.

But here's my favorite work,
wrought with the utmost care and feeling.
This one—it was a summer day, very hot,
and my mind rose to ideal things—
this one came to me in a vision, this young Hermes.

(1992, 32)

Most interesting here is the confluence of cultural elements contributing to
the overall effect of the poem. The imaginary sculptor is from the Greek
East but resides in Rome and works for wealthy Roman patrons (he has
even tried his hand at a statue of Kaisarion—self-reflexively anticipating
Cavafy's own efforts to render this subject). His sculptural repertoire is impressive and includes a number of emperors in addition to stock subjects
from Greek mythology (critics have pointed out the political ironies of the
choice of emperors who were famous both for their Philhellenism and for
their conquest of the Hellenistic kingdoms).[56] The mention of Poseidon
curiously recalls Browning's Duke of Ferrara in "My Last Duchess," who
closes his dramatic monologue by boasting about a similar statue (Cavafy's
poem has a whiff of the Italian Renaissance about it and the humanist fetishization of classical sculpture).[57] Cavafy concludes his poem with the
idealized vision of a youthful god, the beatific ephebe who haunts so many
of his poems and visions. Taking his cue from Pater and inflecting his
compositions with a more daring homoeroticism, Cavafy finds his mature
voice in an unapologetic showcasing of decadent subjects. Both writers
share an immense and pervasive wistfulness stemming from an acute aesthetic sensibility grounded in the thematics of the male romance. Cavafy

emulates this stylized Paterian sublimation of an exquisite but often pain-ful eroticism in his writings by celebrating same-sex desire and extolling it as a legitimate aesthetic subject for twentieth-century poetry.

Cavafy's indebtedness to Victorian aestheticism, rather than diminish-ing his originality as a twentieth-century poet, comprises yet another facet of his unique ability to historicize the past for a contemporary audience. His historicist sensibility thus not only extends to his mastery of ancient history but also encompasses his proficiency with disseminating and inter-preting the Victorian period; indeed, Cavafy remains an important con-duit for channeling his own century, which was, properly speaking, the nineteenth. There is certainly an element of truth to Malanos's observation that after 1900, "his interest in anything new or contemporary gradually dwindled to nothing."[58] Like his contemporary and friend E. M. Forster, who straddled an important fault line of modernism, "managing at once to argue a necessarily backward vision in the face of an increasingly abhor-rent modernity,"[59] Cavafy situated himself to retrieve, preserve, and revise whatever he found valuable from the nineteenth century, making the most of his Victorian literary pedigree and decadent predisposition.

5

CAVAFY'S BYZANTIUM

Historicizing Fantasies of Exquisite Decline

Of the many concepts that resonated with decadent aesthetes, Byzantium most powerfully captured the effete sophistication that fin de siècle writers and artists strove to convey in their creative works and critical writings. Indeed, the epithets "Byzantine" and "decadent" were often used synonymously; Byzantium, as either a historical reality or an aesthetic fantasy, appears frequently in the terminology and subject matter of decadent writers and theorists, who employed it both strategically and provocatively to conjure up notions of sumptuous decay, cruel despotism, and verbal intricacy. These associations were purposefully manipulated to both refract and deflect the Enlightenment's negative critique of Byzantine history, which was viewed variously as a "tissue of revolts, seditions and perfidies" (Montesquieu), "a worthless collection [which] contains nothing but declamations and miracles . . . a disgrace to the human mind" (Voltaire), and a chronicle of "the triumph of barbarism and Christianity" (Gibbon).[1] In short, for Western post-Enlightenment intellectuals and historians (among whom may be included the modern Greek humanist and language reformer Adamantios Koraes), Byzantium stood for oppression, corruption, and decadence (Christodoulou 2010, 445). Although to some extent these negative qualities were grounded in historical fact—the reality of Byzantine "caesaropapism" founded upon theocratic rule in support of religious orthodoxy must be acknowledged—the more notorious attributes of "Byzantinism" (palace intrigue, Orientalizing opulence, perpetual decay, and obscurantist erudition, to name a few) fascinated and seduced many decadent writers. For in Byzantium they found a beguiling looking glass, or rather a distorting mirror, in which they eagerly saw reflected piquantly perverse images of sublime deliquescence, hieratic stasis, and languorous ennui.

Concomitant with this decadent discourse of Byzantinism was a gradually emerging positive countercurrent to the post-Enlightenment's poisonous view, one that sought to rehabilitate the Eastern Roman Empire by presenting it as the cultural repository of classical learning and the sophisticated and legitimate heir to Graeco-Roman civilization. During the second half of the nineteenth century, western European perceptions of Byzantine culture underwent profound changes, largely as a result of the writings of three great popularizers of Byzantine history: E. A. Freeman, Ferdinand Gregorovius, and Gustave Schlumberger.[2] This ideological shift was also occurring in postindependence Greece, where a raging debate was under way regarding the significance of Byzantine history for the evolution and emergence of the modern Greek cultural identity. Largely as a result of the efforts of the Greek historians Spyridon Zambelios (1813–81) and Constantine Paparrigopoulos (1815–91), modern Greeks were encouraged to view the Byzantine Middle Ages as a bridge linking them back to the late-antique, Hellenistic, and classical periods.[3] All these powerful discursive currents acted upon Cavafy in various ways, allowing him to fashion a unique vantage point from which to explore Byzantium in his poetry. Cavafy's position vis-à-vis Byzantine history and lore gave rise to a complex and sustained engagement with Byzantium, extending from his early compositions to his mature and final years; indeed, he would approach Byzantium from various angles—personal, cultural, ethnocentric, nostalgic, ironic, and aesthetic. In his mature phase, Cavafy was particularly attracted to the latter centuries of Byzantium (twelfth to fifteenth) when, paradoxically, gradual political decline gave birth to a final burst of cultural exuberance. As Steven Runciman writes, "If there is any meaning in the concept of decadence, there are few polities in history that better deserve to be called decadent than the East Christian Empire, the once great Roman Empire, during the last two centuries of its existence. . . . Yet was it a period of decadence? In strange contrast with the political decline, the intellectual life of Byzantium never shone so brilliantly as in those two sad centuries" (1970, 1–2).[4]

It is precisely this paradoxical tension between decline and vitality, the supreme flowering of beauty before its final deterioration (what Mallarmé called "the ideal fault of roses" and Baudelaire "a sunset, like the declining daystar . . . glorious, without heat, and full of melancholy")[5] that gave rise to the nineteenth-century cult of "literary Byzantium" that was promoted by decadent poets and writers (Balakian 1977, 199). This chapter explores Cavafy's relation to the complex dialectic between the decadent conceptualization of Byzantium and its simultaneous rehabilitation during the late nineteenth and early twentieth centuries, with a view to appreciating his unique engagement with Byzantium as a decadent topos par excellence.

Although Byzantium as a concept and historical reality remains a highly complex synthesis—a fused identity that was culturally Hellenic, politically Roman, and religiously Christian (Rapp 2008)—it readily afforded poets and artists a countertradition to western Renaissance humanism that, while remaining undeniably medieval, contained the "germs of the modern and its paradoxes," as Jane Spirit notes: "Broadly speaking, from the 1850s onwards, Byzantium was appropriated by an intellectual elite as a symbol of artistic excellence. . . . It was the final impossibility of Byzantium, of satisfactorily separating or uniting the perceived need for artistic creativity with an acknowledgement of personal and political decay, that made it so potent a symbol" (1995, 157, 166).[6] It was this very unique aesthetic that attracted Roger Fry and the Bloomsbury Postimpressionist artists to the subject matter and pictorial formalities of Byzantine art.[7] William Butler Yeats was similarly enamored of the singular contribution made by Byzantine artists to the history of aesthetics, creativity, and spirituality.

Not surprisingly, as a signifier of paradoxical and perverse tastes, Byzantium remained a convenient target for those hostile to avant-garde decadence. A telling illustration of this is the Parisian publication in May–June 1885 of *Les Déliquescences d'Adoré Floupette,* a collection of poems lampooning the decadent manner, which, in keeping with the parody, listed "Byzance" on the title page as its place of publication. That such a publication should appear in France is fitting, since French monarchs, historians, and intellectuals were at the vanguard of all major facets of western European redactions of Byzantium: its codification in the seventeenth century, its vilification during the Enlightenment, its reinvention as a dominant trope of decadence in the nineteenth, and its rehabilitation as the legitimate heir of the Roman Empire in the twentieth.[8]

During the nineteenth century, references to Byzantium were employed strategically in the culture war waged by aesthetes against the bourgeoisie, and the term "Byzantine" was frequently used by decadent writers who wished to evoke either a sumptuous mood, an outré posture, or an intricate arabesque design. Gautier, as noted in chapter 3, lavishly praised (and in doing so radically defined) Baudelaire's decadent style as Byzantine, "already veined with the greenish streaking of decomposition, and the complex refinement of the Byzantine school, the ultimate form of decadent Greek art" (1909, 39–40). Numerous writers followed Gautier's lead. In *À Rebours*, Huysmans's neurotic aesthete Jean des Esseintes expressed a preference for literature that possessed "Byzantine flowers of thought and deliquescent complexities of style" (Huysmans 2003, 165). Apropos of Huysmans's alleged Byzantine qualities, George Moore wrote that he "goes to my soul like a gold ornament of Byzantine workmanship" (quoted in Macleod 2006, 3). Paul Bourget described Huysmans's prose as "the most Byzantine product of our epoch."[9] Vittorio Pica, in his 1891 article on Mallarmé published in *La Revue indépendant*, labeled the poet under the heading "Les Modernes Byzantins."

Several historical novels and plays dealing with Byzantium appeared during the late nineteenth and early twentieth centuries. Paul Adam, who collaborated with Jean Moréas in *Le thé chez Miranda* (1886), wrote *Princesses Byzantines* (1893), *Basile et Sophie* (1900), and *Irène et les eunuques* (1907). Victorien Sardou's widely popular play *Théodora* (1884), starring Sarah Bernhardt, toured Europe and the Levant, and was performed in Alexandria in 1889.[10] Jean Lombard's novel *Byzance* (1890), Jean Lorrain's "La Fin d'un Jour" *(Princesses d'ivoire et d'ivresse,* 1902), Joséphine Péledan's *Le Prince de Byzance* (1895), Gabriele D'Annunzio's *La Gloria* (1899), and François Herczeg's *Byzance: Pièce en Trois Actes* (1912) collectively brought decadent visions of Byzantium before the eyes of an intrigued public and attest to the definitive association made between Byzantium and decadence via the phenomenon of literary Byzantium. Similarly, in England, solid foundations were set by Ruskin's *The Stones of Venice* (1851), in which the Byzantine aesthetic was reevaluated and seen as the "germ" wherein "the Gothic arrangement is already found."[11] Overlapping with Ruskin's revival of the Gothic is a similar focus in the historical novel genre, which largely followed the lead of Sir Walter Scott's *Count Robert of Paris* (1831). Examples of this include J. M. Neale's *Theodora Phranza* (1857), in which, as Spirit notes, "Byzantine characters acknowledged their decadence while the heroine was presented as an emblem of an honorable Byzantine tradition, heroically marrying Mohammed to preserve the city's peace" (1995, 160); and Henry Pottinger's *Blue and Green or, The Gift of God: A Romance of Old Constantinople* (1879), which recounts the story of the Nika rebellion against the emperor Justinian and is a more positive retelling of the role of Empress Theodora as the power behind the throne. In this same formulaic cast of imperious empresses is Frederic Harrison's novel *Theophano: The Crusade of the Tenth Century: A Romantic Monograph* (1904) and its subsequent dramatic adaptation, *Nicephorus: A Tragedy of New Rome* (1906).[12]

In the realm of historiography, some scholars were advancing Byzantine historical studies in a more fair-minded and scholarly direction. In England, the historian George Finlay challenged Gibbon's notion of Byzantine decline and promoted the idea of the continuity of Greek society and politics (Bullen 2003, 131). In France, Charles Diehl, the first holder of the new chair in Byzantine history established at the Sorbonne, composed numerous works on Byzantine history. His *Études byzantines* (1905) offered humanizing portraits of emperors and empresses and would serve as an important source for Cavafy's mature Byzantine-themed poems.[13] In Great Britain, J. B. Bury—the foremost Byzantinist writing in English during this period (Stephenson 2010c, 466)—held chairs in Greek at Trinity College, Dublin, and in modern history at Cambridge, and was responsible for establishing a revisionist view of the Byzantine Empire as a continuous—and legitimate—extension of the Roman Empire. Frederic Harrison also published several essays on Constantinople in the *Fortnightly Review* (1894) and presented his "Rede Lecture" at Cambridge in which he made a strong case for Byzantium as "the surest witness to the unity of history" (Harrison 1900, 5).[14] One could thus point to two currents flowing simultaneously if somewhat contrapuntally: the decadent reification of Byzantium as the consummate paradigm of exuberant decline and aesthetic excess, and the revisionist historicism that sought to rescue Byzantium from its post-Enlightenment abyss and rehabilitate it as the legitimate heir and medieval continuation of both Roman polity and Hellenic culture.

From the select examples of historical and literary Byzantium cited above, it becomes clear that the association between decadence and Byzantium had become highly entrenched, so much so that two prominent twentieth-century critics on decadence—Mario Praz (1970) and Jennifer Birkett (1986)—structured their critiques of the period around chapters that conspicuously feature the word "Byzantium" in their titles. In his concluding chapter to *The Romantic Agony*, simply titled "Byzantium," Praz writes:

> The period of antiquity with which these artists of the *fin de siècle* liked best to compare their own was the long Byzantine twilight, the gloomy apse gleaming with dull gold and gory purple, from which peer enigmatic faces, barbaric yet refined, with dilated neurasthenic pupils. The writers of the first part of the nineteenth century, filled with nostalgia, had re-evoked the Imperial orgies of the Orient and Rome . . . but on the threshold of the present century even this virile personal element seemed to disappear. The Byzantine period was a period of anonymous corruption, with nothing of the heroic about it; only there stand out against the monotonous background figures such as Theodora or Irene, who are static personifications of the female lust for power. . . . The Decadents devoted themselves to living over again the gory annals of the Eastern Empire, torn by dissensions and court hatreds, hemmed in on all sides by barbarian conquerors, a body full of bruises and decay enveloped in the symmetrical folds of a mantle of heavy gold. (1970, 397)

In this same vein, Birkett's opening and closing chapters to *The Sins of the Fathers* are provocatively titled "The Energy of Byzantium: The Enemy Within" and "Crossroads in Byzantium." Building on the work of Praz, she offers her own definition of decadent Byzantium as a place where "all desires meet: private obsessions, fetishes, morbid fears and guilt are the substance of the decadent world" (1986, 4). Its energy is marked by ambition, power, and failure, "eroticizing the urge for power and the failure to

seize it—the source of that archetypal decadent identification of Love and
Death, desire voluntarily locked in paralysis" (6). The decadent imagination is infected with this Byzantine energy, "simultaneously defiant and
submissive, invoking energies which are immediately frozen, framed and
trapped, surrendered to become images of ruin and waste" (5).[15] A further
dimension of decadent Byzantium is adumbrated by Richard Gilman,
who writes that Byzantium, with its "hedonism and gorgeous heavy styles
of architecture and ornament, in time replaced Rome at the center of this
neoromantic longing. This nostalgia was an appetite for what was felt to be
lacking in the present, a strange desire for depravity and corruption seen
as *liberating*; it was a desire for a stasis of the senses and the soul in a grandeur of repletion" (1979, 93–94, emphasis added).

Taken as a whole, these definitions—although admittedly diffuse and
impressionist—offer an invaluable backdrop against which to evaluate
Cavafy's own poetic redaction of Byzantium. For in keeping with the tradition of literary Byzantium, his Byzantine poems are unmistakably colored
by a nostalgic "neoromantic longing" for a more glorious Greek past; they
also manifest a desire for artistic liberation, one inspired in no small part
by the anti-industrialist medievalism of Ruskin and the Pre-Raphaelites.
Moreover, they evince a fascination with palace intrigue, anonymous corruption, and the thwarted lust for power embodied in the static personifications of Byzantine empresses, a motif that Cavafy explores repeatedly.
Yet he approaches these stock decadent tropes with a newfound appreciation for Byzantine culture gleaned from his immersion in revisionist scholarship (namely, Paparrigopoulos, Bury, Karl Krumbacher, and
Diehl) as well as from his increasing familiarity with and mastery of the
primary historical sources themselves (Prokopios, Psellus, Choniates, At-
taleiates, Komnina, Bryennios, Kantakuzinos, Gregoras, and Sphrantzes,
among others).[16] He gradually discovers in the endless court machina-
tions of emperors and empresses, and in the highly dramatic accounts of
the Byzantine historians in which they are recounted, a unique discourse
characterized by a singular blend of duplicitous rhetoric and sycophantic panegyric. Consequently, he is able to inflect into his chosen subjects
a double dose of decadence, as it were, applying recent historiographical
writings about the extraordinary sophistication of Byzantine culture to the
inherited narrative of fin de siècle Byzantine decadence, as is seen from an
analysis of the poems themselves.

Cavafy's Early Forays into Byzantine Lore

Cavafy's relationship to matters Byzantine constitutes perhaps one of the more controversial dimensions of his poetic corpus. Scholars and critics tend to align themselves in opposing camps, reading the Byzantine poems as either highly ironic or, conversely, sentimentally nostalgic compositions. Before we consider the ideological nuances of these schools of interpretation, a brief look at the poet's early exposure to the actual topos of Constantinople as both a geographical place and an imaginary construct will help frame the matter of Byzantium as it evolved in the poet's creative psyche. From a young age, Cavafy was acutely attuned to his Byzantine roots, an awareness that intensified when, in July 1882, he and his family fled the impending British bombardment of Alexandria to stay with relatives in the Ottoman capital. Cavafy was then a nineteen-year-old impressionable youth who was eager to experiment with the newfound freedoms that living with his relatives afforded him—freedoms of both a sexual and an intellectual nature. The family would remain in Constantinople until 1885, and we have several compositions that date from and were inspired by this period: rejected poems dealing with the local topography; an epic titled "Constantinopoliad";[17] various prose essays; and a fictional piece titled "A Night in Kalinderi" (1885–86), discussed in chapter 2 in relation to the flâneur tradition. In addition, we have a published review essay that directly addresses Byzantine culture—"The Byzantine Poets" (1892)—which is an appreciation à la Pater of Karl Krumbacher's *The History of Byzantine Literature*.[18] The opening sentences of this essay, an important text that documents the influence of a major Byzantinist on Cavafy, record the poet's journalistic participation in the rehabilitation of Byzantine culture:

The poets of our Greek middle ages, although not on par with our ancient poets, or with the graceful followers of the Muse who have been exulted for us by the nineteenth century, are not however deserving of the disdain which they have received over such a period by wise men of the West.

Although we Greeks never really disparaged them per se, in fact we hardly even knew them. It is time for this polite forgetfulness to cease. The Byzantine bards interest us most ardently because they demonstrate that, not only did the Greek lyre never fracture, it never ceased producing sweet sounds. Indeed, the Byzantine poets serve as the link between the glory of our ancient poets and the charm and golden hopes of our contemporary Greek poets. (2010, 36)

Much of this newfound enthusiasm for Byzantium was a consequence of Cavafy's exposure to his Phanariot family roots, an interest that prompted his subsequent efforts at documenting his family genealogy and exploring the alleged descent of the Cavafy family from the Byzantine royal Dukas family. Although this connection back to Byzantine royalty was openly agreed to be a Phanariot pretense—John playfully refers to himself as "an unworthy descendent of the imperial house of Doucas" (Ghika 2009, 23)— the impact of this genealogical myth surely added to Cavafy's interest in Byzantine royal families and undoubtedly factored into his decision to write about Anna Komnina, who, through her mother Irene, was likewise a descendent of the imperial house of Doukas. As Katerina Ghika has meticulously shown in her article on Cavafy's family crest, the family— in keeping with the practices of other Greek mercantile families of the period—consciously cultivated aristocratic airs that necessitated a Byzantine imperial lineage, fanciful as this would have been.[19] Cavafy writes of this in his genealogy: "The Cavafy's [*sic*] pedigree, tracing back the family's origin to the emperors of the house of Doucas, I have left out [,] it belonging rather to the region of tradition than of fact" (quoted in Ghika 2009, 24).

We also have a concerted effort on the part of the poet between the years 1888 and 1892—the period during which Cavafy was writing under the full sway of Baudelaire and French decadence—to compose a series of poems grouped under the Parnassian heading "Βυζαντιναί Ημέραι" ("Byzantine Days"). Although Cavafy destroyed most of these poems, their surviving titles allow us to speculate on the possible subject matter and aspects of Byzantium that interested him during this period.[20] The titles of these eleven poems are as follows: "Empress Eudocia's Praise,"[21] "The Restoration of Icons during the Reign of Empress Irene," "Charlemagne the Great," "The Demands of the Pope," "The Reconquest of Crete," "Before the Gates of Jerusalem," "The Siege of Nicaea (or Nikopoulos)," "The Good (or Bad) Knight," "The Greek Warrior," "The Neigh of the Horse," and "I Prefer Death to Living" ("Theophilos Palaiologos"). Scholars have offered varying opinions on these titles and how the poems they represented might be used as thematic indexes charting conceptual thought patterns in Cavafy's evolving view of Byzantine culture and history. George Savidis (1985a) connected them early on with Cavafy's initial engagement with literary Byzantium; according to Savidis, the poet eventually rejected these poems after he read Gibbon between 1896 and 1899, a critical encounter that impelled him to discard his "Parnassian or Decadent Byzantinism."[22] Diana Haas (1983b, 77) furthers Savidis's hypothesis and argues that these poems define two periods that intrigued Cavafy at the time: the eighth-century restoration of icons, and the Crusades; for Haas, these poems significantly chronicle Cavafy's interest in antagonistic relations between Byzantium and the West, in addition to recording Cavafy's growing patriotic identification with Byzantium.[23] Sarah Ekdawi (1996a, 24) dissents somewhat from this view and rejects the Savidis-Haas time frame for Cavafy's reading of Gibbon; she argues instead for an earlier exposure to Gibbon, which she feels contributed to the focus on the "aggressive aspect of Western Christianity" and consequently on a much more negative view of Byzantine Christianity.[24] Along with Anthony Hirst (1989, 2000, 2003), who promotes a rather radical but erudite layered reading of Cavafy's poems—one for the "innocent" and one for the "informed" reader[25]—Ekdawi argues that the ultimate ironic nuances of Cavafy's Byzantine poems reside largely in their thematic sequence and relative placement in printed form. Thus they resonate off one another disruptively in unmistakably ironic and often negative ways.

One could reconcile these divergent critical readings somewhat by reframing Cavafy's Byzantine poems within a decadent and aesthetic context. This would allow for the concurrent presence of the subversive irony initially detected by Alkis Thrylos in 1924 and more recently endorsed by Hirst and Ekdawi, yet still accommodate the unmistakable enthusiasm and passion sanctioned by the sympathetic and patriotic school of critics composed of B. F. Christidis, Savidis, K. T. Dimaras, and Haas. The readings that follow attempt to take into account both schools of interpretation and to synthesize them under the more encompassing category of literary decadence.

"Our Illustrious Byzantinism": Irony, Nostalgia, or Decadence?

Pivotal to any discussion of Cavafy and Byzantium is the poem "In Church," composed in 1892, revised in 1901 and 1906, and printed in 1912.

The poem is one of Cavafy's most direct and significant statements on Byzantine aesthetics:

> I love the church—her gilt six-winged banners,
> her silver vessels, her candelabra,
> her lights, her icons, and pulpit.
>
> Whenever I go inside a Greek church:
> what with the fragrances of incense,
> the liturgical chanting and harmonies,
> the grandeur of the priests' presence
> and the solemn rhythm of their every movement—
> resplendent in their ornate vestments—
> my mind lays hold of the great honors of our race,
> of the glory of our being Byzantine [Byzantinism].
>
> (2013, 76)

What stands out most in this poem is the synesthetic experience conveyed by the speaker's reaction to the gorgeous sensuality characteristic of the Byzantine religious rite. This focus is highly reminiscent of the sensual correlation delineated in Baudelaire's "Correspondences," as would be expected given the date of the poem's composition.[26] The encomiastic aesthetic thrust of "In Church" seems straightforward enough and calls to mind various descriptive religious tableaux out of Huysmans and Pater.[27] The poem seeks to evoke the sublime aura of Byzantine worship. As Biserra Pentcheva writes, "Because the Eastern Orthodox liturgy maintained its late antique tradition of saturation of the senses, the objects embedded in its rite gave rise to a sensorially rich performance" (2010, 2). This richness is clearly what the speaker wishes to evoke, and all remains unequivocally celebratory until the word "Byzantinism" appears, a term that unduly complicates the poem by introducing a concept laden with pejorative connotations. The problematic dimensions of this concept are defined by Dimiter Angelov, who argues that Byzantinism "is an essentialist and negative understanding of a medieval civilization that places it into rigorous analytical categories from a Western and modern viewpoint. . . . Byzantinism, like Balkanism, is a concept of 'otherness' by which Byzantium is turned into the crippled 'other' of the cultural construct of Europe" (2003, 6–7). It is the concluding presence of the word

"Byzantinism" that has polarized critical interpretations of the poem, inducing some to read it as ironic and others as nostalgic. As early as 1924, Greek critic Alkis Thrylos (1924, 185) took the poem to be completely ironic, claiming that it adheres to Cavafy's overall pessimism, which, she argues, could not but have viewed the religious leanings of Byzantine rulers cynically as hypocritical gestures.[28] This reading was later challenged by B. F. Christidis (1958) in his monograph *Cavafy and Byzantium*, where he asserts that Cavafy had nothing but adulation for Byzantium, a line of thinking supported by K. T. Dimaras and George Savidis and later extensively promoted by Diana Haas. Haas in particular has compellingly argued that Cavafy's use of the word "Byzantinism" goes deliberately against the grain of the customary use of the word during this period by reclaiming it to signify a more positive and revisionist conceptualization of Byzantium.[29]

As an undeniable "synonym of decadence and verbal intricacy" (Angelov 2003, 11), the term "Byzantinism" complicates the poem on many levels. More than anything it signals the reader to contextualize the poem's objects within the framework of ecclesiastical decadence, which is how "In Church" should be properly interpreted: squarely within the decadent tradition with its fixation on medieval church aesthetics and ritual. Although this angle does not necessarily impugn the celebratory list of ecclesiastical objects and decor, it does somewhat qualify the panegyric. Indeed, the poem gives off the very same fragrant "odor of Christianity" found in the writings of other decadent aesthetes of the period. (For Nietzsche, of course, Christianity and decadence remain interchangeable philosophies, a fact that lends yet another decadent dimension to Cavafy's fin de siècle interest in Byzantine religiosity.)[30] One has only to read it in tandem with the ambivalent religiosity articulated by Huysmans's Jean des Esseintes in the following passages from *À Rebours* to appreciate this resonance:

> As yet [the Latin Language] had not acquired that special gamey flavour which in the fourth century—and even more in the following centuries—the odour of Christianity was to give to the pagan tongue as it decomposed like venison, dropping to pieces at the same time as the civilization of the Ancient World, falling apart while the Empires succumbed to the barbarian onslaught and the accumulated pus of ages. (Huysmans 2003, 33)

"There's no doubt about it," Des Esseintes said to himself, after a searching attempt to discover how the Jesuit element had worked its way to the surface at Fontenay; "ever since boyhood, and without my knowing it, I've had this leaven inside me, ready to ferment; the taste I've always had for religious objects may be proof of this."

However, he tried his hardest to persuade himself of the contrary, annoyed at finding that he was no longer master in his own house. Hunting for more acceptable explanations of his ecclesiastical predilections, he told himself he had been obliged to turn to the Church, in that the Church was the only body to have preserved the art of past centuries, the lost beauty of the ages. She had kept unchanged, even in shoddy modern reproductions, the goldsmiths' traditional forms ... retained, even in aluminum, in fake enamel, in coloured glass,[31] the grace of the patterns of olden days. . . .

But however much he dwelt on these motives, he could not quite manage to convince himself. It was true that, after careful thought, he still regarded the Christian religion as a superb legend; a magnificent imposture; and yet, in spite of all his excuses and explanations, his skepticism was beginning to crack. (Huysmans 2003, 73–74)

When read in conjunction with these musings, the poem exhibits a similarly conflicted faltering, one that such aesthetic devotion to high church ritual and forms—the "magnificent imposture"—induced in many guilt-ridden aesthetes. Cavafy displayed this very ambivalence on his deathbed when he initially refused to receive Holy Communion from the Patriarch of Alexandria, although he eventually relented (Liddell [1974] 2000, 206). This emotional contradiction, which generates the tension between the speaker's ostensible love of church and the ideologically vexed word "Byzantinism," becomes less problematic when the poem is read in a fully decadent context. Thus the ironic tension many have detected is ultimately situated in this decadent topos of conflicted guilt and devotion, the "dialectic of shame and grace" (Hanson 1997, 27) that well describes the fixation of so many homosexual aesthetes with high church culture, whether Roman Catholic or, in Cavafy's case, Greek Orthodox. Irony and adulation, therefore, are held in perpetual suspension in this poem. Cavafy took his cue from Huysmans and other devout decadents, of whom Jules Barbey d'Aurevilly famously said that the only possible choices were "between the muzzle of a pistol or the foot of the cross" (quoted in Beckson 1966, xxviii). By choosing the Byzantine cross, Cavafy lays claim to a tradition that he felt was doubly his own: the decadent discourse inherent in the word "Byzantinism." He inflects an acute ambivalence into a concept that was itself similarly conflicted, signifying as it did a tainted but undeniably sumptuous and intellectually sophisticated religious sensibility.

The seductive decadent sensuality of Byzantium is foregrounded in "Imenus" (1915/1919), a poem to which Cavafy added a somewhat cosmetic Byzantine overlay (its original title was "Love It More" and had nothing to do with Byzantium). This has led some readers to remove "Imenus" from the category of Byzantine subject matter altogether (Ekdawi 1996a, 21). Yet the fact that Cavafy framed it in the Byzantine reign of the debauched emperor Michael the Third (842–867)—a dissolute figure who indulged in drinking bouts, horse races, and religious burlesques (Kazhdan 1991, 2:1362)—indicates that he wished to connect the erotic pleasure conveyed by the poem's opening letter with the legendary corruption associated by decadent writers with Byzantine court life:

> "   to be loved even more
> the sensual delight realized morbidly and with depravity;
> rarely finding the body that feels delight the way it wants it to—
> that, morbidly and with depravity, rouses
> an erotic intensity that sound health cannot know . . ."
>
> Fragment from a letter
> by the young Imenus (a patrician) well-known
> in Syracuse for his dissipation,
> during the dissipated times of Michael the Third.
>
>   (2013, 132)

This morbidly corrupting erotic intensity unequivocally illustrates the definitions of Byzantine decadence by Praz, Birkett, and Gilman cited above. The setting of Syracuse is also a deliberate touch, as the city was an outpost of empire that had close cultural ties to Constantinople: the bishops of Syracuse were directly under the authority of the patriarch of Constantinople, and many ambitious youth went to the Byzantine capital for their schooling (Kazhdan 1991, 3:1997). The city fell to the Arabs in 878—thus its historical appeal as a sophisticated decadent city with strong cultural ties to the Greek world on the brink of annihilation (Jusdanis 1983, 142), much like Byzantine Alexandria in the unfinished poem "Of the Sixth or Seventh Century" (1927*) set "prior to the onslaught of the powerful Arab nation."

A similar and certainly more familiar subject of imperial depravity is conjured up in the unfinished poem on Justinian, "From *The Secret History*" (1923*), which derives its occult content from the well known account of Prokopios referenced in the title:

> Often the gaze of Justinian
> would induce horror and abhorrence in his servants.
> They suspected something about which they dared not speak:
> when one night, by chance, they were proven right,
> that he was a Demon from hell:
> he emerged late from his room and roamed
> headless in the halls of the palace.
>
> (1994a, 158, my translation)

Like "Imenus," this poem—one of Cavafy's most gothic compositions—introduces the theme of Byzantine corruption, albeit one imbued with demonic elements. Here the occult is not simply a matter of popular superstition, as in other poems that feature the supernatural, but rather derives directly from an anecdote recorded in a primary historical text—perhaps the most notorious of all Byzantine historical narratives: Prokopios's *The Secret History*. The poem raises hermeneutical questions about reading and interpreting Byzantine sources by problematizing the overall integrity and credibility of Byzantine historians, who, as Anthony Kaldellis (2010a, 212, 217) notes, were notoriously "idiosyncratic in subject matter and approach" as well as subversive and insincere in their dramatic rhetoricity. One wonders whether Prokopios was merely slandering Justinian and Theodora out of sheer malice or if there is some coded truth to be teased out of his account. The taint of duplicity perpetually associated with the word "Byzantine" comes into play here, a topic that fascinated Cavafy; he deliberately manipulates textual registers in this and other Byzantine poems in order to interrogate the legitimacy and veracity of his historical and literary sources. Just as "Imenus" gestures intertextually to incorporate an alleged primary document (the letter in this instance is a fictitious one), "From *The Secret History*" functions similarly to present an event narrated in a historical text. This is fully in keeping with Cavafy's attitude toward Byzantine lore, about which he is on record as saying, "For me, the Byzantine period is like a closet with many drawers. If I want something, I know where to find it, into which drawer to look" (quoted in Sareyannis 1983, 113). Regarding Byzantine historians, he believed that "they are not appreciated as they should be. One day they will be discovered and will be admired for their originality. They cultivated a genre of historiography which was never written before and has not been written since. They wrote history dramatically" (ibid.).

These sentiments regarding the uniqueness of Byzantine historical writings certainly shaped Cavafy's choice of the passages he either cites or references in his Byzantine-themed poems. His growing awareness of the levels of complexity inherent in Byzantine accounts of court life is another dimension of Byzantine decadence, one that allowed him to break away somewhat from the received stereotype of fin de siècle literary Byzantium and be more creative and nuanced in his approach. He was clearly developing an appreciation for the singular rhetoricity of this historical tradition (partly what he meant by the Byzantines writing their history dramatically), a quality that was not necessarily seen as a positive attribute. In fact, the opposite was generally held to be true, as Emanuel Bourbouhakis aptly notes: "Byzantine texts have routinely been branded as 'rhetorical' not in a bid to explain them, but to impugn their merit. . . . From its beginnings in antiquity, rhetoric has been under a sort of cultural indictment, charged with insincerity and the provision of an elaborate and ultimately decadent form of verbal theatre, inimical at once to truth and artistic authenticity" (2010, 175). In his poetry, Cavafy attempts quite innovatively to explore aspects of this precious rhetoricity and the duplicitous insincerity that frequently informs it, bringing upon himself in the process much censure and critical abuse from his contemporaries.[32] What makes this rhetorical legacy (one recently labeled the "Third Sophistic")[33] ultimately more decadent and precious is that not only is historiography as practiced by the Byzantines no longer produced, but more tragically, the Byzantine historian-scholars left no real legacy: "They wrote for the most part in a sophisticated language for a sophisticated public which was soon to be wiped out" (Runciman 1977, 97). Once again, there is an implied topos of annihilation here, one that lends an even greater dramatic urgency to all the rarefied topics treated in these historicizing poems.

In the case of Prokopios's *The Secret History*, we have Cavafy writing what remained an unpublished poem based on what was technically an unpublished history—"της ανεκδότου ιστορίας" (Prokopios's text, although known to Byzantine historians, was not recovered by Western scholars until 1623).[34] Added to this is the poem's unspeakable scandalous scenario based on court gossip—episodes witnessed by panic-stricken and oppressed palace servants. These multiple anecdotal layers of narrative complexity and obscurity make for a very subversive and arcane poem, one that challenges the official received history of Justinian's reign by recounting "so many actual nightmares, frightful demonic visitations, and dream-visions of devastation" (Kaldellis 2010b, viii). In this sense, Cavafy's poem, by faithfully adhering to an original Byzantine text, calls attention to a counternarrative of oppression and terror. It is based on a passage from book 2, chapter 12 (lines 18–21), where we are told the following about Justinian:

> And some of those who were present in discussions with him late at night, obviously in the palace, men whose souls were pure, believed they had witnessed some kind of apparition, a strange demonic being that had taken his place. One of them said that Justinian would suddenly rise up from the imperial throne and roam about the hall; for he was not in the habit of staying seated still for long. It seemed his head suddenly disappeared, while the rest of his body continued its perambulations. (Prokopius 2010, 59)

As a defamatory document that defiantly records the failures of Justinian's reign, *The Secret History* serves as a text that counterbalances the other more celebrated aspects of the great Byzantine emperor—the buildings, legal codifications, and military victories. By engaging with it, Cavafy is doing more than simply dabbling in Byzantine phantasmagoria; he presents an alternative account that exposes the nightmarish regime of an oppressive emperor. In choosing Prokopios, he selects a unique writer—the only Roman historian who wrote about the rein of a living emperor, albeit clandestinely (Kaldellis 2010b, x). This fact aligns Prokopios's history with those penned by Anna Komnina and John Kantakuzinos, imperial figures on whom Cavafy focuses precisely because they were actual players in the narratives they produced—imperial historians, so to speak. It bears stating that by turning to the gothic topic of Justinianic demonic excess in the height of his poetic maturity, Cavafy distances himself from any alleged school of realism, a point overlooked by certain critics bent on negating the decadent dimension of Cavafy's oeuvre. The presence of related supernatural themes and occult topics in *The Unfinished Poems* documents how attached Cavafy was to the matter of Byzantine decadence and illustrates how predominant this literary conceit would remain in his creative process.

Byzantine Drama: The Komninos Dynasty

Cavafy's deft appreciation for the complex tension between historical veracity and dramatic rhetoricity in the corpus of Byzantine historiography is evident in his presentation of the imperial women Anna Komnina; her mother, Irene Doukaina; and her grandmother, Anna Dalassene. Along with Anna's nephew Manuel Komninos, these figures form the subject of a cluster of poems that date from Cavafy's second period of engagement with Byzantine lore (1912–32). Given his earlier interest in empresses as revealed in the titles of his "Byzantine Days" poems (Athenais-Eudocia and Irene), along with their prominence in works of literary Byzantium as seen in the previous overview, it comes as no surprise that Cavafy would return to the theme of imperial women (the list also includes Anna of Savoy, Irene Assan, and Theodora Kantakuzinos, who will be discussed below in connection with John Kantakuzinos). Cavafy employs his signature palimpsest technique in "Anna Komnina" (1917/1920), whereby he includes passages from an original Byzantine text and weaves them into his own poem, which subsequently functions as a metacommentary:

> In the prologue to her *Alexiad*,
> Anna Komnina laments her widowhood.
>
> Her soul is all vertigo.
> "And I bathe my eyes," she tells us,
> "in rivers of tears. . . . Alas for the waves" of her life,
> "alas for the revolutions." Sorrow burns her
> "to the bones and the marrow and the splitting" of her soul.

But the truth seems to be this power-hungry woman
knew only one sorrow that really mattered;
even if she doesn't admit it, this arrogant Greek woman
had only one consuming pain:
that with all her dexterity,
she never managed to gain the throne,
virtually snatched out of her hands by impudent John.

(1992, 109)

That Cavafy decided to focus on the period of the Komninoi is significant—surely it was a choice made partly in defiance of Koraes, who, pace Gibbon, viewed the twelfth century as the most inglorious period for Greece (Alexios Komninos, it should be noted, was castigated as a particularly decadent emperor for emulating the trappings of the Persian and Parthian courts [Christodoulou 2010, 446–447]). There was, in addition to this decadent association, a positive revisionist dimension to this choice—the growing appreciation for the high achievement of learning and letters during this period, a point emphasized by Charles Diehl, whose spirit looms large over Cavafy's Komninoi poems. According to Diehl, "Seldom was the taste for literature, and above all for the literature of antiquity, more widespread than in the Byzantium of the Comneni" (1963, 177). This was most evident in the case of Anna, who had "the distinction of being the only secular woman historian of the European Middle Ages, and a historian of the highest caliber" (Laiou 2000, 1). *The Alexiad* was an extraordinary work, a new kind of history in fact: history as epic (Macrides 2000, 67). That Gibbon detracted from Anna's work ("instead of the simplicity of style and narrative which wins our belief, an elaborate affectation of rhetoric and science betrays in every page the vanity of a female author" [Gouma-Peterson 2000b, 110]) could only have made *The Alexiad* more enticing to Cavafy.

Several factors drew Cavafy to Princess Anna. Her mother's family, the Doukai, was older, more glorious and aristocratic than the Komninoi.[35] Cavafy was likely indulging in a bit of genealogical self-aggrandizement by writing about the "Imperial House of Ducas" from which he supposedly hailed. There is also his sheer fascination with the hieratic wielding and bestowal of power at the Byzantine court, the endless process of palace intrigue. Anna's relation to Byzantine power structures—both political and intellectual—is outlined most incisively by Diehl:

She was, to say the least, an altogether remarkable woman, one of the finest feminine intellects ever produced by Byzantium, and far superior to most of the men of her time. And whatever one may think of her character, there is something melancholy about the unfulfilled existence of this Princess who had every right to be ambitious. . . . She came of ambitious stock. Her grandmother, Anna Dalassena, who by sheer tenacity and force of will had placed her family on the throne; her father, the Emperor Alexius, so clever, so crafty, so persevering; her mother, Irene, whose spirit was at once masculine, courageous, and intriguing—all these were immensely ambitious. . . . Her pride, personal, ancestral, and national, was immeasurable. In her eyes Byzantium was still the mistress of the world, of whom all the other nations should be the humble vassals, and her throne the finest of all the thrones of the world. (1963, 197, 180)

Hence the indomitable arrogance and attendant melancholia that, for Cavafy, serve as Anna's dominant psychological traits.

The poem is divided into three stanzas: the first sets up the quote from Anna's prologue to *The Alexiad*; the second gives us a tapestry-like interweaving of Anna's prose text converted into poetry with particular emphasis placed on her anguish; the third comments on this anguish and exposes Anna's histrionics as a cover for the raw pain of her thwarted ambition. Writing her epic in the solitary confinement of the Kecharitomeni convent, she was in essence serving out her life sentence of internal exile from matters of empire, an example of glamorous dispossession and the almost hysterical Byzantine energy defined by Birkett, "simultaneously defiant and submissive, invoking energies which are immediately frozen, framed and trapped, surrendered to become images of ruin and waste" (1986, 5). Cavafy appears to be in full agreement with Diehl regarding the irritating excess of Anna's tears (Diehl concludes that Anna had only herself to blame for her failed attempt to assassinate her brother).[36] Cavafy employs the word "αγέροχη" (arrogant) to convey Anna's particular type of hauteur, a term that, as Hirst (2000, 59) argues, he adapted from Diehl's phrase "l'orgueilleuse princesse."[37] The word implies not simply arrogance but also unbridled ambition; Anna's failed bid for power proved devastating, and she stands as yet another example of sublime defeat, a tragic abject figure who had to live with her misfortune in as dignified a manner as possible. Diehl's words offer a most fitting gloss on the precise nature of her failure and effectively illustrate what Cavafy sought to capture emotionally in the second stanza of the poem:

> It was because she hoped to regain the throne through, and with, Nicephorus Bryennius, that she loved him so much. And it was because she believed herself qualified to reign, by right of seniority, that as long as Alexius lived she plotted, agitated, and used all her influence to push forward her husband, Nicephorus, with the aim of recovering the power that she considered herself unjustly deprived of. This was the constant goal of her ambition, the justification for all her acts; this one, tenacious, dream filled her whole existence— and explains it—up until the day when, having finally failed to attain her goal, she understood that she had, at the same time, wrecked her life. (1963, 185)

Ironically, however, it was through her pen and intellect that she managed to reclaim that power by writing her father's history.[38] This paradoxical dimension of Anna's story must have intrigued Cavafy, who sympathized with her marginalized status as both a thwarted princess and an exiled intellectual. As such, she stands as a veritable case study in Byzantine abjection,[39] depression, and melancholia, an angle Julia Kristeva (2006) explores in her intriguing novel *Murder in Byzantium,* which centers on Anna's legend.[40] Cavafy both admired and pitied Anna and sought through her to highlight not only the elite intellectual tradition she represented but also the tragedy of her failed attempt to usurp the Byzantine throne.

A similar exploration of imperial women and their quest for power may be found in the poem "Anna Dalassini" (1927). In contrast to Anna Komnina and her enervating hysterics, here Anna Dalassini is presented within the context of the august magnanimity and hieratic poise associated with imperial depictions of court life, the much vaunted τάξις (order) that defined the ideal of Byzantine rule:[41]

> In the royal decree that Alexios Komninos
> put out especially to honor his mother—
> the very intelligent Lady Anna Dalassini,
> noteworthy in both her works and her manners—
> much is said in praise of her.
> Here let me offer one phrase only,
> a phrase that is beautiful, sublime:
> "She never uttered those cold words 'mine' or 'yours.'"
>
>   (1992, 145)

The poem has been criticized for its thinness and lack of lyrical depth (according to Greek poet Nasos Vayenas, it is one of Cavafy's weakest).[42] Cavafy's interest in Anna Dalassini doubtless relates to her dual persona as both a ruthless schemer and a devoted mother. Widowed with eight children, she not only emerged to become the power behind the throne but remained absolutely dedicated to her son Alexios. As Diehl comments, she was "an extraordinary woman and an excellent mother" who "by sheer tenacity and force of will had placed her family on the throne. . . . She had a statesman's mind. Her admirable understanding of affairs and her thorough grasp of politics would have qualified her to rule a world. She brought to her task some remarkable natural gifts, such as that of easy, concise speech, never at a loss for the right word, and rising without effort to eloquence. . . . 'Without her intelligence and acumen,' her son said of her, 'the monarchy would have been lost.' And Anna Comnena pronounces her superior to all the statesmen of her times" (1927, 325, 197, 304).

Cavafy's poem focuses on the famous Golden Bull reproduced in *The Alexiad* that granted Anna supreme executive power, specifically on the one "sublime" phrase "Never were those cold words 'mine' and yours' uttered between us" (Komnene 2009, 92). In essence, the bull bears testimony to the closeness shared between Alexios and his mother: "It was well known that one soul animated us, physically separated though we were, and by the grace of Christ that happy state has persisted to this day" (ibid.). In its effort to convey this sublime aesthetic, the poem aspires to a rather stylized static quality, which was no doubt a deliberate attempt on Cavafy's part to emulate the hieratic presentation of imperial figures in Byzantine mosaics, coins, and illuminated manuscripts. As such, it partakes of that decadent feature defined by Praz (1970, 397) as "the static personifications of the female lust of power" and deliberately centers on the two words "mine" and "yours." In the original Greek, the line in which these words are contained ("ου το εμόν ή το σον, το ψυχρόν τούτο ρήμα ερήθην") functions metrically as a dactylic hexameter (Hirst 2000, 65), an epigram of sorts accompanying the rather two-dimensional abstraction of the empress outlined in the poem. If we compare the poem with imperial depictions of empresses holding chrysobulla either in monumental mosaics or in the chrysobull portraits found in illuminated manuscripts, we have a better sense of the aesthetic effect Cavafy was likely trying to achieve in this poem (figure 11).[43] Although the technique of foregrounding select passages from historical sources is standard in Cavafy's poems,

Figure 11. Emperor Alexios III Komnenos of Trebizond and his wife, Theodora. Illustration from the *Chrysobull of Alexios III to the Dionysiou Monastery on Mount Athos*, Greece.

here the streamlining of the two words "mine" and "yours" causes them to leap out and demand attention. Not only is Cavafy drawing attention to the beauty of the Byzantine Greek (the words actually derive from a sermon of John Chrysostom), but he is also illustrating a decadent style of writing. As famously defined by Paul Bourget (2009) in his essay "The Example of Baudelaire," "A decadent style is one in which the unity of the book falls apart, replaced by the independence of the page, where the page decomposes to make way for the independence of the sentence, and the sentence makes way for the word." Cavafy effectively employs a Byzantine aesthetic strategy to present a highly mannered and abstract image of an august empress in the full "grandeur of repletion" who deserves praise for her "works and her manners"; his sublime imperial portrait is at once decadent in its linguistic stylistics and historically scrupulous in its lexical and iconographic resonances.[44]

The third empress connected with the Komninoi court was Irene Doukaina, who is referred to in passing as a "viper" in the poem "A Byzantine Nobleman in Exile Composing Verses" (1921) (the poem was discussed in chapter 3 in the context of exile). The decadent flourishes of the poem are evident from the very first line, which betrays an extreme sense of Byzantine pedantry that culminates in feelings of incredible boredom (the Greek term "ανιών" was deliberately selected for its etymological relationship to the celebrated "ennui" of the decadents):

> The frivolous can call me frivolous.
> I've always been most punctilious about
> important things. And I insist
> that no one knows better than I do
> the Holy Fathers, or the Scriptures, or the Canons of the Councils.
> Whenever he was in doubt,
> whenever he had any ecclesiastical problem,
> Botaniatis consulted me, me first of all.
> But exiled here (may she be cursed, that viper
> Irini Doukaina), and incredibly bored,
> it is not altogether unfitting to amuse myself
> writing six- and eight-line verses,
> to amuse myself poeticizing myths
> of Hermes and Apollo and Dionysus,
> or the heroes of Thessaly and the Peloponnese;

and to compose the most strict iambics,
such as—if you'll allow me to say so—
the intellectuals of Constantinople don't know how to compose.
It must be just this strictness that provokes their disapproval.

(1992, 110)

In his annotation to the poem, George Savidis identifies the speaker as being loosely based on the Byzantine emperor Michael VII, who was dethroned by Alexios Komninos (Cavafy 1992, 237). Although the poem functions mostly as a mock-Parnassian satire that applies as much to Cavafy in his early phase as it does to effete Byzantine poets in general, it does single out the empress Irene as the culprit. Diehl once again provides indispensable psychological insight into this intrepid imperial figure, who was the driving force behind the plot to deprive her son John of the throne in favor of Anna, her favorite. Irene was "a woman, apparently unassuming and discreet but in reality a schemer, clever, cunning, and consumed by ambition—until the day when she was to seek in the cloister, as her daughter Anna Comnena sought in literature, consolation for her frustrated hopes. . . . She offers an interesting example of the Byzantine Princesses of the twelfth century, women at once lettered and political, rather grave and austere, but of impeccable moral behavior, and endowed with a solemn grace that is not without beauty" (1963, 200, 225). This final summation of the Byzantine princesses succinctly defines the critical spirit animating Cavafy's poems as well, influenced as they were by the writings of the period's leading French Byzantinist. Like Diehl's portraits, they are fascinating glimpses into the lives of regal medieval women who not only dominated their husbands "by their beauty, or by their superior intelligence" but who "reigned themselves or, more frequently, have with sovereign power, disposed of the crown and made Emperors" (Diehl 1963, 6).

The final poem in the Komninoi cycle is "Manuel Komninos" (1905/1916):

One dreary September day
Emperor Manuel Komninos
felt his death was near.
The court astrologers—bribed, of course—went on babbling
about how many years he still had to live.

But while they were having their say,
he remembered an old religious custom
and ordered ecclesiastical vestments
to be brought from a monastery,
and he put them on, glad to assume
the modest image of a priest or monk.

Happy all those who believe,
and like Emperor Manuel end their lives
dressed modestly in their faith.

                              (1992, 63)

The composition is based both on the historical narrative account of the Byzantine historian Niketas Choniates (1157–1217) and on visual iconographic depictions of emperors in both secular and religious garb. Not surprisingly, critics are divided over how to interpret the final stanza of the poem—either as an ironic stab at an immoral and lecherous emperor or as a genuine benediction. There is no doubt that Cavafy would have expected his more erudite readers to fault Manuel for his notoriously corrupt court. As Paul Magdalino writes, "According to Choniates, the palace under Manuel was the scene of many 'senseless' love affairs in which the young emperor compounded adultery with incest, and his cousin Andronikos followed suit. This picture of a licentious court atmosphere is confirmed by the many erotic allusions in the imperial encomia of 'Manganeios Prodromos' and by the sexual innuendo in the Ptochoprodromic satires" (2000, 29). The decadence of Manuel's court was indirectly highlighted by Anna in *The Alexiad* as well, as Diehl notes: "In exalting the great figure of Alexius, it did not entirely displease her to lower a little, by inevitable comparison, the successors of this foremost of the Comneni. She also noted, not without some secret satisfaction, what she believed to be the signs of a rapid and irremediable decadence" (1963, 195).[45]

Cavafy's presentation of Manuel as a debauched emperor who sought the foot of the cross in his final days calls to mind the example of many notorious decadent figures who made similar gestures late in their lives (decadent converts to Catholicism include Huysmans, Verlaine, and Wilde).[46] There is no indication that Cavafy is overtly satirizing this longstanding tradition, which, when viewed within a decadent framework, can accommodate both the stigma of debauchery and the belatedness of genuine repentance—the dialectic of sin and expiation. Ironic readings of this poem tend to overlook this central facet of decadence altogether. Hirst (2000, 49), for example, draws attention to some interesting "informed" details in his analysis of the poem, in particular the observation in Choniates that the monastic habit found in haste was too short and exposed the emperor's knees and the "wretchedness of the body."[47] Hirst concludes that the speaker in the poem is the patriarch, whose tone toward the emperor is, if not ironic, then surely smug (54). While there is clearly a note of cynicism in the poem's allusion to the bribed astrologers who played along with the sycophantic court culture of imperial encomia, there is also an aspect of exoneration and escape inherent in the call for monastic garb, a relieved withdrawal from the mandarin court atmosphere into a modest simplicity. In this sense, the theatrics of repentance function as both a psychologically compelling and a politically expedient ploy. Manuel's conversion to monasticism aligns him with the other imperial figure who captured Cavafy's imagination, John Kantakuzinos, an emperor who abdicated the throne and spent the remaining twenty-nine years of his life as the monk Joasaph. (It should be noted that all three Komninoi royal women retired to convents as well.) The famous illuminated manuscript image depicting Kantakuzinos as both emperor and monk (figure 12) bears witness to this imperial tradition and the centrality of monastic retirement in royal Byzantine narratives. It was often standard practice and expected royal protocol; as such, it would hardy qualify for overtly sarcastic treatment at the hands of a poet as attuned to the conventions of Byzantine behavior and etiquette as was Cavafy.

John Kantakuzinos: Irreversible Decline

Emperor John VI Kantakuzinos, who reigned from 1347 to 1354, served Cavafy as the subject of two published and two unfinished poems. A remarkable figure who was unique in being "the only Byzantine emperor to record the events of his own career" (Nicol 1996, 1),[48] Kantakuzinos was, like Cavafy, a historian manqué whose curious life included both a stunningly dramatic usurpation of the Byzantine throne and an equally shocking abdication and retreat into monastic seclusion. The devastating six-year civil war that erupted between Kantakuzinos and Empress Anna

Figure 12. Emperor John VI Kantakuzinos as emperor and monk.
Bibliothèque Nationale de France (Grec 1242).

of Savoy (1341–47) provided Cavafy with a rich period in which to explore the themes of corruption and palace intrigue, particularly as they played out among three imperial women: Theodora Kantakuzine, Anna of Savoy, and Irini Assan, the emperor's mother, adversary, and wife, respectively. In the poem "John Kantakuzinos Triumphs" (1924), we are presented with the plight of an unidentified supporter of Anna of Savoy whose political choice has possibly ruined him:

> He sees the fields that still belong to him:
> the wheat, the animals, the trees laden with fruit;
> and beyond them his ancestral home
> full of clothes, costly furniture, silverware.
>
> They'll take it all away from him—O God—they'll take it all
>   away from him now.
>
> Would Kantakuzinos show pity for him
> if he went and fell at his feet? They say he's merciful,
> very merciful. But those around him? And the army?—
> Or should he fall down and plead before Lady Irini?
>
> Fool that he was to get mixed up in Anna's party!
> If only Lord Andronikos had never married her!
> Has she ever done anything good, shown any humanity?
> Even the Franks don't respect her any longer.
> Her plans were ridiculous, all her plotting farcical.
> While they were threatening everyone from Constantinople,
> Kantakuzinos demolished them, Lord John demolished them.
>
> And to think he'd planned to join Lord John's party!
> And he would have done it, and would have been happy now,
> a great nobleman still, his position secure,
> if the bishop hadn't dissuaded him at the last moment
> with his imposing hieratic presence,
> his information bogus from beginning to end,
> his promises, and all his drivel.
>
> (1992, 131)

The informed or curious reader perhaps knows or will discover that after triumphing, Kantakuzinos proved to be a forgiving and rather lenient victor, so the fears expressed in the poem are likely misplaced.[49] Interestingly

enough, the villainy of the poem centers on the character of Anna, the notoriously corrupt and vindictive empress. This is in keeping with Cavafy's
decadent fixation on Byzantine empresses, although Anna presents a rather
unique case. Diehl relays that the Frankish princess was less Hellenized than
any of the other princesses from the West and that she heartily disliked the
Greeks, was guided by her passions, and had a jealous and evil disposition
(1963, 289–291). She particularly resented the favoritism her husband, the
emperor Andronikos III, had shown his then Grand Domestic John Kantakuzinos: "Like the sovereign, he governed all public affairs, and so highly
was he favored that in the field he and the Emperor occupied the same tent,
and often the same bed, a privilege that etiquette forbade even to the imperial children" (292). Her animus against Kantakuzinos even extended to his
beautiful and intelligent wife, Irini Asan,[50] of whom she was openly jealous, and to his mother, Theodora, whom she and her party gravely abused.

The other two villains in this saga are Anna's accomplices, Alexios Apo-
kaukos (the Grand Domestic) and the patriarch, John Kalekas, referred to
negatively in the previous poem "with his imposing hieratic presence, /
his information bogus from beginning to end, / his promises, and all his
drivel." (He is also the subject of an unfinished poem titled "The Patriarch.")[51] Anna's party was responsible for the persecution, imprisonment,
and cruel starvation of Theodora, who, forbidden medical care, died in
prison on Epiphany in 1342 (Nicol 1996, 54). This is the subject of the unfinished poem fittingly titled "During the Feast of Lights" (1925*):

When, during the Feast of Lights, they planned once again the same things
they had done on Christmas,
when they brought back their thugs,
planning anew to prop up
the child before the rabble (alas
for John, good Lord Andronikos's heir,
who would have fared better with her and her son),

when, during the Feast of Lights, they planned once again the same things;
again the mob's crude profanity,
and the vile slanderous implication about her;
she couldn't take the agony for a second time
and in the dingy room where she was imprisoned,
Lady Kantakuzine gave up her soul.

The demise of Lady Kantakuzine, so wretched,
I gleaned from the History of Nikephoros Gregoras.
In the historical works of the emperor
John Kantakuzinos, it is somewhat differently
recorded; but not with less pity.

(1994a, 214, my translation)

The final stanza introduces a comparison of the historical accounts by the historian Nikephoros Gregoras (1293–1361) and the emperor himself; it praises the uniqueness of Kantakuzinos's treatment of a subject that must have been heartbreaking for him to narrate.

All four Kantakuzinos poems bear witness to how profoundly disastrous the civil war proved for the Byzantine Empire, weakening it to a dangerous degree and ushering in the final period of irreversible decline. This is something that Kantakuzinos himself admitted in his *Histories,* as Donald Nicol notes: "The memoirs of John Cantacuzene do not constitute a panegyric, rather a justification of all his activities through two civil or dynastic wars until he was, with some reluctance, crowned as Emperor in Constantinople in 1347. He then describes in detail his part in the events of his seven-year reign, culminating in his despairing acceptance of the fact that the Empire was beyond repair" (1996, 168–169). Cavafy expressed his admiration for Kantakuzinos in his unfinished poem "The Patriarch" (1925), where he refers to him as "the worthy man that our race possessed at that time, / wise, lenient, patriotic, brave, skillful . . . the venerable, the diligent, the generous " (Cavafy 1994a, 207 [my translation]). The qualities Cavafy shared with the emperor—understatement and restraint both in character and historical writing—have been pointed out by Mendelsohn (Cavafy 2009c, 87). Kantakuzinos was a ruler who maintained the high standards of Byzantine culture even while the culture was decomposing around him.[52] This positive aura is complicated by the fact that, under Kantakuzinos's reign, the Turks established a permanent presence in Thrace and Asia Minor (the emperor married his daughter Theodora to Orhan, the Osmanli emir of Bythinia, in an effort to foster good relations and military alliances between royal families). Diehl's final pronouncement is one with which Cavafy could hardly have taken issue: Kantakuzinos, "in spite of his outstanding qualities, and Anna of Savoy, because of all the mistakes of her rule, were largely responsible for the decadence and final ruin of the Byzantine Empire" (1963, 307).

A salient moment when decline and grandeur dramatically intersect is captured in the poem "Of Colored Glass" (1925). In one of her more notorious acts of spite, Anna emptied the treasury and drained the empire, selling the most beautiful pieces of the imperial treasury, including the crown jewels, which she pawned to the republic of Venice (they were never to be redeemed). Her reasons for doing so were openly known: "If ever Cantacuzene were to be victorious, she said, at least he would not lay hands on all those splendors that enhance the glamor of power" (Diehl 1963, 301). Cavafy dramatizes the poignant coronation of John and Irini by means of theatrics calculated to convey the sublime decline of late Byzantine history:

> I'm quite touched by a single detail
> in the coronation at Blachernae of John Cantacuzenus
> and Irene, daughter of Andronicus Asan.
> Inasmuch as they had very few precious stones
> (our hapless state was extremely poor)
> they wore artificial ones. A pile of glass pieces,
> red, green, or blue. In my view
> there's nothing shameful or undignified
> about those little pieces
> of colored glass. To the contrary, they seem
> but a sad protestation
> against the unfair sorry state of those being crowned.
> They are symbols of what they ought to have,
> of what was without question right for them to have
> at the coronation of a Lord John Cantacuzenus
> and a Lady Irene, daughter of Andronicus Asan.
>   (2013, 166)

The coronation, which should have taken place in Hagia Sophia, had to be held in the less august venue of the Vlahernai palace church, the great church having suffered major damage from a recent earthquake (it remained in disrepair because of the depletion of the imperial treasury). Here once again we encounter Cavafy's interest in mineralogy—the play between artificial and genuine jewels. The few precious stones are set alongside artificial ones, and the result is not simply a sad protest but, more important, a perverse triumph of artifice and deception that allows the imperial spectacle to go on (much like the panoply orchestrated around

Kaisarion in "Alexandrian Kings"). This dynamic partakes of the decadent fascination with artifice and costume, aesthetic touches that Cavafy paints into his historical-poetic narrative of political decay. He strategically chooses the complex persona of Kantakuzinos to illustrate this confluence of decadence and dignity; he likely would have agreed with Alexander Kazhdan's subsequent assessment of the emperor: "The poetry of the heroic defeat in Byzantine literature was invented by Kantakuzinos" (cited in Nicol 1996, 168). The triumph, diffidence, and hesitation shown by the "reluctant emperor," as Nicol refers to him, is a testament to both the high intellectual accomplishments of the period and its tragic vulnerabilities.[53]

As similar exploration of heroic defeat may be found in the poem "Theophilos Palaiologos" (1914), where the final days of Byzantium are foregrounded in an unmistakably melancholy manner:

> This is the last year, this the last
> of the Greek emperors. And, alas,
> how sadly those around him talk.
> Kyr Theophilos Palaiologos
> in his grief, in his despair, says:
> "I would rather die than live."
>
>   Ah, Kyr Theophilos Palaiologos,
> how much of the pathos, the yearning of our race,
> how much weariness
> (such exhaustion from injustice and persecution)
> your six tragic words contained.
>
>   (1992, 201)

Theophilos, cousin of the last emperor of Byzantium, Constantine XI Palaiologos, died defending the city on May 29, 1453, after the walls had been breached at a minor gate called Kerkoporta, which led to the final storming by the Ottoman Turks. Literally throwing himself into the onslaught of armed Turks overtaking the city, he decided that all was lost and cried out his legendary acknowledgment of defeat. Dallas (1986, 174–176) observes that the poem is an example of Cavafy's technique of demythologizing history and presenting an "anti-heroic" interrogation of historical sources. What we ultimately encounter in this poem is another version of the decadent dilemma articulated in "Waiting for the Barbarians," in which the only real "solution" is utter annihilation. Here Cavafy quotes a historical source (George Sphrantzes's *Chronicon Minus*) from which he appropriated the Greek phrase "θέλω θανεῖν" ("I would rather die"), a fragment at once historically accurate and ambiguously modernist.[54] The poem's "six tragic words" mark the political end of the Byzantine era, although not necessarily its cultural end. Cavafy will go on to write two additional poems set in this final Byzantine period: "It Was Taken" (1921*), based on a Pontian folk song on the fall of Constantinople, and the unfinished "After the Swim" (1921*), which features the paradox of the cultural renaissance experienced during the late Palaiologan period just prior to the collapse of Byzantium.

"After the Swim" presents the phenomenon of the revival of learning and the renascent Hellenism that would spark the Italian Renaissance by invoking the spirit of George Gemistos Plethon (ca. 1360–1452), the Neoplatonic philosopher and Byzantine intellectual who advocated a return to paganism:

Both were naked when they emerged from the sea of the Samian
coast; they were slow to dress after their enjoyable swim
(it was a hot summer's day)
and they regretted having to cover the beauty of their statuesque nakedness
that so harmoniously complemented the loveliness of their faces.

What aesthetes the ancient Greeks were,
who presented undiminished
the naked beauty of youth.

Poor Gemistos was not all that wrong
(and let Lord Andronikos and the patriarch suspect him as they will)
when he desired and urged us to return to paganism:
My holy faith—may it always remain sacred—
but Gemistos makes sense to some extent.

Back then George Gemistos's teaching greatly
influenced the young,
that most wise and very eloquent
preacher of Hellenic paideia.

(1994a, 122, my translation)

The poem was inspired largely by Edward Gibbon's account of the Council of Florence in his *Decline and Fall*: "At the Synod of Florence,

Gemistus Pletho said, in familiar conversation to George of Trebizond, that in a short time mankind would unanimously renounce the Gospel and the Koran, for a religion similar to that of the Gentiles [i.e. pagans]" (Cavafy 1994a, 121n). The events of the poem occur shortly after the philosopher's death and touch upon the numerous cultural crises that riddled the Byzantine world—namely, the Hellenic inheritance, theological heresies, and the encroaching humanism of the Renaissance, which was very much indebted to Plethon.[55] As C. M. Woodhouse writes, Plethon "was the first competent interpreter of both Platonism and Aristotelianism to address Latin audiences for a thousand years. . . . The philosophical study of Plato, as distinct from the literary task of translation . . . began with Gemistos' arrival" (1986, x). Cavafy's poem, while foregrounding the sensuality of the swimmers, is unmistakably caught up in a historic moment when a nascent neo-Hellenism rears its rather statuesque head. For Cavafy, these young Byzantine Greeks are aesthetically connected to their forbears; a mere glance at Greek sculpture will suffice to prove their racial continuity. We have here not only another example of Paterian aesthetic homoeroticism but also a bold claim for the uninterrupted succession of the Greek race. For Cavafy, Plethon was not merely a preacher of Hellenic paideia but a lover (ἐραστής, *erastes*) of it as well, as an earlier version of the poem reads. (An earlier variation of line six reads "the view of their erotic parts," which emphasizes the sensual aspect of Plethon the lover's revival of paganism [Cavafy 1994a, 117]). The word *erastes* takes on a heightened meaning when we keep in mind that the reestablishment of Platonism in the West would lead to the belated legitimization of Greek homosexuality as an area of literary inspiration and academic study. Thus in the poem, the two Hellenic components of eros and paideia, so fundamental to the Victorian sense of Hellenism in both its decadent-aesthetic and liberal-humanist facets, are stridently celebrated. Even Orthodox Christianity ("my Holy Faith") is duly integrated into the equation, another instance of Cavafy's Paterian allegiance to the aesthetic forms and cultural formulas of Christianity. The poem masterfully brings together all the various decadent strains that appear throughout Cavafy's work and serves as a liminal composition marking the historical transition from decadent late Byzantium to the new phase of cultural Hellenism in Renaissance Italy, where it will in turn gradually ripen into its own state of sophisticated deliquescence. "After the Swim" effectively bridges the chasm between western and eastern decadence by means of Byzantine Hellenism and stands as Cavafy's consummate (albeit private) statement on the profound importance of Byzantine culture to the western literary tradition in both its high humanist and its subversively decadent strains.

Epilogue

DECADENCE'S GAY LEGACY

Although Cavafy's erotic verse may no longer be labeled decadent solely by virtue of its homosexual content, this was largely the case when he first wrote and published. Nowhere is this more apparent than in the two extant comments by Cavafy himself that come closest to referencing the subject of decadence. The first, cited in the prologue, was made to George Valasso-poulo and is recorded in Forster's letter to Cavafy (July 1, 1917), in which Cavafy allegedly expressed the view that "the artist must be depraved." The second exists in a private commentary in which Cavafy writes, "η διαστροφή" (inversion) is a "πηγή μεγαλείου" (source of greatness). Both statements should be read within the homosexual context demarcated by the two touchstones of decadence: the notion of degeneration[1] on one end of the spectrum and the countermanding idea of an elitist gay exceptionalism on the other.[2] Homosexual decadents and aesthetes effectively pivoted between these binaries, deftly employing variations of each in their creative contributions to the decadent literary tradition. As Richard Kaye notes, "The sexual ambiguity of so much aestheticist ideology often appears to be a cagey avowal of elitist homoerotics, which, like aestheticism, proclaimed that what was 'unnatural' was more beautiful and therefore preferable to that which was found in mundane nature" (1995, 2). Not only was decadent aestheticism linked to homosexuality because of the sexual tastes of so many of its key advocates, but the arguments regarding amorality in art and literature were frequently thinly veiled attempts by fin de siècle homosexuals at justifying same-sex relations.[3] In this decadent context, moral distinctions are rendered subservient to the search for the beautiful; sexuality, like taste, involves a heightened sensitivity to beauty.[4]

Decadence's antibourgeois valorization of an ideal, artificial, and amoral world over the reality of conventional respectability proved foundational for the ongoing affiliation between decadence and homosexuality. As the chapters of this book have argued, Cavafy's work was informed at every step by the decadent aesthetic in its various pictorial and literary manifestations, beginning with the Pre-Raphaelites and the discourse of homosexual legitimacy that emerged from their work, then engaging more directly with the French decadent poets and writers, who would in turn animate the writings of the late Victorian British homosexual apologists on whom Cavafy relied heavily for inspiration. The fin de siècle thus constitutes a pivotal period during which homosexual male culture—via decadence—becomes a "visible part of the mainstream literary world" (Vicinus 1999, 84). Cavafy's writings emerge from this cultural milieu, and the gradual "gaying" of critical studies of his poetry, abetted by the unflagging and expanding loyalty of his gay readership, remains linked to this decadent legacy.[5] His ability to portray the gay cruising culture of his day and the bold manner by which he features the homoerotic at a time when few poets had the courage to do so, are factors that continue to generate queer readings of his work.[6] One of the earliest critics to comment on Cavafy's daring portrayal of homosexuality (Forster, it should be noted, while fully appreciating this openness, refrained from commenting on it publicly)[7] was W. H. Auden, who wrote: "The erotic world he depicts is one of casual pickups and short-lived affairs. Love, there, is rarely more than physical passion, and when tenderer emotions do exist, they are almost always one-sided. At the same time, he refuses to pretend that his memories of moments of sensual pleasure are unhappy or spoiled by feelings of guilt" (1989, xvii).[8] This notable absence of shame distinguishes

Cavafy from many "pre-Stonewall" gay writers, whose work is often marked by feelings of abjection and excessive sentimentality.[9] His contribution to the gay tradition is thus unique in that it offers a spectrum of poetry that includes both the aesthetic sublimation of desire through art and the open expression of sexual passion, a corpus that effectively transcends the mutually exclusive tension between these two elements frequently found in twentieth-century gay culture.

David Halperin's (2012) highly provocative study of gay subjectivity offers an interesting point of entry into this facet of Cavafy's work, providing as it does a valuable context for appraising the poet's position in queer culture. Halperin points to the critical impasse that developed in twentieth-century gay culture between ironic camp humor on the one hand and the obsession with sex and physical beauty[10] on the other (gay identity vs. gay eroticism), one that led to the post-Stonewall rejection of hyperrefined culture, femininity, abjection, and shame in favor of masculinity, sex, and pride. As Halperin puts it, "As queen was to butch, so culture was to sex"; post-Stonewall gay liberation favored "a model of gay identity that focused on sex at the expense of culture—and that excluded the feminine identifications that had informed and defined much of traditional gay male culture" (8). Cavafy managed to navigate between these two extremes in his erotic poetry, largely by channeling the classical tradition of the Greek cult of male beauty in which culture and sensuality fully coalesce, balanced by poems that dramatize casual sexual encounters. With his own variation of art for art's sake, he offers what Christopher Robinson terms "the erotic moment for its own sake, linking to a specifically homoerotic context the experience of unstable relationships, the transience of human beauty and the need for art to preserve and give meaning to the fragmented experience of reality" (2005, 267–268).

Central to this delicate balance between culture and sexuality is the ascendancy of male beauty in Cavafy's poems, a subject that aligns him with an uninterrupted gay literary tradition stretching back to antiquity.[11] For some readers, this overriding obsession with male beauty remains problematic, dominant though it is in gay culture.[12] Mark Lilly, for one, points out that in Cavafy's love poems, too much importance is attached to physical beauty: "It is one thing . . . to celebrate the body and the pleasures of sexuality. . . . But it is certainly another thing to exalt beauty to such an extent, to confer on it such a premium, that it is represented as an indispensable attribute for a successful human life" (1993, 48–49).[13] And in a similar but less censorious vein, Gregory Woods comments on how Cavafy exalts "the soaring beauty of what so many others dismiss as degenerate and unnatural":

> It is as if he embodies homosexuality in some way that is physically different from–both aesthetically and erotically superior to—the bodies of heterosexual boys. This refined form of homoerotic beauty is perceptible only to those whom it will attract—namely, fellow homosexual boys and men. . . . There is an ideal masculinity, in other words, which is specifically homosexual. Transgression intensifies both beauty and the pleasure one takes in it. . . . This is Cavafy's triumph. It justifies his attention to sex and represents a strong line of defense against rejection itself. The rejection is taken for granted. If it is shaming, shame is accepted with pride. (1998, 191)

This aesthetic and erotic superiority partakes of that aforementioned ideal strain of gay exceptionalism that runs through so much decadent writing. In this sense, a certain portion of Cavafy's erotic poems remain very true to the fin de siècle and illustrate "the peculiar merging of eroticism and aestheticism that is distinctive to gay male culture" as defined by Halperin: "By mingling the rapt transports of sexual idolatry with a distant, almost clinical appreciation of beauty, gay men achieve a kind of disinterestedness in their relation to erotic objects that brings their experience of sexual desire very close to that of pure aesthetic contemplation" (2012, 230). This very "mingling" channels a particular facet of the decadent tradition, namely, the aesthetic privileging of the cerebrally erotic over the physically sexual. Jean Pierrot documents a significant articulation of this deviant position by one of the central figures of the period: "In his *Certains* of 1890, Huysmans reprinted a fairly long article on Félicien Rops that is in fact a fascinating study of the relationship between eroticism and the fine arts. In it he demonstrates that eroticism is the fruit of pure and self-sufficient imagination, and that real sexual pleasure destroys it. Seen in this way, decadent eroticism becomes just one of the forms taken by an exacerbated imagination. . . . Huysmans is here expressing one of the principal facts about decadent eroticism: this it was a purely intellectual and cerebral activity" (1981, 135). Cavafy, as a conscious inheritor of this tradition, promotes a variation of this intellectual eroticism in numerous poems. In

"When They Stir in Your Mind" (1913/1916), he effectively dramatizes Huysmans's view:

> Try to watch over them, poet,
> however few there are that can be stayed.
> The visions of your erotic life.
> Slip them, half-hidden, into your phrases.
> Try to hold on to them, poet,
> when they stir in your mind
> at night or in the noonday glare.
>
> (2013, 98)

Similarly, in "So They'll Come—" (1920), we have another version of "poetic necromancy" (as George Savidis termed it),[14] where erotic ghosts return to haunt the poet:

> A single candle will do.   Its faint light
> will be just right,   will be more tender
> for when they come,   when Love's Shades come.
>
> A single candle will do.   The room tonight
> needn't have much light.   In a deep reverie
> and suggestive mood,   and with the light very low—
> thus in my reverie   I'll frame a vision
> so they will come,   so Love's Shades will come.
>
> (2013, 140)

Featured in these poems are "delectations that were half real, / half wrought by my own mind" ("I Went" [Cavafy 1992, 48]) that are summoned to return through memory, the dominant motif in "Return" (1909/1912):

> Return often and take me,
> beloved feeling return and take me—
> when the body's memory awakes,
> and old desire runs through the blood again,
> when lips and skin remember,
> and hands feel as if they touch once more.
>
> Return often and take me at night,
> when lips and skin remember. . . .
>
> (2013, 75)

In addition to expressing an almost Proustian aesthetic predilection for memory as the mediating faculty between fulfillment and loss, these poems vent a psychological frustration with the suffocating circumstances of gay cruising in urban Alexandria in the early twentieth century. This is quite evident in the poem "September, 1903" (1903/1904), in which the speaker has little recourse but to willingly deceive himself despite having come so close to acting on his erotic impulses:

> At least let me now deceive myself with illusions
> so as not to feel my empty life.
>
> And yet I came so close so many times.
> And yet how paralyzed I was, how cowardly;
> why did I keep my lips sealed
> while my empty life wept inside me,
> my desires wore robes of mourning?
>
> To have been so close so many times,
> to those sensual eyes, those lips,
> to that body I dreamed of, loved.
> To have been so close so many times.
>
> (1992, 189)

And one of the most poignant poems from this category, one that speaks across time to a twenty-first-century audience, is "Half an Hour" (1917*), in which the poet admits to the deficiencies of his decadent-aesthetic strategy, yet refuses to abandon it:

> Never made it with you and don't expect
> I will. Some talk, a slight move closer,
> as in the bar yesterday, nothing more.
> A pity, I won't deny. But we artists
> now and then by pushing our minds
> can—but only for a moment—create
> a pleasure that seems almost physical.
> That's why in the bar yesterday—with the help
> of alcohol's merciful power—I had
> a half-hour that was completely erotic.
> I think you knew it and
> stayed on purpose a little longer.

That was really necessary. Because
with all my imagination and spell of the drinks,
I just had to see your lips,
had to have your body near.

(2013, 114)

Apart from its emotive appeal, "Half an Hour" bears witness to how indispensable this particular dimension of the decadent sensibility—the erotic sublime, as it were—remained to Cavafy's art and creative process. Many of Cavafy's remarkably daring expressions of gay passion involved this distinctive aesthetic sublimation of sexuality.

Balancing out these poems of erotic sublimation are others that openly celebrate the physical and embrace the sexual, "Their Beginning" (1915/1921) serving as one of the most powerful examples. In Cavafy's erotic poems, there is a "clear effort to de-romanticise relationships" (Lilly 1993, 49), a quality that appealed to some readers (Gore Vidal [2001, xvii] called Cavafy "the Pindar of the one-night stand between males") but displeased others. Auden, for example, was troubled, as noted above, by the absence of any deep emotional connection. Although Auden appreciated the remarkable absence of guilt or shame in Cavafy's poetry, he held a private view of the erotic poems that was less adulatory. According to Auden's friend Nikos Stangos,[15] though Auden "admired Cavafy's historical poems, he thought the erotic poems 'kitsch.' . . . [Nikos] did not disagree" (Plante 2009, 128).[16] Auden never committed this comment to writing, nor did he explain precisely what he meant by the word "kitsch." Nevertheless, one may safely speculate that his use of the term alludes to that certain excess of sentimentality that most definitions of kitsch include.[17] (It is unlikely that Auden meant to imply that the erotic poems were "bad art" in the extreme sense of the word "kitsch.") The Auden circle, of course, was highly attuned to the gay aesthetic of camp, which is not unrelated to kitsch, terms that have both positive and negative connotations, depending on how they are employed.[18] This dual perspective is aptly described by Calinescu, who notes that kitsch remains "one of the most bewildering and elusive categories of modern aesthetics": "The possibility of the avant-garde's using kitsch elements and, conversely, of kitsch's making use of avant-garde devices is just an indication of how complex a concept kitsch is. . . . Like art itself, of which it is both an imitation and a negation, kitsch cannot be defined from a single vantage point. And again like art—or for

that matter antiart—kitsch refuses to lend itself even to a negative definition, because it simply has no single compelling, distinct counterconcept"
(Calinescu 1987, 232).

Auden's introduction of the kitsch aesthetic to Cavafy criticism invites
further consideration of what might be termed the ongoing "kitchifica-
tion" of Cavafy's work as a significant and increasingly relevant aspect
of his global popularity. In today's world, "no one is safe from kitsch"
(Calinescu 1987, 262), and though a comprehensive analysis of the concept
of kitsch is beyond the scope of this epilogue, the term offers a unique
perspective on the phenomenon of Cavafy's mass appeal.[19] Historically
rooted in the bourgeois realism of the salon paintings and sculptures of
the nineteenth century,[20] kitsch and the debate surrounding its aesthetic
value effectively reprise many of the tropes of decadence that had played
out decades earlier, especially as regards the notion of degeneracy. As Ruth
Holliday and Tracey Potts point out, "The division between art and kitsch
was mobilised by the Nazis but compounded by so many subsequent critics seeking to rescue modern art from the Nazi charge of degeneracy. In
a classic reverse discourse, however, these critics applied the same charge
of degeneracy to kitsch" (2012, 63). Most critics agree that sentimentality
is the common denominator of kitsch subjects; indeed, "decoration and
sentimentality have become key abjects of artistic discourse" (45). Initially
the term was associated with premodernist figurative depictions in art that
were rendered retrograde by the ascendency of modernism with its valorization of abstract impressionism.[21] Gradually the foundational opposition between the avant-garde and kitsch broke down with the postmodern
appropriation of kitsch in the name of pop art, as Roger Scruton argues:
"Having recognized that modernist severity is no longer acceptable—
for modernism begins to seem like the same old thing and therefore
not modern at all—artists began not to shun kitsch but to embrace it,
in the manner of Andy Warhol, Alan Jones, and Jeff Koons" (1999).[22]
More recently there has been a movement to rehabilitate the term and
to rescue kitsch from its debased position as the rear-guard repository of
bad art and the demonized "other" of modernism. One such advocate of
the more positive dimension of kitsch is Norwegian artist Odd Nerdrum,
who maintains that "we cannot simply call Kitsch bad art.... Kitsch forms
its own autonomous system by striving for beauty rather than truth.
Any gesture towards beauty always opens the door to kitsch" (Nerdrum

2011, 68). Similarly, Celeste Olalquiaga, in her book-length study on kitsch, points out that it is "the leftover of modernity's own dreams of transcendence, a remnant loaded simultaneously with hopes and the impossibility of their realization, a ruin. . . . Kitsch is the attempt to repossess the experience of intensity and immediacy through an object" (1998, 84, 291).

For Cavafy critics, the term offers an encompassing way to incorporate a heightened appreciation of what might otherwise be dismissed as obsolescent qualities—the sentimental, pictorial "Victorian" elements that unmistakably animate so many of his poems—and to factor them into a critical consideration of his appeal to a popular audience. His attempt to repossess intensity and immediacy through an object—the evanescent lover—renders his poems melancholic erotic souvenirs,[23] as in "Days of 1903":"I never found them again—that were so quickly lost . . . / the poetic eyes, the pallid/face . . . in the street's nightfall" (2013, 112). In "The Afternoon Sun" (1918/1919), the speaker waxes nostalgic for the room where he and his erstwhile lover used to meet and reminisces about the objects once contained within it: the sofa, the Turkish rug, the vases, table, chairs and bed: "They still must be around somewhere, poor old things. // Beside the window was the bed / the reach of the afternoon sun divided in half. //. . . At four o'clock one afternoon, we were separating / for just a week . . . And oh, / that week became forever" (2013, 129). In "Before Time Could Change Them" (1924), two lovers are forced to part because of economic and social circumstances that are given a sentimental gloss: "Or maybe Destiny / came on like an artist separating them now / before their feeling turned off, before Time could change them: / each one for the other to remain forever / the twenty-four-year old beautiful young boy" (2013, 161). In "One Night" (1907/1915), the recollection of a one-night stand becomes so overwhelming "that even now/as I write, after so many years!/in my lonely house, I am drunk again" (2013, 90). And in "The Mirror in the Vestibule" (1930), the mirror—rejoicing at having caught the image of a handsome delivery boy—itself becomes a metaphor for the rather Romantic act of reflecting upon emotion in tranquility: "But the old mirror that had seen so much / during the long years of its existence, / thousands of things and faces, that old mirror was now overjoyed, / and filled with pride at having taken on / perfect beauty for a few moments" (2013, 201).

The imbrication of the pictorial and the nostalgic in these poems creates a unique sentimentality[24] that is just saved from bathos by the intervention of the agency of art and creative memory. This very sentimental strain with its focus on the representational is a clear vestige of what could be termed a Victorian sensibility; indeed, the presence of such emotional elements in Cavafy's erotic poems (nothing could distinguish them further from Eliot's high modernist insistence on the impersonal separation between emotion and creativity) allows Cavafy to break ground by rehabilitating the senti-mental, which, according to Eve Kosofsky Sedgwick (1990), constitutes an important gay male project. Sedgwick identifies what she terms the prefig-uring "modernist aesthetic according to which sentimentality inheres less in the object figured than in a prurient vulgarity associated with figuration itself." Postmodernism, she notes, is "in this view, the strenuous rematch between the reigning champ, modernist abstraction, and the deposed chal-lenger, figuration, would thus *necessarily* have kitsch and sentimental-ity as its main spaces of contestation." Thus the figuration that had to be "abjected from modernist self-reflexive abstraction was not the figuration of just *any* body, the figuration of figurality itself, but, rather, that repre-sented in a very particular body, the desired male body. So as kitsch or sentimentality came to mean representation itself, what represented 'rep-resentation itself' came at the same time signally to be a very particular, masculine object and subject of erotic desire" (166–167). Cavafy's decadent indulgence in the figuration of the male body necessarily occupies this very space of contestation, where sentimental kitsch both lingers in the residual Victorian aestheticism that the poet refused to abandon while also emerg-ing as part of a radical gay strategy reconfiguring queer desire.

Regarding the kitschification of Cavafy, two pictorial examples from the world of artistic photography serve as apt illustrations; in each case, kitsch operates on various levels to accentuate sentimental elements from Cavafy's work while simultaneously offering sophisticated parodies of it by calling attention to itself as kitsch ("kitsch in quotations" as it were).[25] In his highly fanciful and campy work of "staged photography,"[26] *The Adventures of Constantine Cavafy*, art-photographer Duane Michals (2007) creates a series of provocative imaginary portraits accompanied by eleven poems as well as some of his own philosophical reflections. The series of what Michals terms "little fables of my imaginary theatrics" features actor Joel Grey portraying Cavafy in various voyeuristic scenarios involving stunning young men reading poetry, stripping, and posing in cafés and bedrooms. The immediate camp association of Grey with his iconic role as master of ceremonies in Bob Fosse's movie musical *Cabaret* lends the entire series of photos an unmistakable element of kitsch. This is evident in the tableau "Cavafy Cheats at Playing Strip Poker," where Michals capriciously transgresses the boundaries of heteronormative taste by presenting an almost lecherous Cavafy ogling and swindling a buff blond youth. Included in the series are ersatz poems by Michals written in the manner of Cavafy—one to God ("Cavafy Abandons God to His Fate"), another about old friends who "chit chat of this and that" with Michals posing as the Greek intellectual Dimitris Michaleides. Throughout, Cavafy is shown in various mock-sentimental poses: as an old poet lusting after young poets reading his work; a nurse tending to a wounded student; a priest hearing confessions of young men; and a masseuse rubbing down a youth with massage oil. The work concludes with an epilogue in which the poet "decorates his muse with verse" (figure 13). The inclusion of actual facsimiles of Cavafy's Greek original manuscripts in this highly kitschified tableau illustrates what Calinescu (1987, 236) defines as the kitsch combination effect of using "genuine great art as mere ostentatious decoration."

In this same tradition of art photography, Greek photographer Dimitris Yeros (2010) offers a series of portraits illustrating an anthology of Cavafy poems that involve close-up portraits of famous personalities and

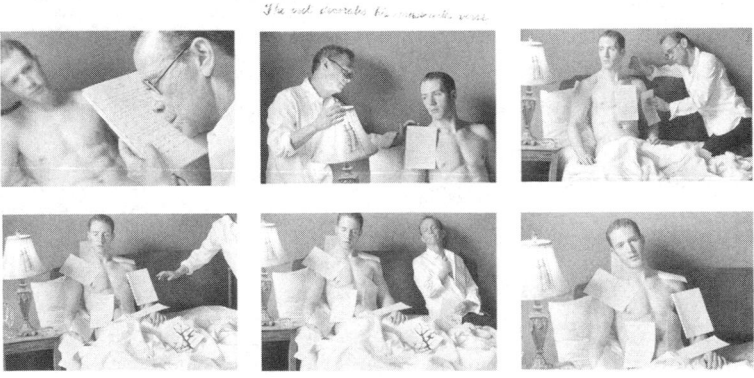

Figure 13. Duane Michals, *The Old Poet Decorates His Muse with Verse, 2003–05*
(6 gelatin silver prints, 5×7″) from *The Adventures of Constantine Cavafy*.
© Duane Michals. Courtesy of DC Moore Gallery, New York.

handsome models. The emphasis here pivots from the striking physiognomies of eminent artists[27] captured in provocative poses to the faces and bodies of young men (models and dancers, none of whom, according to Yeros, had the slightest interest in the poems for which they were posing or even knew who Cavafy was!). Edward Albee introduces the book with the following quote: "In whatever readings, I found his poetry so vivid, so personal, so powerful that I was aware of being in the presence of a great poet, one whose concerns echoed mine and whose mastery was thrilling" (11). Notwithstanding this high artistic praise from a fellow artist, the series includes photos that vary in their manipulation of the sentimental, ranging from Jeff Koons shown holding inflated pool animals (a self-reflexive nod to avant-garde kitsch) to a mantilla-covered Olympia Dukakis posing as the mother in the poem "Supplication" (figure 14). Included in the series of portraits are Carlos Fuentes, Naguib Mahfouz, Jean Baudrillard, Quentin Crisp, Gabriel Garcia Marquez, and Edmund White (Duane Michals is shown posing while seated in a café next to a shirtless youth in a three-part photo series that replicates his own work). Like Michals, Yeros openly indulges in sentimental aspects of Cavafy's poems while managing to achieve a high level of artistry, capturing that paradoxical dynamic of kitsch identified by Calinescu to both animate and negate art.

Such fine homoerotic photographic tributes to Cavafy reveal how appealing his work remains to audiences outside the confines of academia and serve as revealing indexes of his ever-expanding popularity. To date, the most global moment for Cavafy (leaving aside the collective events, articles, and celebratory memorabilia surrounding the 2013 "Year of Cavafy") remains the highly dramatic but overwhelmingly sentimental moment at the funeral of Jacqueline Kennedy Onassis (May 23, 1994) when Maurice Tempelsman read "Ithaka" to a viewing audience that surely numbered in the tens of millions. The occasion of the death of "America's tragic twentieth-century empress," in the words of Gore Vidal (2001, xix), brought Cavafy to a global audience that he could never have imagined even in one of his most outré historicizing fantasies. The juxtaposition of the poem with the persona of "Jackie O," American royalty famously commodified by Warhol as a pop icon, brings together several strands of kitsch, beginning with the fact that Tempelsman added two verses of his own to the poem, sentimentalizing it even further.[28] "Ithaka," essentially a poetic expression of art for art's sake, becomes in this context a tribute to

Figure 14. Dimitris Yeros, *Supplication*, with Olympia Dukakis as the mother of the drowned sailor. From *Shades of Love: Photographs Inspired by the Poems of C. P. Cavafy.* Used with permission of the photographer.

the refined cultural tastes[29] (and decadent shopping habits) of one of the world's most famous women. The moment is Cavafian on numerous levels, notably the funereal use of a poem and the subtle decadent implication of its inscribed Paterian message. It is rendered kitsch both by its climactic inclusion in a public display of national emotion and by the ironic infusion of the elements of commodity fetishism introduced by its association with Jacqueline Kennedy Onassis and her indelible Warholian aura.[30] (The fact that it was read in its English translation should not be overlooked, as the disseminating role played by translation remains crucial to Cavafy's global appeal.)[31] Additionally it becomes political kitsch by virtue of its association with the Kennedy legacy and Camelot.[32]

What Cavafy might have made of such sensational settings for his poems and the current global celebration of his fame is a matter for speculation. One imagines his reaction would be akin to the amazement he wrote about in his unfinished poem "The Seven Children of Ephesus," who wake up two centuries after their mystical slumber in the third century to a converted world in the fifth. Doubtless like them, he would be quite pleased ("θα χαίρονταν") to see certain changes in the cultural landscape that have allowed for a deeper appreciation of his poetry; and likewise, he would be somewhat bewildered at how, in the twenty-first century, all is so different ("ήσαν όλα τόσο διαφορετικά") from the nineteenth, in which he was born, and from the early twentieth, during which he found his mature poetic voice. Despite so many differences, the one unchanging factor with which he would be exceedingly familiar is the recurring pattern of decline and rebirth, a transhistorical dynamic about which he remains the poet par excellence. He inscribes himself into this cycle quite ingeniously with his poem "Very Seldom" (1911/1913):

> He's an old man. Run down and bent.
> Crippled by age and overindulgence,
> he walks slowly down the narrow street.
> But when he enters his house to hide
> his misery and old age, he thinks about
> the share in youth he still retains.
>
> Young men quote his verse now.
> His visions pass into their lively eyes.
> His expression of beauty stirs

their healthy sensual minds,
their well-built shapely bodies.
(2013, 77)

This proleptic sentiment offers an ideal *mise en abyme* image with which
to conclude a study of Cavafy's decadent poetics: that of an aging poet
anticipating his own posthumous rebirth through future appreciations of
his aesthetic vision—the framing and reframing of the exquisite imaginary portraits he has bequeathed to us some 150 years after his birth.

BIBLIOGRAPHY

Agapitos, Panagiotis A. 1994. "Byzantium in the Poetry of Kostis Palamas and C. P. Cavafy." *Kambos: Cambridge Papers in Modern Greek* 2:1–20.

Aghion, Irène, Claire Barbillon, and François Lissarrague. 1994. *Gods and Heroes of Classical Antiquity.* Paris: Flammarion.

Aillagon, Jean-Jacques. 2008. "The Barbarians and Rome." In *Rome and the Barbarians: The Birth of a New World.* Edited by Jean-Jacques Aillagon, 42–53. Milan: Skira Editore.

Alexiou, Margaret. 1983. "Eroticism and Poetry." *Journal of the Hellenic Diaspora* 10 (1–2): 45–65.

Alkalay-Gut, Karen. 2000. "Aesthetic and Decadent Poetry." In *The Cambridge Companion to Victorian Poetry.* Edited by Joseph Bristow, 228–254. Cambridge: Cambridge University Press.

Anderson, Ronald, and Anne Koval. 1995. *James McNeill Whistler: Beyond the Myth.* New York: Carroll and Graf.

Andreadi, Effi. 2003. *Κ.Π. Καβάφης, ο κόσμος του και οι εικαστικές μορφές της εποχής του.* Athens: Greek Ministry of Culture.

Angelov, Dimiter G. 2003. "Byzantinism: The Imaginary and Real Heritage of Byzantium in Southeastern Europe." In *New Approaches to Balkan Studies.* Edited by

Dimitris Keridis, Ellen Elias Bursac, and Nicholas Yatromanolakis, 3–22. Everett, MA: Fidelity Press.

Arabatzidou, Eleni. 2000. "Καβαφικές Συνάφειες Αισθητισμού." In *Η Ποίηση του Κράματος.* Edited by Michalis Pieris, 29–36. Heraklion: University of Crete.

———. 2013. Το Διακείμενο του Αισθητισμού στην Ποιητική του Κ.Π. Καβάφη. Thessalonica: Kyriakidis Publishing.

Athanasopoulou, Maria. 2003. "Κ.Π. Καβάφη, 'Εις το φως της ημέρας' (1896): το Υπερρωτικό ως Εκδήλωση του Νεωτερικού." *Νέα Εστία* 1761 (November): 652–665.

Attwood, Philip. 1986. "Maria Zambaco: *Femme Fatale* of the Pre-Raphaelites." *Apollo* (July): 31–37.

Auden, W. H. 1989. Introduction to *The Complete Poems of Cavafy,* xv–xxiii. Translated by Rae Dalven. New York: Harcourt Brace.

Balakian, Anna. 1977. *The Symbolist Movement: A Critical Appraisal.* New York: New York University Press.

Bann, Stephen. 2004a. Introduction to *The Reception of Walter Pater in Europe.* Edited by Stephen Bann, 1–18. New York: Thoemmes Continuum.

———, ed. 2004b. *The Reception of Walter Pater in Europe.* New York: Thoemmes Continuum.

Barrow, Rosemary Julia. 2007. *The Use of Classical Art and Literature by Victorian Painters, 1860–1912.* Lewiston, NY: Edwin Mellen Press.

Bassett, Sharon. 1999. "Golden Mediocrity: Pater's Marcus Aurelius and the Making of Decadence." In *Perennial Decay: On the Aesthetics and Politics of Decadence.* Edited by Liz Constable, Dennis Denisoff, and Matthew Potolsky, 254–267. Philadelphia: University of Pennsylvania Press.

Bate, Percy. 1905. *The English Pre-Raphaelite Painters.* London: George Bell and Sons.

Baudelaire, Charles. 1964. *Baudelaire as a Literary Critic: Selected Essays.* Introduced and translated by Lois Boe Hyslop and Francis E. Hyslop, Jr. University Park: Pennsylvania State University Press.

———. 1965. *Art in Paris: 1845–1862. Salons and Other Exhibits. Reviewed by Charles Baudelaire.* Translated by Jonathan Mayne. London: Phaidon Press.

———. 1989. *Baudelaire: The Poems in Prose.* Translated by Francis Scarfe. London: Anvil Press.

———. 1995. *The Painter of Modern Life and Other Essays.* Edited and translated by Jonathan Mayne. London: Phaidon Press Ltd.

———. 1998. *The Flowers of Evil.* Translated by James McGowan. London: Oxford University Press.

Beaumont, Matthew. 2010. Introduction to *Studies in the History of the Renaissance.* Edited by Matthew Beaumont, vii–xxix. New York: Oxford University Press.

Beckson, Karl. 1966. Introduction to *Aesthetes and Decadents of the 1890's: An Anthology.* Edited by Karl Beckson, xvii–xl. New York: Random House.

Benjamin, Walter. 2006. *The Writer of Modern Life: Essays on Charles Baudelaire.* Edited by Michael W. Jennings. Cambridge: Harvard University Press.

Benson, Bruce Ellis. 2008. *Pious Nietzsche: Decadence and Dionysian Faith.* Bloomington: Indiana University Press.

Bernheimer, Charles. 2002. *Decadent Subjects*. London: Johns Hopkins University Press.

Bertrand, Louis. 1994. *Louis Aloysius Bertrand's Gaspart de la Nuit*. Translated by John L. Wright. London: University Press of America.

Bien, Peter. 1990. "Cavafy's Homosexuality and His Reputation Outside of Greece." *Journal of Modern Greek Studies* 8 (2): 197–211.

Bingen, Jean. 2007. *Hellenistic Egypt: Monarchy, Society, Economy, Culture*. Edinburgh: Edinburgh University Press.

Birkett, Jennifer. 1986. *The Sins of the Fathers: Decadence in France 1870–1914*. London: Quartet Books.

———. 1990. "*Fin-de-siècle* Painting." In *Fin de Siècle and Its Legacy*. Edited by Mikulas Teich and Roy Porter, 147–169. Cambridge: Cambridge University Press.

———. 1998. "Masochistic Inscriptions: Politics, Fetishism, and Form in the Work of Joséphin Péladan (1859–1916)." In *The Decadent Reader: Fiction, Fantasy and Perversion from Fin de Siècle France*. Edited by Asti Hustvedt, 842–851. New York: Zone Books.

Bizzotto, Elisa. 2002. "The Imaginary Portrait: Pater's Contribution to a Literary Genre." In *Walter Pater: Transparencies of Desire*. Edited by Laurel Brake, Lesley Higgins, and Carolyn Williams, 213–223. Greensboro, NC: ELT Press.

Bloom, Harold, ed. 1985. *Walter Pater*. Modern Critical Views. New York: Chelsea House.

Blunt, Wilfred. 1975. *England's Michelangelo: A Biography of George Frederic Watts*. London: Hamish Hamilton.

Boardman, John. 1968. *Engraved Gems: The Ionides Collection*. Evanston, IL: Northwestern University Press.

Boletsi, Maria. 2013. *Barbarism and Its Discontents*. Stanford: Stanford University Press.

Bolus-Reichert, Christine. 2009. *The Age of Eclecticism: Literature and Culture in Britain, 1815–1885*. Columbus: Ohio State University Press.

Boubly, Mark. 1979. "Nietzsche and the *Finis Latinorum*." In *Studies in Nietzsche and the Classical Tradition*. Edited by James C. O'Flaherty, 214–233. Chapel Hill: University of North Carolina Press.

Bourbouhakis, Emmanuel C. 2010. "Rhetoric and Performance." In *The Byzantine World*. Edited by Paul Stephenson, 175–187. London: Routledge.

Bourget, Paul. 2009. "The Example of Baudelaire." Translated by Nancy O'Connor. *New England Review* 30:2. http://cat.middlebury.edu/~nereview/30-2/Bourget.htm.

Bowersock, G. W. 1981. "The Julian Poems of C.P. Cavafy." *Byzantine and Modern Greek Studies* 7:89–104.

———. 1996a. "Late Antique Alexandria." In *Alexandria and Alexandrianism*. Edited by John Walsh, 263–272. Malibu, CA: J. Paul Getty Museum.

———. 1996b. "The New Cavafy: Unfinished Poems 1918–1932." *American Scholar* 65 (2): 243–257.

———. 2000. "The Vanishing Paradigm of the Fall of Rome." In *Glen W. Bowersock: Selected Papers on Late Antiquity*, 187–197. Bari, It.: Edipuglia.

———. 2009. *From Gibbon to Auden: Essays on the Classical Tradition*. London: Oxford University Press.

Boyiopoulos, Kostas. 2012. "The Darkening of the Mirror: Cavafy's Variations on *The Picture of Dorian Gray.*" *Journal of Modern Greek Studies* 30 (1): 21–43.

Brake, Laurel. 1994a. *Subjugated Knowledges: Journalism, Gender and Literature in the Nineteenth Century.* London: Macmillan.

———. 1994b. *Walter Pater.* Plymouth, UK: Northcote House.

———. 2000. "'The Profession of Letters': Walter Pater and Greek Studies." In *Journalism, Literature and Modernity: From Hazlitt to Modernism.* Edited by Kate Campbell, 121–140. Edinburgh: Edinburgh University Press.

———. 2002. "The Entangling Dance: Pater after Marius, 1885–1891." In *Walter Pater: Transparencies of Desire.* Edited by Laurel Brake, Lesley Higgins, and Carolyn Williams, 24–36. Greensboro, NC: ELT Press.

Brake, Laurel, and Ian Small, eds. 1991. *Pater in the 1990s.* Greensboro, NC: ELT Press.

Brake, Laurel, Lesley Higgins and Carolyn Williams, eds. 2002. *Walter Pater: Transparencies of Desire.* Greensboro, NC: ELT Press.

Brant, Pierre. 2002. "History and Ideology: The Greeks and 'Persian Decadence.'" Translated by Antonia Nevill. In *Greeks and Barbarians.* Edited by Thomas Harrison, 193–210. Edinburgh: Edinburgh University Press.

Bristow, Joseph, ed. 2000. *The Cambridge Companion to Victorian Poetry.* Cambridge: Cambridge University Press.

Brix, Michel. 2001. "Modern Beauty versus Platonic Beauty." Translated by Tony Campbell. In *Baudelaire and the Poetics of Modernity.* Edited by Patricia Ward, 1–14. Nashville: Vanderbilt University Press.

Bruder, Anne. 2004. "Constructing Artists and Critic between J. M. Whistler and Oscar Wilde: 'In the Best Days of Art There Were No Art-Critics.'" *English Literature in Transition* 47 (2): 161–180.

Bryant, Barbara. 1996. "G. F. Watts at the Grosvenor Gallery: 'Poems Painted on Canvas' and the New Internationalism." In *The Grosvenor Gallery: A Palace of Art in Victorian England.* Edited by Susan P. Casteras and Colleen Denney, 109–128. New Haven: Yale Center for British Art.

———. 1997. "G. F. Watts and the Symbolist Vision." In *The Age of Rossetti, Burne-Jones and Watts: Symbolism in Britain (1860–1910).* Edited by Andrew Wilton and Robert Upstone, 65–87. London: Tate Gallery Publishing.

———. 2011. "The Grosvenor Gallery, Patronage and the Aesthetic Portrait." In *The Cult of Beauty: The Aesthetic Movement, 1860–1900.* Edited by Stephen Calloway and Lynn Federle Orr, 158–177. London: V&A Publishing.

Buckler, William E. 1987. *Walter Pater: The Critic as Artist of Ideas.* New York: New York University Press.

Bullen, J. B. 1991. "The Historiography of *Studies in the History of the Renaissance.*" In *Pater in the 1990s.* Edited by Laurel Brake and Ian Small, 155–167. Greensboro, NC: ELT Press.

———. 1998. *The Pre-Raphaelite Body: Fear and Desire in Painting, Poetry and Criticism.* Oxford: Clarendon Press.

———. 2003. *Byzantium Rediscovered.* London: Phaidon.

———. 2010. "Pater and Contemporary Visual Art." In *Victorian Aesthetic Conditions: Pater Across the Arts.* Edited by Elicia Clements and Lesley J. Higgins, 33–46. New York: Palgrave Macmillan.

Bulwer-Lytton, Edward George. (1834) 1979. *The Last Days of Pompeii*. London: Sidgwick and Jackson.

——. (1871) 2005. *The Coming Race*. Middletown, CT: Middlebury University Press.

Buruma, Ian. 2011. "Le Divorce: Why Belgium, Home of the European Union, Has Never Been More Disunited." *New Yorker* January 10, 36–40.

Butler, John Davis. 1967. *Jean Moréas: A Critique of his Poetry and Philosophy*. Paris: Mouton.

Calinescu, Matei. 1987. *Five Faces of Modernity*. Durham, NC: Duke University Press.

Calloway, Stephen. 2011. "'Tired Hedonists': The Decadence of the Aesthetic Movement." In *The Cult of Beauty: The Aesthetic Movement, 1860–1900*. Edited by Stephen Calloway and Lynn Federle Orr, 224–235. London: V&A Publishing.

Calloway, Stephen and Lynn Federle Orr, eds. 2011. *The Cult of Beauty: The Aesthetic Movement, 1860–1900*. London: V&A Publishing.

Carter, A. E. 1958. *The Idea of Decadence in French Literature 1830–1900*. Toronto: University of Toronto Press.

——. 1977. *Charles Baudelaire*. Boston: Twayne Publishers.

Cassavetti, Eileen. 1989. "The Fatal Meeting, The Fruitful Passion." *Antique Collector* 60 (3): 34–45.

Casteras, Susan P., ed. 1995a. *Pre-Raphaelite Art in Its European Context*. London: Associated University Presses.

——. 1995b. "The Pre-Raphaelite Legacy to Symbolism." In *Pre-Raphaelite Art in Its European Context*. Edited by Susan Casteras and A. E. Faxon, 33–49. London: Associated University Presses.

——. 2002. "'The Prime Hours of First—and Subsequent—Initiations': Henry James on Pre-Raphaelite Art and Artists." In *Henry James Review* 23 (3): 304–317.

Casteras, Susan P., and Colleen Denney, eds. 1996. *The Grosvenor Gallery: A Palace of Art in Victorian England*. New Haven: Yale Center for British Art.

Catsaouni, Helen. 1983. "Cavafy and the Theatrical Presentation of History." *Journal of the Hellenic Diaspora* 10 (1–2): 105–116.

Cavafy, C. P. 1963. *Πεζά*. Edited by George Papoutsakis. Athens: Phexi.

——. 1982. *Καβάφης Άπαντα. Άρθρα και Κριτικές*. Vol. 5. Edited by Pantazis Fykires. Athens: Fykires Publishers.

——. 1983. *Αποκηρυγμένα Ποιήματα και Μεταφράσεις (1886–1898)*. Edited by George Savidis. Athens: Ikaros.

——. 1989. *The Complete Poems of Cavafy*. Translated by Rae Dalven. New York: Harcourt Brace.

——. 1992. *C. P. Cavafy: Collected Poems*. Translated by Edmund Keeley and Philip Sherrard. Princeton: Princeton University Press.

——. 1993. *Κρυμμένα Ποιήματα*. Edited by George Savidis. Athens: Ikaros.

——. 1994a. *Ατελή Ποιήματα: 1918–1932*. Edited by Renata Lavagnini. Athens: Ikaros Press.

——. 1994b. "Constantinopoliad an Epic." Edited by Diana Haas. In *Ζητήματα Ιστορίας των Νεοελληνικών Γραμμάτων*, 281–304. Thessaloniki: Paratiritis.

——. 2001. *Before Time Could Change Them: The Complete Poems of Constantine P. Cavafy*. Translated by Theoharis C. Theoharis. New York: Harcourt.

———. 2003a. *C. P. Cavafy: 154 Poems*. Translated by Evangelos Sachperoglou. Athens: Evangelos Sachperoglou.

———. 2003b. *C. P. Cavafy: Sixty-Three Poems Translated by J. C. Cavafy*. Athens: Ikaros.

———. 2003c. *Τα Πεζά (1882–1931)*. Edited by Michael Pieris. Athens: Ikaros.

———. 2009a. "Cavafy Anthology." Translated by George Valassopoulo. In *The Forster-Cavafy Letters: Friends at a Slight Angle*. Edited by Peter Jeffreys, 123–184. Cairo: American University in Cairo Press.

———. 2009b *C. P. Cavafy: Collected Poems*. Translated by Daniel Mendelsohn. New York: Knopf.

———. 2009c. *C. P. Cavafy: The Unfinished Poems*. Translated by Daniel Mendelsohn. New York: Knopf.

———. 2010. *Selected Prose Works*. Translated and annotated by Peter Jeffreys. Ann Arbor: University of Michigan.

———. 2013. *Complete Plus: The Poems of C. P. Cavafy in English*. Translated by George Economou with Stavros Deligiorgis. Emersons Green, UK: Shearsman Books.

Cevasco, G. A. 2001. *The Breviary of the Decadence: J.-K. Huysmans's* A Rebours *and English Literature*. New York: AMS Press.

Chapman, Mary, and Glenn Hendler, eds. 1999. *Sentimental Men: Masculinity and the Politics of Affect in American Culture*. Berkeley: University of California Press.

Charlesworth, Barbara. 1965. *Dark Passages: The Decadent Consciousness in Victorian Literature*. Madison: University of Wisconsin Press.

Chauncey, George. 2009. "The Trouble with Shame." In *Gay Shame*. Edited by David M. Halperin and Valerie Traub, 277–282. Chicago: University of Chicago Press.

Cheeke, Stephen. 2008. *Writing for Art: The Aesthetics of Ekphrasis*. Manchester, UK: Manchester University Press.

Cheney, Liana De Girolami, ed. 1992. *Pre-Raphaelitism and Medievalism in the Arts*. Lewiston, NY: Edwin Mellen Press.

Choniates, Niketas. 1984. *O City of Byzantium: Annals of Niketas Choniates*. Translated by Harry J. Magoulias. Detroit: Wayne State University Press.

Christensen, Allan Conrad. 1976. *Edward Bulwer Lytton: The Fiction of New Regions*. Athens: University of Georgia Press.

Christensen, Peter G. 1995. "C. P. Cavafy." In *The Gay and Lesbian Literary Heritage*. Edited by Claude J. Summers, 149–151. New York: Henry Holt.

Christides, B. F. 1958. *Ο Καβάφης και το Βυζάντιο*. Athens: Biohart Editions.

Christodoulou, Despina. 2010. "Byzantium in Nineteenth-Century Greek Historiography." In *The Byzantine World*. Edited by Paul Stephenson, 445–461. London: Routledge.

Christophides, Loucas. 1983. *Ο Φιλολογικός Περιοδικός Τύπος (1890–1919)*. Athens: Byron.

Cioran, E. M. 1998. *A Short History of Decay*. Translated by Richard Howe. New York: Arcade Publishing.

Clements, Elicia, and Lesley J. Higgins, eds. 2010. *Victorian Aesthetic Conditions: Pater across the Arts*. New York: Palgrave Macmillan.

Clements, Patricia. 1985. *Baudelaire and the English Tradition*. Princeton: Princeton University Press.

Cleto, Fabio, ed. 1996. *Camp: Queer Aesthetics and the Performing Subject: A Reader.* Edinburgh: Edinburgh University Press.

Cocks, Anna Somers. 1980. *The Victoria and Albert Museum: The Making of a Collection.* London: Windward.

Collier, Peter, and Robert Lethbridge, eds. 1994. *Artistic Relations: Literature and the Visual Arts in Nineteenth-Century France.* New Haven: Yale University Press.

Comfort, Kelly, ed. 2008. *Art and Life in Aestheticism.* New York: Palgrave Macmillan.

Conlon, John J. 1982. *Walter Pater and the French Tradition.* East Brunswick, NJ: Associated University Presses.

Connolly, David. 2002. "The Least Satisfying Form of Writing: Seferis on Translation." *Journal of Modern Greek Studies* 20 (1): 29–46.

———, ed. 2003. *The Dedalus Book of Greek Fantasy.* Translated by David Connolly. Cambs, UK: Dedalus.

Constans, Claire. 1996. *La Grèce: Delacroix en révolte, et les peintres français.* Paris: Éditions de la Réunion des musées nationaux.

Cook, Peter. 2000. "Text and Image, Allegory and Symbol in Gustave Moreau's Jupiter et Sémélé." In *Symbolism, Decadence and the Fin De Siècle.* Edited by Patrick McGuinness, 122–143. Exeter, UK: University of Exeter Press.

Cooper, Suzanne Fagence. 2003. *Pre-Raphaelite Art in the Victoria and Albert Museum.* London: Harry N. Abrams.

Cork, Richard. 2003. "The Greek Bearing Gifts." *London Times,* November 22, 23.

Cornell, Kenneth. 1970. *The Symbolist Movement.* Hamden, UK: Archon Books.

Cruise, Colin. 2010. "Critical Connections and Quotational Strategies. Allegory and Aestheticism in Pater and Simeon Solomon." In *Victorian Aesthetic Conditions: Pater Across the Arts.* Edited by Elicia Clements and Lesley J. Higgins, 68–82. New York: Palgrave Macmillan.

Cruise, Colin, ed. 2005. *Love Revealed: Simeon Solomon and the Pre-Raphaelites.* London: Merrell.

Culler, Jonathan. 1998. Introduction to *Charles Baudelaire: The Flowers of Evil,* xiii–xlviii. Translated by James McGowan. Oxford: Oxford University Press.

Dallas, Ioannis. 1984. *Ο Καβάφης και η Δεύτερη Σοφιστική.* Athens: Stigmi.

———. 1986. *Καβάφης και Ιστορία.* Athens: Hermes.

Dalven, Rae. 1972. *Anna Comnena.* New York: Twayne Publishers.

Damrosch, David. 2003. *What Is World Literature?* Princeton: Princeton University Press.

Daskalopoulos, Dimitris. 1988. *Κ.Π. Καβάφης: Σχέδια στο Περιθώριο.* Athens: Diatton.

———. 1990. *Λογοτεχνικά Περιοδικά της Αλεξάνδρειας (1904–1953).* Athens: Diatton.

———. 1999. "Ο Ποιητής Κ.Π. Καβάφη (1983–1933)." In *Συμπαθητική Μελάνη.* Edited by Dimitris Daskalopoulos, 45–49. Athens: Hermes.

———. 2005. "Ο Κ.Π. Καβάφης και οι Εικαστικοί Καλλιτέχνες: Μια Αμφίδρομη Σχέση." In *Κ.Π. Καβάφης: Ποιήματα.* Edited by Dimitris Daskalopoulos, 7–16. Athens: Kastaniotis Editions.

Daskalopoulos, Dimitris, and Maria Stasinopoulou. 2001. *Ο Βίος και το Έργο του Κ.Π. Καβάφη.* Athens: Metaichmio.

David, Marie-France. 2001. *Antiquité Latine et Décadence*. Paris: Honoré Champion Éditeur.

Davidson, James. 2007. *The Greeks and Greek Love: A Radical Reappraisal of Homosexuality in Ancient Greece*. London: Weidenfeld & Nicolson.

Davis, Michael F. 2002. "Walter Pater's 'Latent Intelligence' and the Conception of Queer 'Theory.'" In *Walter Pater: Transparencies of Desire*. Edited by Laurel Brake, Lesley Higgins, and Carolyn Williamson, 261–285. Greensboro, NC: ELT Press.

Dawson, Gowan, Richard Noakes, and Jonathan R. Topham. 2004. Introduction to *Science in the Nineteenth-Century Periodical*. Edited by Gowan Dawson, Richard Noakes, and Jonathan R. Topham, 1–34. Cambridge: Cambridge University Press.

Debaisieux, Renée-Paule. 1995. *Le Décantisme Grec dans les Oeuvres en Prose 1894–1912*. Paris: Editions L'Harmattan.

——. 1997. *Le Décantisme Grec une Esthétique de la Déformation*. Paris: L'Harmattan.

Delille, Edward. 1891. "French Authors on Each Other." *The Nineteenth Century* 30 (177): 783–798.

Dellamora, Richard. 1990. *Masculine Desire: The Sexual Politics of Victorian Aestheticism*. Chapel Hill: University of North Carolina Press.

——. 1994. *Apocalyptic Overtures: Sexual Politics and the Sense of an Ending*. New Brunswick, NJ: Rutgers University Press.

——. 1999. "Introduction to *Victorian Sexual Dissidence*. Edited by Richard Dellamora, 1–17. Chicago: University of Chicago Press.

——. 2010. "Greek Desire and Modern Sexualities." In *Imagination and Logos: Essays on C.P. Cavafy*, 121–142. Edited by Panagiotis Roilos. Cambridge, MA: Harvard University Press.

Denney, Colleen. 1997. "Acts of Worship at the Temple of Art: The Grosvenor Gallery and the Second-Generation Pre-Raphaelites." In *Collecting the Pre-Raphaelites: the Anglo-American Enchantment*. Edited by Margaretta Frederick Watson, 65–75. Aldershot, UK: Scholar Press.

——. 2000. *At the Temple of Art: The Grosvenor Gallery, 1877–1890*. London: Associated University Presses.

Denisoff, Dennis. 1995. "Decadence." In *The Gay and Lesbian Literary Heritage*. Edited by Claude J. Summers, 187–191. New York: Henry Holt.

——. 2008. "The Dissipating Nature of Decadent Paganism from Pater to Yeats." *Modernism/Modernity* 15 (3): 431–446.

Denommé, Robert T. 1972. *The French Parnassian Poets*. London: Feffer & Simons.

Des Cars, Laurence. 1998. "Edward Burne-Jones and France." In *Edward Burne-Jones: Victorian Artist-Dreamer*. Edited by Stephen Wildman and John Christian, 25–39. New York: Metropolitan Museum of Art.

Desmarais, Jane, and Chris Baldick. 2012. Introduction to *Decadence: An Annotated Anthology*. Edited by Jane Desmarais and Chris Baldick, 1–11. Manchester, UK: Manchester University Press.

Diehl, Charles. 1927. *Byzantine Portraits*. Translated by Harold Bell. New York: Knopf.

——. 1957. *Byzantium: Greatness and Decline*. Translated by Naomi Walford. New Brunswick, NJ: Rutgers University Press.

——. 1963. *Byzantine Empresses*: Translated by Harold Bell and Theresa de Kerpely. New York: Knopf.

Dijkstra, Bram. 1986. *Idols of Perversity: Fantasies of Feminine Evil in Fin-de-Siècle Culture.* New York: Oxford University Press.

Dimaras, K. T. 1982. *Greek Romanticism.* Athens: Hermes.

———. 1992. *Σύμμικτα, Γ': Περί Καβάφη.* Edited by George Savidis. Athens: Gnosi.

Dimiroulis, Dimitris. 1983. "Cavafy's Imminent Threat: Still Waiting for the Barbarians." *Journal of the Hellenic Diaspora* 10 (102): 89 –103.

———. 2005. *Εμμανουήλ Ροΐδης: Η Τέχνη του Ύφους και της Πολεμικής.* Athens: Metechmio.

Donoghue, Denis. 1995. *Walter Pater: Lover of Strange Souls.* New York: Knopf.

Dorfles, Gillo, ed. 1969. *Kitsch: An Anthology of Bad Taste.* London: Studio Vista.

Dorment, Richard, and Margaret F. Macdonald. 1994. *James McNeill Whistler.* London: Tate Gallery Publications.

Dorra, Henri, ed. 1994. *Symbolist Art Theories: A Critical Anthology.* Berkeley: University of California Press.

Doulis, Thomas. 2003. *Out of the Ashes: The Emergence of Greek Fiction in the Nineteenth Century.* Philadelphia: Xlibris.

Dowling, Linda. 1986. *Language and Decadence in the Victorian Fin de Siècle.* Princeton: Princeton University Press.

———. 1994. *Hellenism and Homosexuality in Victorian England.* Ithaca: Cornell University Press.

———. 1996. *The Vulgarization of Art: The Victorians and Aesthetic Democracy.* Charlottesville: University of Virginia Press.

Dowling, Theodore E. 1915. *Hellenism in England.* London: Faith Press.

Droulia, Lucia. 2005. *Ο Ελληνικός Τύπος: 1783 ως Σήμερα: Ιστορικές και Θεωρητικές Προσεγγήσεις. Πρακτικά Διεθνούς Συνεδρίου, Αθήνα, 23–24 Μαΐου, 2002.* Athens: Institut de Recherches Néohelléniques.

Duffy, John. 1995. "Reactions of Two Byzantine Intellectuals to the Theory and Practice of Magic: Michael Psellos and Michael Italikos." In *Byzantine Magic.* Edited by Henry Maguire, 83–97. Washington, DC: Dumbarton Oaks.

Dutton, Denis. 2009. "Kitsch." *MoMA Art Terms—Grove Art Online.* Oxford University Press. http://www.moma.org/collection/theme.php?theme_id=10104.

Eagle, Dorothy, and Paul Harvey, eds. 1967. *The Oxford Companion to English Literature.* 4th ed. Oxford: Oxford University Press.

Easson, Angus. 2004. "'At Home' with the Romans: Domestic Archaeology in *The Last Days of Pompeii.*" In *The Subverting Vision of Bulwer Lytton.* Edited by Allan Conrad Christensen, 100–115. Newark: University of Delaware Press.

Eells, Emily. "'Influence Occulte': The Reception of Pater's Works in France before 1922." In *The Reception of Walter Pater in Europe.* Edited by Stephen Bann, 87–116. New York: Thoemmes Continuum.

Ekdawi, Sarah. 1993a. "Days of 1895, '96 and '97: The Parallel Prisons of C. P. Cavafy and Oscar Wilde." *Modern Greek Studies Yearbook* 9:297–305.

———. 1993b. "The Erotic Poems of C. P. Cavafy." *Kambos: Cambridge Papers in Modern Greek* 1:23–46.

———. 1996a. "Cavafy's Byzantium." *Byzantine and Modern Greek Studies* 20:17–34.

———. 1996b. "Cavafy's Mythical Ephebes." In *Ancient Greek Myth in Modern Greek Poetry.* Edited by Peter Mackridge, 33–44. Portland, OR: F. Cass.

———. 1997. "Cavafy's English Poems." *Byzantine and Modern Greek Studies* 21:223–230.

———. 2000–2001. "The Passions File: Cavafy's Private Collection?" *Modern Greek Studies Yearbook* 16–17:159–175.

———. 2011. "'Missing Dates': The 'Μέρες' Poems of C. P. Cavafy." *Byzantine and Modern Greek Studies* 35 (1): 70–91.

Ellmann, Richard. 1983. *The Uses of Decadence: Wilde, Yeats, and Joyce*. Bennington, VT: Bennington Chapbooks in Literature.

———. 1988. *Oscar Wilde*. New York: Knopf.

Evans, Helen C., ed. 2004. *Byzantium: Faith and Power (1261–1557)*. New York: Metropolitan Museum of Art.

Fahmy, Khaled. 2004. "Towards a Social History of Modern Alexandria." In *Alexandria, Real and Imagined*. Edited by Anthony Hirst, 281–306. Aldershot: Ashgate.

Federle Orr, Lynn. 2011. "The Cult of Beauty: The Victorian Avant-Garde in Context." In *The Cult of Beauty: The Aesthetic Movement, 1860–1900*. Edited by Stephen Calloway and Lynn Federle Orr, 24–37. London: V&A Publishing.

Ferguson, Niall. 2011. *Civilization: The West and the Rest*. New York: Penguin.

Fischer, Klaus P. 1989. *History and Prophecy: Oswald Spengler and the Decline of the West*. New York: Peter Lang.

Flanders, Judith. 2005. *A Circle of Sisters*. New York: Norton.

Fletcher, Ian. 1973. *Swinburne*. London: Longman Group.

Fletcher, Pamela M. 2003. *Narrating Modernity: The British Problem Picture, 1895–1914*. Aldershot, UK: Ashgate.

Forster, E. M. 2004. *Alexandria: A History and a Guide and Pharos and Pharillon*. Edited by Miriam Allott. London: Andre Deutsch.

Frankopan, Peter. 2009. Introduction to *The Alexiad*, by Anna Komnene, ix–xxiv. Translated by E. R. A. Sewter. New York: Penguin Books.

Fraser, G. S. 1968. "Walter Pater: His Theory of Style, His Style in Practice, His Influence." In *The Art of Victorian Prose*. Edited by George Levine and William Madden, 201–223. London: Oxford University Press.

Fraser, Hilary. 2000. "Victorian Poetry and Historicism." In *The Cambridge Companion to Victorian Poetry*. Edited by Joseph Bristow, 114–136. Cambridge: Cambridge University Press.

Frier, Bruce W. 2010. "Making History Personal: Constantine Cavafy and the Rise of Rome." Cavafy Forum: University of Michigan. http://www.lsa.umich.edu/modgreek/wtgc/c.p.%20cavafyforum.

Frisby, David. 1994. "The Flâneur in Social Theory." In *The Flâneur*. Edited by Keith Tester, 81–110. London: Routledge.

Fröhlich, Fabian. 2009. "The Mirror of Venus." In *Edward Burne-Jones: The Earthly Paradise*. Edited by Staatsgalerie Stuttgart, 97–101. Ostfildern, Ger.: Hatje Cantz Verlag.

Ftyaras, Konstantinos. 1983. "Το 1928 ή '29 μ.Χ. στην Αλεξάνδρια." *Χάρτης* 5–6: 545–547.

Gagnier, Regenia. 2010. *Individualism, Decadence and Globalization*. New York: Palgrave Macmillan.

Garelick, Rhonda K. 1998. *Rising Star: Dandyism, Gender, and Performance in the Fin de Siècle*. Princeton: Princeton University Press.

Gautier, Théophile. 1903. *Art and Criticism: The Magic Hat; Enamels and Cameos and Other Poems. The Complete Works of Théophile Gautier.* Vol. 12. Edited and translated by Frederick C. de Sumichrast. Boston: C. T. Brainard.

——. 1909. "Charles Baudelaire." In *The Complete Works of Théophile Gautier.* Vol. 2. Edited and translated by Frederick C. de Sumichrast. London: Athenaeum Press.

——. 1968. *Emaux et Camées avec une iconographie rassemblée et commentée par Madeleine Cottin.* Paris: Lettres Modernes/Minard.

Gentzler, Edwin. 2001. *Contemporary Translation Theories.* Toronto: Multilingual Press.

Gere, Charlotte. 2010. *Artistic Circles: Design & Decoration in the Aesthetic Movement.* London: V & A Publishing.

Ghika, Katerina. 2009. "«Τοις Ρωμαίων έμμενε»: εμβλήματα του Κωνσταντίνου Καβάφη." *Νέα Εστία* 165:18–53.

Giannakopoulou, Liana. 2001. "Moulded by Eros with Skill and Experience: Sculpture of the Male Body in the Poetry of Cavafy." In *Dialogos: Hellenic Studies Review.* Edited by David Ricks and Michael Trapp, 78–98. London: Frank Cass.

Giannaris, George. 1984. *Jean Moréas ο Έλληνας.* Athens: Cactus.

Gilbert, Elliot L. 1983. "Tumult of Images: Wilde, Beardsley and *Salome.*" *Victorian Studies* 26 (2): 133–159.

Gilman, Richard. 1979. *Decadence: The Strange Life of an Epithet.* New York: Farrar, Straus and Giroux.

Glick, Elisa. 2009. *Materializing Queer Desire. Oscar Wilde to Andy Warhol.* New York: SUNY Press.

Goldhill, Simon. 2002a. *The Invention of Prose.* Oxford: Oxford University Press.

——. 2002b. *Who Needs Greek: Contests in the Cultural History of Hellenism.* Cambridge: Cambridge University Press.

——. 2011. *Victorian Culture and Classical Antiquity.* Princeton: Princeton University Press.

Gouma-Peterson, Thalia. 2000. "Gender and Power: Passages to the Maternal in Anna Komnene's *Alexiad.*" In *Anna Komnene and Her Times.* Edited by Thalia Gouma-Peterson, 107–124. New York: Garland.

Gourmont, Rémy de. 1966. "Stephen Mallarmé and the Idea of Decadence." In *Selected Writings.* Translated by Glenn Burne, 67–76. Ann Arbor: University of Michigan Press.

——, ed. 1994. *An Anthology of French Symbolist and Decadent Writing Based upon* The Book of Masks *by Remy de Gourmont.* Translated by Andrew Mangravite. London: Atlas Press.

Goysdotter, Moa. 2013. *Impure Vision: American Staged Photography of the 1970s.* Lund, Swed.: Nordic Academic Press.

Graham, Wendy. 1999. "Henry James and British Aestheticism." *Henry James Review* 20 (3): 265–274.

Grant, Richard B. 1975. *Théophile Gautier.* Boston: Twayne Publishers.

Greenberg, Clement. 1939. "Avant-Garde and Kitsch." http://www.sharecom.ca/greenberg/kitsch.html.

Grigorian, Natasha. 2004. "The Writings of J.-K. Huysmans and Gustave Moreau's Painting: Affinity or Divergence?" *Nineteenth-Century French Studies* 32 (3–4): 282–297.

Gutzwiller, Kathryn. 2003. "Visual Aesthetics in Meleager and Cavafy." *Classical and Modern Literature* 23 (2): 67–87.

Haarer, F. K. 2007. "Writing Histories of Byzantium: The Historiography of Byzantine History." In *A Companion to Byzantium*. Edited by Liz James, 9–21. Malden, MA: Wiley Blackwell.

Haas, Diana. 1982. "Cavafy's Reading Notes on Gibbon's *Decline and Fall*." *Folia Neohellenica* 4:25–96.

———. 1983a. "«Αι Αρχαί του Χριστιανισμού»: Ένα Θεματικό Κεφάλαιο του Καβάφη." *Χάρτης* 5–6:589–608.

———. 1983b. "«Στόν ένδοξό μας Βυζαντινισμό»: σημειώσεις για ένα στίχο του Καβάφη." *Διαβάζω* 78:76–81.

———. 1984. "Early Cavafy and the European 'Esoteric Movement.'" *Journal of Modern Greek Studies* 2 (2): 209–223.

———. 1996. *Le Problème Religieux Dans L'Oeuvre de Cavafy*. Paris: Presses de l'Université de Paris-Sorbonne.

Hagstrum, Jean H. 1958. *The Sister Arts: The Tradition of Literary Pictorialism and English Poetry from Dryden to Gray*. Chicago: University of Chicago Press.

Hall, Jason David, and Alex Murray. 2013. Introduction to *Decadent Poetics: Literature and Form at the British Fin de Siècle*. Edited by Jason David Hall and Alex Murray, 1–25. New York: Palgrave Macmillan.

Halperin, David M. 2012. *How to Be Gay*. Cambridge, MA: Harvard University Press.

Hanson, Ellis. 1997. *Decadence and Catholicism*. Cambridge, MA: Harvard University Press.

Hares-Stryker, Carolyn, ed. 1997. *An Anthology of Pre-Raphaelite Writings*. Sheffield, UK: Academic Press.

Harms, Alvin. 1975. *José-Maria de Heredia*. Boston: Twayne Publishers.

Harrison, Frederic. 1900. *Byzantine History in the Early Middle Ages*. London: Macmillan.

———. 1904. *Theophano: The Crusade of the Tenth Century: A Romantic Monograph*. London: Chapman and Hall.

Harvey, Denise, ed. 1983. *The Mind and Art of C. P. Cavafy: Essays on His Life and Work*. Athens: Denise Harvey.

Head, Constance. 1977. *Imperial Twilight: The Palaiologos Dynasty and the Decline of Byzantium*. Chicago: Nelson-Hall.

Heilmann, Ann, and Mark Llewellyn. 2010. *Neo-Victorianism: The Victorians in the Twenty-First Century, 1999–2009*. New York: Palgrave Macmillan.

Heintzelman, Arthur W. 1956. "Legros' Illustrations for Poe's *Tales*." *Boston Public Library Quarterly* 8:43–48.

Helsinger, Elizabeth K. 2008. *Poetry and the Pre-Raphaelite Arts: Dante Gabriel Rossetti and William Morris*. New Haven: Yale University Press.

Herczeg, François. 1912. *Byzance: Pièce en Trois Actes*. Paris: Honoré Champion, Libraire-Éditeur.

Herzfeld, Michael. 1982. *Ours Once More: Folklore, Ideology, and the Making of Modern Greece*. Austin: University of Texas Press.

Hiddleston, J. A. 1999. *Baudelaire and the Art of Memory*. Oxford: Clarendon Press.

Higgins, Lesley. 2002. "No Time for Pater: The Silenced Other of Masculine Modernism." In *Walter Pater: Transparencies of Desire*. Edited by Laurel Brake, Lesley Higgins, and Carolyn Williams, 37–54. Greensboro, NC: ELT Press.

———. 2007. "Walter Pater: Painting in the Nineteenth Century." *ELT* 50 (4): 415–453.

Hill, Barbara. 1996. "Alexios I Komnenos and the Imperial Women." In *Alexios I Komnenos: Papers of the Second Belfast Byzantine International Colloquium, 14–16 April 1989*. Edited by Margaret Mullett, 37–54. Belfast: Belfast Byzantine Enterprises.

———. 2000. "Actions Speak Louder Than Words: Anna Komnene's Attempted Usurpation." In *Anna Komnene and Her Times*. Edited by Thalia Gouma–Peterson, 45–62. New York: Garland.

Hirst, Anthony. 1998. "Two Cheers for Byzantium: Equivocal Attitudes in the Poetry of Palamas and Cavafy." In *Byzantium and the Modern Greek Identity*. Edited by David Ricks, 105–117. Aldershot, UK: Ashgate.

———. 2000. "C. P. Cavafy: Byzantine Historian?" *Kambos: Cambridge Papers in Modern Greek* 8:45–74.

———. 2003. "Cavafy and Cantacuzenus: Allies or Enemies?" *Kambos: Cambridge Papers in Modern Greek* 11:51–81.

———, ed. 2004. *Alexandria, Real and Imagined*. Aldershot, UK: Ashgate.

Hitchens, Christopher. 2011. "Widow of Opportunity." *Vanity Fair*, December 4. http://www.vanityfair.com/culture/features/2011/12/hitchens-201112.

Ho, Elizabeth. 2012. *Neo-Victorianism and the Memory of Empire*. London: Continuum.

Holleran, Andrew. 1996. *The Beauty of Men*. New York: William Morrow.

Holliday, Ruth, and Tracey Potts. 2012. *Kitsch! Cultural Politics and Taste*. New York: Manchester University Press.

Hollinghurst, Alan. 2005. Introduction to *Bruges-la-Morte*, by Georges Rodenbach, 11–19. Translated by Mike Mitchell and Will Stone. Cambs, UK: Dedalus.

Hönnighausen, Lothar. 1988. *The Symbolist Tradition in English Literature: A Study of Pre-Raphaelitism and Fin de Siècle*. Translated by Giesla Hönnighausen. Cambridge: Cambridge University Press.

Houston, John Porter, and Mona Tobin Houston, trans. 1980. *An Anthology of French Symbolist Poetry*. Bloomington: Indiana University Press.

Howard-Johnston, James. 1996. "Anna Komnene and the *Alexiad*." In *Alexios I Komnenos: Papers of the Second Belfast Byzantine International Colloquium, 14–16 April 1989*. Edited by Margaret Mullett, 260–302. Belfast: Belfast Byzantine Enterprises.

Howgate, Sarah, ed. 2006. *David Hockney Portraits*. New Haven: Yale University Press.

Humphreys, Karen. 2003. "Dandyism, Gems, and Epigrams: Lapidary Style and Genre Transformation in Barbey's *Les Diaboliques*." *Nineteenth-Century French Studies* 31 (3–4): 259–277.

Hustvedt, Asti. 1998. "The Art of Death: French Fiction at the Fin de Siècle." In *The Decadent Reader: Fiction, Fantasy and Perversion from Fin-de-Siècle France*. Edited by Asti Hustvedt, 10–29. New York: Zone Books.

————, ed. 1998. *The Decadent Reader: Fiction, Fantasy and Perversion from Fin-de-Siècle France*. New York: Zone Books.

Huyghe, René. 1971. *Delacroix and Greece*. Athens: Macris Graphic Arts.

Huysmans, Joris-Karl. 2003. *Against Nature*. Translated by Robert Baldick. London: Penguin Books.

Hyder, Clyde K. 1970. Introduction to *Swinburne: The Critical Heritage*. Edited by Clyde K. Hyder, i–xxix. London: Routledge and Kegan Paul.

Ilinskaya, Sonia. 1983. *Κ Π Καβάφης: οι δρόμοι προς το ρεαλισμό στην ποίηση του 20ου αιώνα*. Athens: Kedros.

Ince, W. N. 1979. *Heredia*. London: Athlone Press.

Ionides, Alexander C. Jr. 1927. *Ion: A Grandfather's Tale*. Dublin: Cuala Press.

Ionides, Julia. 1995. "The Greek Connection: The Ionides Family and Their Connections With Pre-Raphaelite and Victorian Art Circles." In *Pre-Raphaelite Art in Its European Context*. Edited by Susan Casteras and Alicia Craig Faxon, 160–174. London: Associated University Presses.

Ionides, Luke. (1925) 1996. *Memories*. Reprint, Ladlow, UK: Dog Rose Press.

Iser, Wolfgang. 1987. *Walter Pater: The Aesthetic Moment*. Translated by David Henry Wilson. London: Cambridge University Press.

Jagot, Hélène. 2008. "The 'Great Invasions' in Nineteenth-century Painting." In *Rome and the Barbarians: The Birth of a New World*. Edited by Jean-Jacques Aillagon, 588–591. Milan: Skira Editore.

James, Henry. 1989. *The Painter's Eye: Notes and Essays on the Pictorial Arts by Henry James*. Edited by John L. Sweeney. Wisconsin: University of Wisconsin Press.

Jamison. Anne. 2001. "Any Where Out of this Verse: Baudelaire's Prose Poetics and the Aesthetics of Transgression." *Nineteenth-Century French Studies* 29 (3–4): 256–286.

Jeffreys, Peter. 2002. "Dünya Güseli: Cavafy's Folkloric Odalisque." *Byzantine and Modern Greek Studies* 26:218–246.

————. 2005. *Eastern Questions: Hellenism and Orientalism in the Writings of C. P. Cavafy and E. M. Forster*. Greensboro, NC: ELT Press.

————, ed. 2009. *The Forster-Cavafy Letters: Friends at a Slight Angle*. Cairo: American University in Cairo Press.

Jenkyns, Richard. 1991. *Dignity and Decadence: Victorian Art and the Classical Inheritance*. New York: Harper Collins.

Joannides, Paul. 1980. *The Victorians and Ancient Greece*. Cambridge, MA: Harvard University Press.

————. 2001. "Delacroix and Modern Literature." In *The Cambridge Companion to Delacroix*. Edited by Beth S. Wright, 130–153. London: Chaucer Press.

Johnson, Barbara. 1980. *The Critical Difference*. Baltimore: Johns Hopkins University Press.

Johnson, Dorothy. 2001. "Delacroix's Dialogue with the French Classical Tradition." In *The Cambridge Companion to Delacroix*. Edited by Beth S. Wright, 108–129. London: Chaucer Press.

Joyce, Simon. 2007. *The Victorians in the Rearview Mirror*. Athens, OH: Ohio University Press.

Jullian, Philippe. 1971. *Dreamers of Decadence: Symbolist Painters of the 1890s*. New York: Praeger.

Jusdanis, Gregory. 1982. "Cavafy, Tennyson and the Overcoming of Influence." *Byzantine and Modern Greek Studies* 8:123–130.

———. 1983. "The Modes of Reading; or Why Interpret? A Search for the Meaning of 'Imenos.'" *Journal of the Hellenic Diaspora* 10 (1–2): 137–148.

———. 1987. *The Poetics of Cavafy: Textuality, Eroticism, History.* Princeton: Princeton University Press.

———. 2003. "World Literature: The Unbearable Lightness of Thinking Globally." *Diaspora* 12(1): 103–130.

Kahn, Annette. 1987. *J.-K. Huysmans: Novelist, Poet and Art Critic.* Ann Arbor: UMI Research Press.

Kaiser, Matthew. 2002. "Marius at Oxford: Paterian Pedagogy and the Ethics of Seduction." In *Walter Pater: Transparencies of Desire.* Edited by Laurel Brake, Lesley Higgins, and Carolyn Williamson, 189–201. Greensboro: ELT Press.

Kakavas, Yiorgos, ed. 2002. *Ελλήνων κειμήλια, δωρεές στον καθεδρικό ναό της Αγίας Σοφίας του Λονδίνου.* Athens: Byzantine and Christian Museum.

Kaldellis, Anthony. 2007. *Hellenism in Byzantium.* Cambridge: Cambridge University Press.

———. 2010a. "The Corpus of Byzantine Historiography: An Interpretative Essay." In *The Byzantine World.* Edited by Paul Stephenson, 211–222. London: Routledge.

———. 2010b. Introduction to *The Secret History*, by Prokopios, vii–lix. Edited and translated by Anthony Kaldellis. Indianapolis: Hackett.

Kaplan, Edward K. 1990. *Baudelaire's Prose Poems.* Athens: University of Georgia Press.

Kaplan, Fred. 1987. *Sacred Tears: Sentimentality in Victorian Literature.* Princeton: Princeton University Press.

Kapsalis, S. D. 1983. "'Privileged Moments': Cavafy's Autobiographical Inventions." *Journal of the Hellenic Diaspora* 10 (1–2): 67–88.

Karagiannis, Vangelis. 1983. *Σημειώσεις από την Γενεαλογία του Καβάφη.* Athens: Greek Literary and Historical Archive.

Karampini-Iatrou, Michaela. 2003. *Η Βιβλιοθήκη Κ.Π. Καβάφη.* Athens: Hermes.

———. 2005. "Οι τρείς χάριτες: Ελληνίδες ζωγράφοι και μοντέλα στον κύκλο των Προραφαηλητών." In *Όσο κρατάει η ανάγνωση,* 661–674. Thessaloniki.

Katsigianni, Anna. 2000. "Πτυχές του Καβαφικού Μοντερνισμού: Τα 'Αποσιωπημένα' Πεζά Ποιήματα." In *Η Ποίηση του Κράματος.* Edited by Michalis Pieris, 81–102. Herakleion: University Publications of the University of Crete.

Kavafis, Constantino. 1979. "'Εις το φως της ημέρας': *Un Racconto inedito a cura di Renata Lavagnini."* Pelermo.

Kaye, Richard. 1995. "Aestheticism." In *The Gay and Lesbian Literary Heritage.* Edited by Claude J. Summers, 2–5. New York: Henry Holt.

Kazantzakis, Nikos. 1975. *Journeying: Travels in Italy, Egypt, Sinai, Jerusalem and Cyprus.* Translated by Themis and Theodora Vasils. Boston: Little, Brown.

———. 1965. *Ταξιδεύοντας.* Athens: Helen Kazantzakis Ltd.

Kazhdan, Alexander P., ed. 1991. *The Oxford Dictionary of Byzantium.* 3 vols. New York: Oxford University Press.

Kearns, James. 2007. *Théophile Gautier, Orator to the Artists: Art Journalism in the Second Republic.* London: Maney Publishing.

Keeley, Edmund. 1976. *Cavafy's Alexandria: A Study of Myth in Progress.* Cambridge, MA: Harvard University Press.

——. 2000. *On Translation: Reflections and Conversations.* Amsterdam: Harwood Academic Publishers.

Kelley, David. 1994. "Transpositions." In *Artistic Relations: Literature and the Visual Arts in Nineteenth-Century France.* Edited by Peter Collier and Robert Lethbridge, 178–191. New Haven: Yale University Press.

Kestner, Joseph A. 1989. *Mythology and Misogyny: The Social Discourse of Nineteenth-Century British Classical-Subject Painting.* Madison: University of Wisconsin Press.

Kitromilides, Paschalis M. 1998. "On the Intellectual Content of Greek Nationalism: Paparrigopoulos, Byzantium and the Great Idea." In *Byzantium and the Modern Greek Identity.* Edited by David Ricks, 25–33. Aldershot, UK: Ashgate.

Klewitz, Vera. 2009. "Goddess or Femme Fatale? The Sculptress Maria Cassavetti-Zambaco." In *Edward Burne-Jones: The Earthly Paradise.* Edited by Staatsgalerie Stuttgart, 79–83. Ostfildern, Ger.: Hatje Cantz Verlag.

Knight, Philip. 1986. *Flower Poetics in Nineteenth-Century France.* Oxford: Clarendon Press.

Komnene, Anna. 2009. *The Alexiad.* Translated by E.R.A. Sewter. New York: Penguin Books.

Kopidakis, M. Z. 1983. "Άνθη του Κακού: Από το Περιβόλι του Άτταλου." *Χάρτης* 5–6: 630–633.

——. 2000. *Ιστορία της Ελληνικής Γλώσσας.* Τρίτη Έκδοση. Athens: ELIA.

Kopp, Robert, and George Poulet. 1969. *Baudelaire: The Artist and His World.* Translated by Robert Allen and James Emmons. Geneva: Editions d'Art Albert Skira.

Kostis, Nikolas, trans. 2006. *Beyond the Broken Statues: Modern Greek Short Stories.* River Vale, NJ: Cosmos Publishing.

Krieger, Murray. 1992. *Ekphrasis: The Illusion of the Natural Sign.* Baltimore: Johns Hopkins Press.

Kristeva, Julia. 2006. *Murder in Byzantium.* Translated by C. Jon Delogu. New York: Columbia University Press.

Kureishi, Hanif. 2010. "The Decline of the West." In *Collected Stories.* London: Faber and Faber.

Lacambre, Geneviève. 1999. "Gustave Moreau and Exoticism." In *Gustave Moreau: Between Epic and Dream.* Edited by G. Lacambre, 15–20. Chicago: Art Institute of Chicago.

Laiou, Angeliki. 2000. "Introduction: Why Anna Komnene?" In *Anna Komnene and Her Times.* Edited by Thalia Gouma-Peterson, 1–14. New York: Garland.

Lambert-Charbonnier, Martine. "Poetics of *Ekphrasis* in Pater's 'Imaginary Portraits.'" In *Walter Pater: Transparencies of Desire.* Edited by Laurel Brake, Lesley Higgins, and Carolyn Williamson, 202–212. Greensboro, NC: ELT Press.

Lambourne, Lionel. 1996. *The Aesthetic Movement.* London: Phaidon.

Lambropoulos, Vassilis. 1983. "The Violent Power of Knowledge: The Struggle of Critical Discourses for Domination over Cavafy's 'Young Men of Sidon, A.D. 400.'" *Journal of the Hellenic Diaspora* 10 (1–2): 149–166.

——. 2003–4. "The Greeks of Art and the Greeks of History." *Modern Greek Studies: A Journal for Greek Letters* 11–12: 66–74.

Langlois, Walter G., ed. 1971. *The Persistent Voice: Essays on Hellenism in French Literature Since the 18th Century.* New York: New York University Press.

Latham, David, ed. 2003. "Haunted Texts: The Invention of Pre-Raphaelite Studies." In *Haunted Texts: Studies in Pre-Raphaelitism*. Edited by David Latham, 1–33. Toronto: University of Toronto Press.

Lathia, Eleni. 1978. "Παραστάσεις Αγγείων και Καβαφικοί Στίχοι." *Κριτικά Φύλλα* 8: 101–109.

Lavagnini, Renata. 2003. "Ένα Διήγημα του Καβάφη." *Το Δέντρο* 125–126 (April-June): 75–87.

Lechonitis, George. 1942. *Καβαφικά Αυτοσχόλια*. Alexandria, Egypt.

Leontis, Artemis, ed. 2002. *"What These Ithakas Mean." Readings in Cavafy*. Athens: Hellenic Literary and Historical Archive.

Levine, George, and William Madden. 1968. *The Art of Victorian Prose*. London: Oxford University Press.

Liddell, Robert. (1974) 2000. *Cavafy: A Critical Biography*. Reprint, London: Duckworth.

Lilly, Mark. 1993. *Gay Men's Literature in the Twentieth Century*. London: Macmillan.

Livingstone, Marco, and Kay Heymer. 2003. *Hockney's People*. Boston: Bulfinch Press.

Lloyd, Rosemary. 1981. *Baudelaire's Literary Criticism*. Cambridge: Cambridge University Press.

——. 2002. *Baudelaire's World*. Ithaca: Cornell University Press.

——. 2008. *Charles Baudelaire*. London: Reaktion Books.

Long, Basil Somerset. 1925. *Catalogue of the Constantine Alexander Ionides Collection*. London: Victoria and Albert Museum.

Lugg, Catherine A. 1999. *Kitsch: From Education to Public Policy*. New York: Falmer Press

MacCarthy, Fiona. 2012. *The Last Pre-Raphaelite: Edward Burne-Jones and the Victorian Imagination*. Cambridge: Harvard University Press.

Mackridge, Peter. 1985. *The Modern Greek Language*. Oxford: Oxford University Press.

Macleod, Dianne Sachko. 1996. *Art and the Victorian Middle Class: Money and the Making of Cultural Identity*. Cambridge: Cambridge University Press.

Macleod, Kristin. 2006. *Fictions of British Decadence: High Art, Popular Writing, and the Fin de Siècle*. New York: Palgrave.

Macrides, Ruth. 2000. "The Pen and the Sword: Who Wrote the *Alexiad?*" In *Anna Komnene and Her Times*. Edited by Thalia Gouma-Peterson, 63–81. New York: Garland.

Magdalino, Paul. 1993. *The Empire of Manue I Komnenos, 1143–1180*. Cambridge: Cambridge University Press.

——. 2000. "The Pen of the Aunt: Echoes of the Mid-Twelfth Century in the *Alexiad*." In *Anna Komnene and Her Times*. Edited by Thalia Gouma-Peterson, 15–43. New York: Garland.

Maguire, Henry, ed. 1995. *Byzantine Magic*. Washington, DC: Dumbarton Oaks.

——. 1997. "Images of the Court." In *The Glory of Byzantium: Art and Culture of the Middle Byzantine Era, A.D. 843–1261*. Edited by Helen C. Evans and William D. Wixom, 183–191. New York: Metropolitan Museum of Art.

Majewski, Henry F. 2002. *Transposing Art into Texts in French Literature*. Chapel Hill: University of North Carolina.

Malanos, Timos. 1942. "Introductory Note." *Καβαφικά Αυτοσχόλια*. Edited by George Lechonitis, 9–16. Alexandria, Egypt.

——. 1957. *Ο Ποιητής Κ.Π. Καβάφης.* Athens: Difros.

Maliaras, Barbara. 1992. "Love and Death: The Function of the Grotesque in the Paintings of Edward Burne-Jones." In *Pre-Raphaelitism and Medievalism in the Arts.* Edited by Liana De Girolami Cheney, 127–142. Lewiston, NY: Edwin Mellen Press.

Mancoff, Debra N. 1998. *Burne-Jones.* San Francisco: Pomegranate.

Mango, Cyril, ed. 2002. *The Oxford History of Byzantium.* 3 vols. Oxford: Oxford University Press.

Marsh, Jan, and Pamela Gerrish Nunn. 1989. *Women Artists and the Pre-Raphaelite Movement.* London: Virago Press.

McGann, Jerome J. 1972. *Swinburne: An Experiment in Criticism.* Chicago: University of Chicago Press.

——. 2004. Introduction to *Major Poems and Selected Prose: Algernon Charles Swinburne.* Edited by Jerome McGann and Charles L. Sligh, xv–xxviii. New Haven: Yale University Press.

McGuinness, Patrick, ed. 2000. *Symbolism, Decadence and the Fin De Siècle.* Exeter, UK: University of Exeter Press.

——. 2003. Introduction to *Against Nature,* by Joris-Karl Huysmans, xiii–xxxvi. Translated by Robert Baldick. London: Penguin Books.

McMullen, Roy. 1973. *Victorian Outsider: A Biography of J. A. M. Whistler.* New York: Dutton.

Mellor, Ronald. 2008. "*Graecia Capta*: The Confrontation between Greek and Roman Identity." In *Culture, Identity and Ethnicity from Antiquity to Modernity.* Edited by Katarina Zacharia, 79–125. Aldershot, UK: Ashgate.

Meltzer, Francoise. 1998. "*Fatal Attraction* Redux: 'La Faënza.'" In *The Decadent Reader: Fiction, Fantasy and Perversion from Fin-de-Siècle France.* Edited by Asti Hustvedt, 752–764. New York: Zone Books.

Mendelsohn, Daniel. 2009. Introduction to *C. P. Cavafy: Collected Poems,* xv–lix. Translated by Daniel Mendelsohn. New York: Knopf.

Merrill, Linda. 1992. *A Pot of Paint: Aesthetics on Trial in Whistler v. Ruskin.* Washington, DC: Smithsonian Institution Press.

——. 1998. *The Peacock Room: A Cultural Biography.* New Haven: Yale University Press.

Merritt, James D. 1966. Introduction to *The Pre-Raphaelite Poem.* Edited by James D. Merritt, 9–31. New York: Dutton.

Merritt, Travis R. 1968. "Taste, Opinion, and Theory in the Rise of Victorian Prose Stylism." In *The Art of Victorian Prose.* Edited by George Levine and William Madden, 3–38. London: Oxford University Press.

Metaxas, Constantine. 1974. *Κ. Καβάφης Ανέκδοτα Στοιχεία της Οικογενείας του Ποιητού.* London: N.p.

Michals, Duane. 2007. *The Adventures of Constantine Cavafy.* Santa Fe: Twin Palms Publishers.

Michaelidis, Eugenios. 1964. *Μητρώον του Δημοσιογραφικού Περιοδικού Τύπου της Αιγύπτου υπό Αιγυπτιωτών Ελλήνων (1862–1963).* Alexandria: Center for Greek Studies.

Miller, J. Hillis. 2003. "Whistler/Swinburne: 'Before the Mirror'" In *Haunted Texts: Studies in Pre-Raphaelitism.* Edited by David Latham. Toronto: University of Toronto Press.

Mitsakis, K. 1983. "Ο Κ. Π. Καβάφης και η παρακμή του δυτικού κόσμου." In *Μέρες του Ποιητή Κ.Π. Καβάφη*, 137–147. Athens: Τετράδια Ευθύνης.

Moffat, Wendy. 2010. *A Great Unrecorded History: A New Life of E. M. Forster.* New York: Farrar, Straus and Giroux.

Monsman, Gerald Cornelius. 1967. *Pater's Portraits: Mythic Pattern in the Fiction of Walter Pater.* Baltimore: Johns Hopkins University Press.

———. 1977. *Walter Pater.* Boston: Twayne Publishers.

———. (1885) 2008. Introduction to *Marius the Epicurean: His Sensations and Ideas*, by Walter Pater, vii–xxiii. Edited by Gerald Monsman. Kansas City: Valancourt Books.

Montesquieu, Charles de Secondat. 1965. *Consideration on the Causes of the Greatness of the Romans and Their Decline.* Translated by David Lowenthal. New York: Free Press.

Moran, Maureen. 2002. "Pater's 'Great Change': *Marius the Epicurean* as Historical Conversion Romance." In *Walter Pater: Transparencies of Desire.* Edited by Laurel Brake, Lesley Higgins, and Carolyn Williamson, 170–188. Greensboro, NC: ELT Press.

Morley, Neville. 2005. "Decadence as a Theory of History." *New Literary History* 35:573–585.

Morris, Mowbray. 1886. "An Alexandrian Age." *Macmillan's Magazine* 55 (November): 27–35.

Mullett, Margaret, ed. 1996. *Alexios I Komnenos: Papers of the Second Belfast Byzantine International Colloquium, 14–16 April 1989.* Belfast: Belfast Byzantine Enterprises.

Munro, John M. 1970. *The Decadent Poetry of the Eighteen-Nineties.* Beirut: American University of Beirut.

Murphy, Margueritte. 2008. "The Critic as Cosmopolite: Baudelaire's International Sensibility and the Transformation of Viewer Subjectivity." In *Art and Life in Aestheticism.* Edited by Kelly Comfort, 25–41. New York: Palgrave Macmillan.

Nerdrum, Odd, ed. 2011. *Kitsch: More Than Art.* Oslo: Schibsted Forlag.

Neville, Leonora. 2010. "Strong Women and Their Husbands in Byzantine Historiography." In *The Byzantine World.* Edited by Paul Stephenson, 72–82. London: Routledge.

Newall, Christopher. 1995. *The Grosvenor Gallery Exhibitions: Change and Continuity in the Victorian Art Word.* Cambridge: Cambridge University Press.

———. 1997. "Themes of Love and Death in Aesthetic Painting of the 1860's." In *The Age of Rossetti, Burne-Jones and Watts: Symbolism in Britain (1860–1910).* Edited by Andrew Wilton and Robert Upstone, 35–46. London: Tate Gallery Publishing, Ltd.

Nicol, Donald M. 1993. *The Last Centuries of Byzantium, 1261–1453.* Cambridge: Cambridge University Press.

———. 1994. *The Byzantine Lady: Ten Portraits, 1250–1500.* Cambridge: Cambridge University Press.

———. 1996. *The Reluctant Emperor: A Biography of John Cantacuzene, Byzantine Emperor and Monk, c. 1295–1383.* Cambridge: Cambridge University Press.

North, Julian. 1999. "Defining Decadence in Nineteenth-Century French and British Criticism." In *Romancing Decay: Ideas of Decadence in European Culture.* Edited by Michael St. John, 83–94. Brookfield, UK: Ashgate.

Norton, Rictor. 1997. *The Myth of the Modern Homosexual: Queer History and the Search for Cultural Unity.* London: Cassell.

Oberholzer, Simon. 2009. "Edward Burne-Jones' Pygmalion." In *Edward Burne-Jones: The Earthly Paradise*. Edited by Staatsgalerie Stuttgart, 67–77. Ostfildern, Ger.: Hatje Cantz Verlag.

Olalquiaga, Celeste. 1998. *The Artificial Kingdom: A Treasury of the Kitsch Experience.* New York: Pantheon Books.

Ostermark-Johansen, Lene. 2002. "The Death of Euphues: Euphuism and Decadence in Late-Victorian Literature." *English Literature in Transition* 45 (1): 4–25.

Owens, Susan. 2011. "Literature and the Aesthetic Movement." In *The Cult of Beauty: The Aesthetic Movement, 1860–1900*. Edited by Stephen Calloway and Lynn Federle Orr, 40–59. London: V&A Publishing.

Paglia, Camille. 1991. *Sexual Personae.* New York: Vintage Books.

Papaleontiou, Lefteris. 1998. *Λογοτεχνικές Μεταφράσεις του Μείζονος Ελληνισμού Μικρασία, Κύπρος, Αίγυπτος, 1880–1930.* Thessalonica: Center for the Greek Language.

Pagoulatos, Andreas. 2010. "Η Επίδραση του Νίτσε στην Ποίηση του Κ.Π. Καβάφη." *Οδός Πανός* 17: 69–73.

Pandelodemos, Dimitris. 1983. "Ο Καβάφης μεταφράζει και ερμηνεύει Baudelaire." *Nea Estia* 114: 1499–1505.

Papanikolaou, Dimitris. 2005. "Words That Tell and Hide": Revisiting C. P. Cavafy's Closets." *Journal of Modern Greek Studies* 23 (1): 235–260.

———. 2014. *Σάν κ'εμένα καμωμένο : ο ομοφυλόφιλος Καβάφης και η ποιητική της σεξουαλικότητας.* Athens: Pataki.

Papoutsakis, George P. 1963. "Πρόλογος." In *Κ.Π. Καβάφη Πεζά.* Edited by George P. Papoutsakis, 9–14. Athens: Phexi.

Pater, Walter. 1925. *Greek Studies: A Series of Essays.* London: Macmillan.

———. 1980. *The Renaissance: Studies in Art and Poetry: The 1893 Text.* Edited by Donald L. Hill. Berkeley: University of California Press.

———. 1986. *Walter Pater: Three Major Texts: (The Renaissance, Appreciations, and Imaginary Portraits).* Edited by William E. Buckler. New York: New York University Press.

———. (1885) 2008. *Marius the Epicurean: His Sensations and Ideas.* (1885). Edited by Gerald Monsman. Kansas City: Valancourt Books.

———. 2010. *Studies in the History of the Renaissance* (1873). Edited by Matthew Beaumont. New York: Oxford University Press.

Pearson, Keith Ansell, and Duncan Large, eds. 2006. *The Nietzsche Reader.* Malden, MA: Blackwell.

Pentcheva, Bissera V. 2010. *The Sensual Icon: Space, Ritual, and the Senses in Byzantium.* University Park: Pennsylvania State University Press.

Peranthis, Michael. 1970. *Ο Αμαρτολός.* Athens: Estia.

Perides, Michalis. 1963. "Εισαγωγή." In *Κ.Π. Καβάφη Ανέκδοτα Πεζά Κείμενα.* Athens: Phexi.

Peyre, Henri. 1980. *What Is Symbolism?* Translated by Emmett Parker. Tuscaloosa: University of Alabama Press.

Philostratus and Callistratus. 1931. *Imagines and Descriptions.* Translated Arthur Fairbanks. Loeb Classical Library. New York: William Heinemann.

Pieris, Michalis. 1992. *Χώρος, Φως και Λόγος*. Athens: Kastaniotis.

——. ed. 2000. *Η Ποίηση του Κράματος*. Herakleion: University Publications of the University of Crete.

——. 2003. "Εισαγωγικό Σημείωμα του Επιμελητή." In *Κ.Π. Καβάφη: Τα Πεζά (1882–1931)*. Athens: Ikaros.

Pierrot, Jean. 1981. *The Decadent Imagination: 1880–1900*. Translated by Derek Coltman. Chicago: University of Chicago Press.

Pittock, Murray G. H. 1993. "Swinburne and the 'Nineties." In *The Whole Music of Passion: New Essays on Swinburne*. Edited by Rikky Rooksby and Nicholas Shrimpton, 120–135. Aldershot, UK: Scolar Press.

Plante, David. 2009. "Poems (1935 and Later) by Constantine Cavafy." In *Fifty Gay and Lesbian Books Everybody Must Read*. Edited by Richard Canning, 127–137. New York: Alyson Books.

Poe, Edgar Allan. 1992. *The Complete Tales and Poems of Edgar Allan Poe with Selections from his Critical Writings*. New York: Barnes and Noble Books.

Pogglioli, Renato. 1983. "*Qualis Artifex Pereo!* Or Barbarism and Decadence." In *The Mind and Art of C. P. Cavafy. Essays on his Life and Work*. Edited by Denise Harvey, 127–156. Athens: Denise Harvey.

Polemis, Demetrios I. 1968. *The Doukai: A Contribution to Byzantine Prosopography*. London: Athlone Press.

Politou-Marmarinou, Eleni. 1983. "Ο Καβάφης και ο Γαλλικός Παρνασσισμός." In *Πρακτικά Τρίτου Συμποσίου Ποίησης, Αφιέρωμα στον Κ.Π. Καβάφη*. Edited by S. Skartsis, 315–346. Athens: Gnosi.

Polykandrioti, Ourania. 2005. "Εφημερίδες και Λογοτεχνία από την Ίδρυση του Ελληνικού Κράτους ως Σήμερα." In *Ο Ελληνικός Τύπος: 1783 ως Σήμερα: Ιστορικές και Θεωρητικές Προσεγγήσεις. Πρακτικά Διεθνούς Συνεδρίου, Αθήνα, 23–24 Μαΐου, 2002*. Edited by Lucia Droulia, 168–177. Athens: Institut de Recherches Néohelléniques.

Pontani, Filippo Mari. 1991. *Επτά Δοκίμια & Μελετήματα για τον Καβάφη*. Athens: Education Foundation of the National Bank of Greece.

Potolsky, Matthew. 1999. "Pale Imitations: Walter Pater's Decadent Historiography." In *Perennial Decay: On the Aesthetics and Politics of Decadence*. Edited by Liz Constable, Dennis Denisoff, and Matthew Potolsky, 235–253. Philadelphia: University of Pennsylvania Press.

——. 2013. *The Decadent Republic of Letters: Taste, Politics, and Cosmopolitan Community from Baudelaire to Beardsley*. Philadelphia: University of Pennsylvania Press.

Powell, Kirsten. 1992. "Burne-Jones, Swinburne, and *Laus Veneris*." In *Pre-Raphaelitism and Medievalism in the Arts*. Edited by Liana De Girolami Cheney, 221–235. Lewiston, NY: Edwin Mellen Press.

Praz, Mario. 1970. *The Romantic Agony*. Translated by Angus Davidson. London: Oxford University Press.

Prettejohn, Elizabeth, ed. 1999. *After the Pre-Raphaelites*. Manchester, UK: Manchester University Press.

——. 1999. "Walter Pater and Aesthetic Painting." In *After the Pre-Raphaelites*. Edited by Elizabeth Prettejohn, 36–58. Manchester, UK: Manchester University Press.

——. 2000. *The Art of the Pre-Raphaelites*. London: Tate Gallery Publishing.

——. 2007. *Art for Art's Sake: Aestheticism in Victorian Painting*. New Haven: Yale University Press.

Prokopios. 2010. *The Secret History*. Edited and translated by Anthony Kaldellis. Indianapolis: Hackett Publishing.

Purton, Valerie. 2012. *Dickens and the Sentimental Tradition*. London: Anthem Press.

Ransome, Arthur. 1913. *Oscar Wilde: A Critical Study*. London: Methuen.

Raap, Claudia. 2008. "Hellenic Identity, *Romanitas*, and Christianity." In *Hellenisms: Culture, Identity and Ethnicity from Antiquity to Modernity*. Edited by Katerina Zacharia, 127–147. Aldershot, UK: Ashgate.

Reed, Christopher. 2004. *Bloomsbury Rooms: Modernism, Subculture, and Domesticity*. New Haven: Yale University Press.

Reed, John R. 1985. *Decadent Style*. Athens, OH: Ohio University Press.

Rees, William, ed. 1990. *The Penguin Book of French Poetry 1820–1950*. Edited and translated by William Rees. New York: Penguin Books.

Reinsch, Diether R. 2000. "Women's Literature in Byzantium? The Case of Anna Komnene." In *Anna Komnene and Her Times*. Edited by Thalia Gouma-Peterson, 83–105. New York: Garland.

Rambaud, Alfred N. 1891. "Empereurs et Impératrices d'Orient." *Revue des Deux Monde* (February 1891): 814–839.

Ricks, David. 2001. "Cavafy and the Body of Christ." *Journal of the Hellenic Diaspora* 27:19–32.

——. 2003. "How It Strikes a Contemporary: Cavafy as a Reviser of Browning." *Kambos: Cambridge Papers in Modern Greek* 11:131–152.

——. 2004. Cavafy's Alexandrianism." In *Alexandria, Real and Imagined*. Edited by Anthony Hirst and Michael Silk, 337–351. Aldershot, UK: Ashgate.

Ricks, David, and Paul Magdalino, eds. 1998. *Byzantium and the Modern Greek Identity*. Aldershot, UK: Ashgate.

Riede, David G. 1978. *Swinburne: A Study in Romantic Mythmaking*. Charlottesville: University of Virginia Press.

Rigopoulos, Yiannis. 1991. *Ut Pictura Poesis: Το "Εκφραστικό" Σύστημα της Ποίησης και Ποιητικής του Κ. Καβάφη*. Athens: Smili.

Rivière, Yann. 2008a. "The 'Portonaccio' Sarcophagus (Rome)." In *Rome and the Barbarians: The Birth of a New World*. Edited by Jean-Jacques Aillagon, 170–171. Milan: Skira Editore.

——. 2008b. "Sarcophagi with Battle Scenes." In *Rome and the Barbarians: The Birth of a New World*. Edited by Jean-Jacques Aillagon, 166–169. Milan: Skira Editore.

Robinson, Christopher. 2005. "Cavafy, Sexual Sensibility, and Poetic Practice: Reading Cavafy through Mark Doty and Cathal O'Searcaigh." *Journal of Modern Greek Studies* 23 (1): 261–279.

Rodenbach, Georges. 2005. *Bruges-la-Morte*. Translated by Mike Mitchell and Will Stone. Cambs, UK: Dedalus.

Roilos, Panagiotis. 2009. *C. P. Cavafy: The Economics of Metonymy*. Chicago: University of Illinois Press.

Rooksby, Rikky, and Nicholas Shrimpton, eds. 1993. *The Whole Music of Passion: New Essays on Swinburne*. Aldershot, UK: Scolar Press.

Runciman, Steven. 1970. *The Last Byzantine Renaissance.* Cambridge: Cambridge University Press.

——. 1977. "Gibbon and Byzantium." In *Edward Gibbon and the Decline and Fall of the Roman Empire.* Edited by G. W. Bowersock, John Clive, and Stephen Gaubard, 53–60. Cambridge: Harvard University Press.

Rutland, William R. 1931. *Swinburne: A Nineteenth Century Hellene.* Oxford: Basil Blackwell.

Sachinis, Apostolos. 1981. *Η Πεζογραφία του Αισθητισμού.* Athens: Estia.

Said, Edward. 2006. *On Late Style: Music and Literature against the Grain.* New York: Pantheon Books.

Salines, Emily. 1994. *Alchemy and Amalgam: Translation in the Works of Charles Baudelaire.* New York: Rodopi.

Salmon, Richard. 2000. "'A Simulacrum of Power': Intimacy and Abstraction in the Rhetoric of the New Journalism." In *Nineteenth-Century Media and the Construction of Identities.* Edited by Laurel Brake, 27–39. New York: Palgrave.

Sareyannis, J.A. 1983. "What Was Most Precious—His Form." *Grand Street* 2 (3): 108–126.

Savidis, George. 1983. "Πρόλογος του Επιμελητή." In *Κ.Π. Καβάφης Τα Αποκηρυγμένα.* Edited by George Savidis, 11–14. Athens: Ikaros.

——. 1985a. "Cavafy, Gibbon and Byzantium." In *Μικρά Καβαφικά Α.*, 93–99. Athens: Hermes.

——. 1985b. *Μικρά Καβαφικά Α.* Athens: Hermes.

——. 1987a. *Μικρά Καβαφικά Β.* Athens: Hermes.

——. 1987b. "Ο Καβάφης Συντάκτης Μαθητικής Ανθολογίας Δημοτικών Τραγουδιών." In *Μικρά Καβαφικά Β.* Edited by George Savidis, 205–246. Athens: Hermes.

——. 1991. *Οι Καβαφικές Εκδόσεις: 1891–1932.* Athens: Ikaros.

Savidis, Lena. 1983. *Λεύκωμα Καβάφη 1863–1910.* Athens: Stamou and Sons.

Savidis, Manuel. 2003. Introduction to *C. P. Cavafy: Sixty-Three Poems Translated by J. C. Cavafy,* ix–x. Athens: Ikaros.

Schaffer, Aaron. 1929. *Parnassus in France.* Austin: University of Texas Press.

——. 1944. *The Genres of Parnassian Poetry.* Baltimore: Johns Hopkins University Press.

Schulte, Rainer, and John Biguenet, eds. 1992. *Theories of Translation: An Anthology of Essays from Dryden to Derrida.* Chicago: University of Chicago Press.

Scott, Clive. 1976. "The Prose Poem and Free Verse." In *Modernism: A Guide to European Literature, 1890–1930.* Edited by Malcolm Bradbury and James McFarlane, 349–368. London: Penguin Books.

——. 2000. "The Poetry of Symbolism and Decadence." In *Symbolism, Decadence and the Fin De Siècle.* Edited by Patrick McGuinness, 57–71. Exeter, UK: University of Exeter Press.

Scott, David. 1977. *Sonnet Theory and Practice in Nineteenth-Century France: Sonnets on the Sonnet.* Hull, UK: University of Hull Publications.

——. 1988. *Pictorialist Poetics: Poetry and the Visual Arts in Nineteenth-Century France.* Cambridge: Cambridge University Press.

——. 1994. "Writing the Arts: Aesthetics, Art Criticism and Literary Practice." In *Artistic Relations: Literature and the Visual Arts in Nineteenth-Century France.* Edited by Peter Collier and Robert Lethbridge, 61–75. New Haven: Yale University Press.

———. 2001. "Painting/Literature: The Impact of Delacroix on Aesthetic Theory, Art Criticism, and Poetics in Mid-Nineteenth-Century France." In *The Cambridge Companion to Delacroix.* Edited by Beth S. Wright, 170–186. London: Chaucer Press.

Scott, Jacqueline. 1998. "Nietzsche and Decadence: The Revaluation of Morality." *Continental Philosophy Review* 31:59–78.

Scruton, Roger. 1999. "Kitsch and the Modern Predicament." *City Journal* (Winter). http://www.city-journal.org/html/9_1_urbanities_kitsch_and_the.html.

Sedgwick, Eve Kosofsky. 1990. *Epistemology of the Closet.* Berkeley: University of California Press.

Seed, David. 2005. Introduction to *The Coming Race,* by Edward Bulwer-Lytton, iii–xxxviii. Middletown, CT: Wesleyan University Press.

Seferis, George. 1983. "Cavafy and Eliot—A Comparison." Translated by Rex Warner. In *The Mind and Art of C. P. Cavafy: Essays on his Life and Work.* Edited by Denise Harvey, 60–88. Athens: Denise Harvey.

Seiler, R. M., ed. 1980. *Walter Pater: The Critical Heritage.* London: Routledge & Kegan Paul.

Ševčenko, Ihor. 2002. "Palaiologan Learning." In *The Oxford History of Byzantium.* Edited by Cyril Mango, 284–293. Oxford: Oxford University Press.

Shattuck, Roger. 1983. "Vibratory Organism: *Crise de prose.*" In *The Prose Poem in France: Theory and Practice.* Edited by Mary Ann Caws, 21–35. New York: Columbia University Press.

Showalter, Elaine. 1990. *Sexual Anarchy: Gender and Culture at the Fin de Siècle.* New York: Viking.

Shrimpton, Nicholas. 1993. "Swinburne and the Dramatic Monologue." In *The Whole Music of Passion: New Essays on Swinburne.* Edited by Rikky Rooksby and Nicholas Shrimpton, 52–72. Aldershot, UK: Scolar Press.

Shryock, Richard. 1998. "Reaction within Symbolism: The Ecole Romane." *The French Review* 71 (4): 577–584.

Shugart, Helene A., and Catherine E. Waggoner. 2012. *Making Camp.* Tuscaloosa: University of Alabama Press.

Shuter, William F. 1997. *Rereading Walter Pater.* Cambridge: Cambridge University Press.

Siewert, John. 2004. "Rhetoric and Reputation in Whistler's Nocturnes." In *After Whistler: The Artist and His Influence on American Painting.* Edited by Linda Merrill, 64–73. New Haven: Yale University Press.

Silk, Michael. 2005. "Nietzsche, Decadence, and the Greeks." *New Literary History* 35: 587–606.

Snell, Robert. 1982. *Théophile Gautier: A Romantic Critic of the Visual Arts.* Oxford: Clarendon Press.

Snyder, Martin D. 2002. "Endymion." In *GLBTQ: An Encyclopedia of Gay, Lesbian, Bisexual, Transgender, and Queer Culture.* Edited by Claude J. Summers. www.glbtq.com/arts/subjects_endymion.html.

Sontag, Susan. 1964. "Notes on Camp." *Partisan Review* 31 (4): 515–530.

Spalding, Frances. 1979. *Whistler.* London: Phaidon Press.

Spatharakis, Ioannis. 1976. *The Portrait in Byzantine Illuminated Manuscripts.* Leiden, Neth.: E. J. Brill.

Spawforth, A. J. S. 2012. *Greece and the Augustan Cultural Revolution.* Cambridge: Cambridge University Press.

Spencer, Michael Clifford. 1969. *The Art Criticism of Theophile Gautier.* Geneva: Libraire Droz.

Spencer, Robin. 1972. *The Aesthetic Movement: Theory and Practice.* London: Studio Vista.

———. 1999. "Whistler, Swinburne, and Art for Art's Sake." In *After the Pre-Raphaelites.* Edited by Elizabeth Prettejohn, 59–89. Manchester, UK: Manchester University Press.

Spirit, Jane. 1995. "Emerging Views of Byzantium, 1850–1930: Germs of the Modern and Its Paradoxes." *English Literature in Transition* 38 (2): 156–167.

St. John, Michael, ed. 1999. *Romancing Decay: Ideas of Decadence in European Culture.* Brookfield, UK: Ashgate.

Stableford, Brian. 1990. Introduction to *The Dedalus Book of Decadence: Moral Ruins.* Edited by Brian Stableford, 1 110. Cambs, UK: Dedalus.

Stanford, Derek, ed. 1973. *Pre-Raphaelite Writing: An Anthology.* London: J. M. Dent & Sons.

Steiner, Wendy. 1982. *The Colors of Rhetoric: Problems in the Relation between Modern Literature and Painting.* Chicago: University of Chicago Press.

Stephan, Philip. 1974. *Paul Verlaine and the Decadence: 1892–90.* Manchester, UK: University of Manchester Press.

Stephenson, Paul, ed. 2010a. *The Byzantine World.* London: Routledge.

——— 2010b. Introduction to *The Byzantine World.* Edited by Paul Stephenson, xxi–xxv. London: Routledge.

———. 2010c. "Pioneers of Popular Byzantine History: Freeman, Gregorovius, Schlumberger." In *The Byzantine World.* Edited by Paul Stephenson, 462–480. London: Routledge.

———. 2010d. "The World of Byzantine Studies." In *The Byzantine World.* Edited by Paul Stephenson, 429–433. London: Routledge.

Stevens, Mary Anne. 1997. "Symbolism—A French Monopoly?" In *The Age of Rossetti, Burne-Jones and Watts: Symbolism in Britain (1860–1910).* Edited by Andrew Wilton and Robert Upstone, 47–64. London: Tate Gallery Publishing.

Stevenson, Lionel. 1972. *The Pre-Raphaelite Poets.* New York: Norton.

Stillman, W. J. 1891. "Journalism and Literature." *Atlantic Monthly* 68:687–695.

Stone, Will. 2005. Introduction to "The Death Throes of Towns." In *Bruges-la-Morte,* by Georges Rodenbach, 135–140. Translated by Mike Mitchell and Will Stone. Cambs, UK: Dedalus.

Stubbs, Burns A. 1950. *James McNeill Whistler: A Biographical Outline.* Washington, DC: Freer Gallery of Art.

Swinburne, Algernon Charles. 2000. *Poems and Ballads and Atalanta in Calydon.* Edited by Kenneth Hayes. London: Penguin Books.

———. 2004. *Major Poems and Selected Prose.* Edited by Jerome McGann and Charles L. Sligh. New Haven: Yale University Press.

Sykes, Christopher Simon. 2011. *David Hockney: The Biography, 1937–1975. A Rake's Progress.* New York: Doubleday.

Symons, Arthur. 1958. *The Symbolist Movement in Literature.* New York: Dutton.

Syrimis, George. 2003. "Promiscuous Texts and Abandoned Readings in the Poetry of C. P. Cavafy." *Modern Greek Literature: Critical Essays.* Edited by Gregory Nagy, 99–118. New York: Routledge.

Teukolsky, Rachel. 2002. "The Politics of Formalist Art Criticism: Pater's 'School of Giorgione.'" In *Walter Pater: Transparencies of Desire.* Edited by Laurel Brake, Lesley Higgins, and Carolyn Williamson, 151–188. Greensboro, NC: ELT Press.

Thomas, Donald. 1993. Introduction to *The Everyman Book of Victorian Verse.* Edited by Donald Thomas. London: Charles E. Tuttle.

Thornton, R. K. R. 1983. *The Decadent Dilemma.* London: Edward Arnold.

Thorpe, Nigel, ed. 2006. The Correspondence of James McNeill Whistler. University of Glasgow Center for Whistler Studies. http://www.whistler.arts.gla.ac.uk.

Thrylos, Alkis. 1924. "Κ. Καβάφης." *Κριτικές Μελέτες III.* Athens: Sarivaxevani Publishers.

Todd, Pamela. 2001. *The Pre-Raphaelites at Home.* London: Pavilion Books.

Tombrou, Maria. 2004. "Καβάφης και Μπράουνιγκ." *Νέα Εστία* 1756:787–809.

Trapp, M. B. 2004. "Images of Alexandria in the Writings of the Second Sophistic." In *Alexandria, Real and Imagined.* Edited by Anthony Hirst and Michael Silk, 113–132. Aldershot, UK: Ashgate.

Tsimbidaros, Vasos. 1974. *Οι Έλληνες στην Αγγλία.* Athens: Alkaios.

Tsirkas, Stratis. 1958. *Ο Καβάφης και η Εποχή του.* Athens: Kedros.

———. 1971. *Ο Πολιτικός Καβάφης.* Athens: Kedros.

———. 1983. "Κ.Π. Καβάφη. Σχεδιάσματα Χρονογραφίας του Βίου του." *Επιθεώρηση Τέχνης* 108:676–706.

Tsoutsoura, Maria. 1993. "'Αλληλουχία κατά τον Βωδελαίρον': ένα κρίσιμο κείμενο του Κ.Π. Καβάφη." *Εποπτεία* (October): 77–94.

Tucker, Paul. 1991. "Pater as a 'Moralist.'" In *Pater in the 1990s.* Edited by Laurel Brake and Ian Small, 107–125. Greensboro, NC: ELT Press.

Tufescu, Florina. 2008. *Oscar Wilde's Plagiarism: The Triumph of Art over Ego.* Portland, OR: Irish Academic Press.

Turner, Mark W. 2003. *Backward Glances: Cruising the Queer Streets of New York and London.* London: Reaktion Books.

Tziovas, Dimitris. 1986a. "Cavafy's Barbarians and their Western Genealogy." *Byzantine and Modern Greek Studies* 10:161–178.

———. 1986b. *The Nationism of the Demoticists and Its Impact on Their Literary Theory (1888–1930).* Amsterdam: Adolf M. Hakkert.

Valaoritis, Nanos. 1983. "Κ. Π. Καβάφης και Ε. Α. Πόε, μεταξύ άλλων." *Χάρτης* 5/6: 650–657.

Vance, Norman. 1997. *The Victorians and Ancient Rome.* Cambridge, MA: Blackwell.

Vasiliev, A.A. 1958. *History of the Byzantine Empire.* Vols. 1 and 2. Madison: University of Wisconsin Press.

Vassiliadi, Martha. 2008. *Les Fastes de la Décadence chez Constantin Cavafy.* Athens: Nepheli.

Vicinus, Martha. 1999. "The Adolescent Boy: Fin-de-Siècle Femme Fatale?" *Victorian Sexual Dissidence.* Edited by Richard Dellamora, 83–106. Chicago: Chicago University Press.

Victoria and Albert Museum. Nd. *The Ionides Collection.* London: Victoria and Albert Museum.

Vidal, Gore. 2001. Introduction to *Before Time Could Change Them: The Complete Poems of Constantine P. Cavafy,* xv–xxi. Translated by Theoharis C. Theoharis. New York: Harcourt.

Vlasto, Petros. 1933. *Greek Bilingualism and Some Parallel Cases.* Athens: Estia.

Wakefield, David. 2007. *The French Romantics: Literature and the Visual Arts 1800–1840.* London: Chaucer Press.

Walder, Anne. 1976. *Swinburne's Flowers of Evil: Baudelaire's Influence on Poems and Ballads, First Series.* Uppsala, Swed.: University of Uppsala.

Ward, Patricia, ed. 2001. *Baudelaire and the Poetics of Modernity.* Nashville: Vanderbilt University Press.

Waters, William, and Peter Nahum. 2009. "Past and Present: Edward Burne-Jones, His Medieval Sources and Their Relevance to His Personal Journey." In *Edward Burne-Jones: The Earthly Paradise,* Edited by Staatsgalerie Stuttgart, 179–203. Ostfildern, Ger.: Hatje Cantz Verlag.

Watson, Margaretta Frederick, ed. 1997. *Collecting the Pre-Raphaelites: The Anglo-American Enchantment.* Aldershot, UK: Scholar Press.

Webb, Peter. 1988. *Portrait of David Hockney.* New York: Dutton.

Weir, David. 1996. *Decadence and the Making of Modernism.* Amherst: University of Massachusetts Press.

Werner, James V. 2004. *American Flâneur: The Cosmic Physiognomy of Edgar Allan Poe.* New York: Routledge.

Whistler, James Abbot McNeill. 1892. *The Gentle Art of Making Enemies.* London: William Heinemann.

White, Andrew Dickson. 1959. *The Diaries of Andrew D. White.* Edited by Robert Morris Ogden. Ithaca: Cornell University Press.

Wildman, Stephen, and John Christian, eds. 1998. *Edward Burne-Jones: Victorian Artist-Dreamer.* New York: Metropolitan Museum of Art.

Williams, Carolyn. 1989. *Transfigured World: Walter Pater's Aesthetic Historicism.* Ithaca: Cornell University Press.

Williamson, Audrey. 1976. *Artists and Writers in Revolt: The Pre-Raphaelites.* London: David and Charles.

Wilton, Andrew. 1997. "Symbolism in Britain." In *The Age of Rossetti, Burne-Jones and Watts: Symbolism in Britain (1860–1910).* Edited by Andrew Wilton and Robert Upstone, 11–28. London: Tate Gallery Publishing.

Wilton, Andrew, and Robert Upstone, eds. 1997. *The Age of Rossetti, Burne-Jones and Watts: Symbolism in Britain (1860–1910).* London: Tate Gallery Publishing.

Wissen, Thomas Reed. 1989. *The Devil's Advocates: Decadence in Modern Literature.* New York: Greenwood Press.

Wood, Christopher. 1998. *Burne-Jones: The Life and Works of Sir Edward Burne-Jones (1833–1898).* London: Weidenfeld and Nicolson.

Woodhouse, C. M. 1986. *George Gemistos Plethon.* Oxford: Clarendon Press.

Woods, Gregory. 1998. *A History of Gay Literature.* New Haven: Yale University Press.

Wright, Beth S. 2001. "Painting Thoughts: An Introduction to Delacroix." In *The Cambridge Companion to Delacroix.* Edited by Beth S. Wright, 1–7. Cambridge: Cambridge University Press.

Yeros, Dimitiris. 2010. *Shades of Love: Photographs Inspired by the Poems of C.P. Cavafy.* San Raphael, CA: Insight Editions.

Young, Andrew McLaren, Margaret MacDonald, and Robert Spencer, eds. 1980. *The Paintings of James McNeill Whistler.* 2 vols. New Haven: Yale University Press.

Yourcenar, Marguerite. 1984. "A Critical Introduction to Cavafy." In *The Dark Brain of Piranesi and Other Essays.* Translated by Richard Howard, 154–197. New York: Farrar, Straus, Giroux.

Zacharia, Katerina, ed. 2008. *Hellenisms: Culture, Identity and Ethnicity from Antiquity to Modernity.* Aldershot, UK: Ashgate.

Zagona, Helen Grace. 1960. *The Legend of Salome and the Principle of Art for Art's Sake.* Paris: Librairie Minard.

NOTES

Prologue

1. The dates following the poem titles indicate the year the poem was either printed in one of Cavafy's privately circulated broadsheet volumes or published in a literary journal or newspaper. An asterisk beside a single date signifies that the poem was never published or circulated and marks the year in which it was written. When multiple dates appear, the earlier date or dates record the year or years of composition followed by the final year of printed publication.

2. Charles Bernheimer argues that no totalizing definition of decadence is possible but finds a "peculiar dynamism" in the term's "frustrating epistemological irresolution" (2002, 28). For overviews of the definition and its history, see Weir (1996, chap. 1); Stableford (1990); and Hall and Murray (2013).

3. See Daskalopoulos (1988, 148). The overstated notion of Cavafian "realism" that this school of interpretation has given rise to (D.N. Maronitis and Sonia Ilinskaya being the most persistent advocates of this critical approach) not only is more properly suited to narrative fiction but, more problematically, uncritically negates Cavafy's pervasive aestheticism and ongoing engagement with decadent subject matter. A critical response against repetitive philological/ethnocentric readings by Greek critics who, in a similar vein, sought to appropriate Cavafy for the national canon was launched by Margaret Alexiou in a special double issue of the *Journal of the Hellenic Diaspora* in which articles by Alexiou, Vassilis Lambropoulos, and Gregory Jusdanis in particular broke new critical ground by inaugurating post-structuralist theoretical readings.

4. Cited in Dowling (1986, 151). On Moréas's abandonment of the term "decadence," see Meltzer (1998, 752–753). Symons, in an 1897 essay on George Meredith cited in Beckson (1966),

defines decadence as "that learned corruption of language by which style ceases to be organic, and becomes, in the pursuit of some new expressiveness or beauty, deliberately abnormal" (xxxix). As Guy Michaud notes, "Decadence and symbolism were not two schools, as one is generally led to think, but two successive phases of one and the same movement, two stages in the poetic revolution" (cited in Meltzer 1998, 755). See also Balakian, who defines symbolism not in dichotomous relation to decadence but as part of a decadence that did not end with the turn of the century: "What gave symbolism, in its generalized sense, longevity and a power of radiation was that quality called 'decadence,' and the ability to convey via the symbol-image the mood of mysterious, metaphysical restlessness and the lyrical sense of doom, by a European association of poetic talents, surrounding the French coterie in the final years of the century" (1977, 199, 100).

5. The term "Phanariot" refers to the sophisticated wealthy class of Greeks who lived in the Phanar district of Constantinople. Phanariot scholars and poets composed in a highly purist and archaizing form of Greek marked by a rather Byzantine emphasis on erudition, artifice, and heavy rhetoric.

6. The Asia Minor Catastrophe of 1922, the result of which was the compulsory exchange of Greek and Turkish populations following the defeat of Greek forces in Turkey, is in many ways comparable to the French defeat of 1870 by the Germans, which ushered in an era of despair and self-conscious decline that many scholars view as the impetus for France's decadent movement.

7. Jeffreys (2009, 35). George Valassopoulo, an Alexandrian lawyer and intimate friend of Cavafy, was the poet's first English translator and collaborated with Forster in an effort to bring out the first English edition of the poems (one that, sadly, was never realized).

1. "Aesthetic to the point of affliction"

1. As Lionel Lambourne writes, the Grosvenor Gallery "came to symbolize the Aesthetic movement for the general public" (1996, 92). For the historic significance of this gallery, see Casteras and Denney (1996). J. B. Bullen notes that the Grosvenor Gallery "was more like a boudoir than a conventional exhibition space. It was set out with fine furniture, plants, wall hangings and, a little later, electric lighting, and in the summer exhibitions pictures were hung, for the first time, in the modern way, where, instead of crowding the walls from floor to ceiling, there were just a few chosen canvases, each with its own breathing-space. In this configuration every picture appeared like a shrine, a shrine to art in the new cult of beauty" (1998, 151).

2. Casteras writes that the "supposed 'unwholesome' lethargy and androgyny of Burne-Jones's figures offended James, but it was the implied sexual behavior itself—and the cultural decadence which allegedly encouraged such tendencies—and not the art which was at the core of his objections" (2002, 315).

3. After Peter Cavafy's death in 1870, his wife, Hariclea, moved with her family to Liverpool to join her sons, probably in 1872. In 1874 the family returned to London, where they lived the high life, attending social events and maintaining "visiting relations with the leading Greek families of London" (Liddell [1974] 2000, 26). In 1876 the family's finances crashed, and they were forced to liquidate the company. Eventually they returned to Alexandria in September of 1877, and it is highly likely that they attended the opening of the Grosvenor Gallery in May of 1877 (the social event of the season). Some family members may also have attended the second Grosvenor opening of 1878. John Cavafy maintained close relations with his London cousins, spending summers there (Karagiannis 1983, 144). John and Constantine visited London again in the summer of 1897.

4. See Lambourne (1996, 214). As James Merritt writes, "The definition of Pre-Raphaelitism has been a problem to everyone who has dealt with it. . . . [The Pre-Raphaelite poets] are, in a sense, 'Decadent' Romantics, just as the 'Aestheticism' of the Nineties is, in a sense, 'Decadent Pre-Raphaelitism'" (1966, 10, 13).

5. See Julia Ionides (1995, 160–174), and Dianne Sachko Macleod, who writes, "England, by the middle of the nineteenth century, had become a middle-class nation. . . . Buoyant and optimistic, its [the bourgeoisie's] aims were to consolidate its position in society and to celebrate its accomplishments by redefining culture in its image" (1996, 210).

6. See Karagiannis (1983, 21–57), Tsirkas (1958, 46–72), and Metaxas (1974).

7. For the Ionides family history, see Alexander C. Ionides (1927) and Luke Ionides ([1925] 1996). For an overview of the history of the Greek diaspora in Great Britain, see T. Dowling (1915) and Tsimbidaros (1974).

8. On the great aesthetic houses of the day, see Macleod (1996, 273), who notes that these "Palaces of Art" served as havens of reverie and retreats from the world of Mammon, and Gere (2010).

9. L. Savidis (1983, 30). On Watts, see also A. Ionides (1927, 6). George Frederick Watts, who was often called the "Victorian Michelangelo," painted portraits of George Cavafy as well as many of the Ionides children—some fifty, according to Julia Ionides (1995, 161). He was a passionate Hellenist who installed casts of the Elgin Marbles in his studio and displayed them throughout his home; he considered himself a "pupil of Phidias," whose Parthenon sculptures were "the abiding passion of his life" (Jenkyns 1991, 291, 297). His paintings were seen as "poems painted on canvas" (Bryant 1996, 109), and he proved to be a powerful influence on the second-generation Pre-Raphaelites as well as a source of inspiration for decadent writers. J.-K. Huysmans refers to him in *À Rebours* as "a dreamy erudite Englishman haunted by fantasies of atrocious colors" (quoted in Des Cars 1998, 28). In France, Watts and Burne-Jones were the most celebrated contemporary English painters by the end of the nineteenth century (25).

10. See Young (1980, 1:31, 20) for the interesting details of the acquisition and selling of these paintings. John Cavafy is acknowledged in Whistler (1892, 322), although the relationship between Whistler and the Cavafy family became strained as a result of protracted disagreements about the loaning of canvases for exhibitions and Whistler's unheeded offer to buy back the paintings. For the letters exchanged between Whistler and the Ionides and Cavafy families, see Thorpe (2006). Anderson and Koval (1995, 97) write that Whistler had become infatuated with Aglaia Ionides, but to no avail. Whistler's brother's wedding to Helen Ionides took place in April 1877, just one month prior to the opening of the Grosvenor Gallery. It is quite possible that Cavafy's family was in attendance. In 1877, Whistler and the Coronios family were neighbors, Whistler living at No. 2 and his patrons at No. 1 Lindsey Row (Young 1980, 1:26). For George Cavafy's patronage, see McMullen (1973, 106). I am grateful to Artemis Leontis for bringing the Cavafy-Whistler connection to my attention, and to Anne Antippas for sharing her vast knowledge on Whistler and his relations with the Ionides family.

11. For a description and photographs of the Holland Park house, one of the great aesthetic houses of the day, see Spencer (1972, 61–64), Merrill (1998, 164–168), Lambourne (1996, 51), and Gere (2010, 126–129). The Ionides home neighbored that of Frederick Leighton, the "grandest of the Victorian classical painters" and the most "thoroughgoing in his Hellenism" (Jenkyns 1991, 201–202).

12. The bequest consisted of 300 drawings and watercolors, 750 prints, and 90 paintings, the latter of which had to hang together as a collection according to the terms of the will. The refurbished Ionides Gallery opened in November 2003. See Cork (2003), Boardman (1968), Cooper (2003), and Long (1925).

13. These "stunners," as they were called in the lingo of the day, feature prominently as artists and models in most literature on the Pre-Raphaelites. See Marsh and Nunn (1989) and Wildman and Christian (1998), who quote a contemporary observer: "Theirs was a lofty beauty, gracious, and noble; the beauty worshipped in Greece of old, yet with a wistful tenderness of poise" (1998, 268). Swinburne was reputed to have said of Marie Spartali (a pupil of Ford Madox Brown), "She is so beautiful that I want to sit down and cry" (quoted in Spencer 1999, 84).

14. This painting, in which Maria is cast as Nimuë, the femme fatale who lures Merlin to his death, was inspired by Tennyson's *Idylls of the King* and caused a sensation during the 1877 Grosvenor Gallery opening. It is one of many that express Burne-Jones's complex emotions for Maria Zambaco. Other canvases featuring Zambaco include *Phyllis and Demophoön, Flora, Love among the Ruins, The Wine of Circe, Venus Epithalamia, The Garden of the Hesperides, Beatrice, The Mill, Pygmalion and the Image, The Tree of Forgiveness, Merlin and Vivian, Portrait of Mary Zambaco, Cupid Finding Psyche*, and *Laus Veneris*. See Klewitz (2009, 79–83).

15. See Merrill (1998) for a detailed study of this room and its aesthetic relation to Holland Park.

16. Mancoff writes, "Zambaco made herself a constant presence in Burne-Jones's studio, and he soon became infatuated. . . . The pervasive appearance of this distinctively beautiful woman in Burne-Jones's art of the late 1860s demonstrates his passionate obsession with her. . . . [In January of 1869] she caused a scandal, threatening suicide in public and brandishing a vial containing enough laudanum for two at least. She then attempted to drown herself in the Regent's Canal; in Burne-Jones's attempt to stop her, Rossetti wrote, he wrestled her to the ground" (1998, 50–51). For other alleged details of this fiasco, see Wood (1998, 49), Kestner (1989, 82–100), Flanders (2005, 119–122), and MacCarthy (2012, 199–243). On Zambaco as a sculptress in her own right, see Attwood (1986) and J. Ionides (1995, 164–166).

17. See Graham (1999, 265) and Cooper (2003, 159–160).

18. In a letter to Whistler, Swinburne wrote that he found in this picture "the metaphor of the rose and the notion of sad and glad mystery in the face languidly contemplative of its own phantom and all other things seen by their phantoms" (Spencer 1999, 62).

19. A letter from Edwin Edwards to Henri Fantin-Latour (Spencer 1999, 68–69). As Spencer writes, "There is an unavoidable association of two girls in an interior with the lesbian subjects of Swinburne's verse and current fiction" (68). The association of the "three graces" with the three women of Whistler's *The White Symphony: Three Girls* would have furthered this connection. The storm over Swinburne refers to the hostility that broke out in the press after the publication of *Poems and Ballads*.

20. See Powell (1992, 228), who notes that *Poems and Ballads* was condemned as decadent, unclean, and the product of a putrescent imagination. The book was withdrawn by its first publisher over threats for prosecution on grounds of obscenity.

21. In a letter from John Cavafy to Constantine dated November 15, 1883, John thanks his brother for referencing verses by Swinburne in a letter sent on November 5. http://cavafy.com/ archive/texts/content.asp?id=64. Cavafy's library contained a French volume on the London art scene, Gabriel Mourey's *Passé le détroit. La vie l'art à Londres* (1895), as documented by Karampini-Iatrou (2003, 101).

22. See Williamson (1976) and Hyder, who writes, "In the nineties Swinburne's position as the leading English poet was clearly recognized. Articles on the poet-laureateship after the death of Tennyson mention Swinburne as deserving the honour" (1970, xli). As Riede argues, "He broke in on that rather agreeably tedious Victorian tea-party with the effect of some pagan creature, at once impish and divine, leaping on the sleek lawn, to stamp its goat-foot in challenge" (1978, 41).

23. Pittock notes, "The sea, an agent of that transience . . . is the natural force which, in its perpetual restlessness under the moon, symbolizes the change brought by Time to history and places. . . . The Swinburnean sea dominates all moods. . . . Swinburne's vision of the sea's role [is] that of an echo or symbol of the interior world of imagination and emotion, or the vanished world of history, a watery 'ou-boum'" (1993, 127–129). The sea illustrates the "central historical doctrine of *Poems and Ballads*" which is "continual change without progress" (Riede 1978, 72). See H. Fraser, who writes that Swinburne "offers a view of the tides of history in which regret for the ebb of pagan faith with the establishment of Christianity is framed by an acceptance of Heraclitean flux" (2000, 121).

24. See Jenkyns (1991, 264). The word "ἄλγος" appears in numerous uncanonical poems: "Dünya Güzeli" (line 15), "Night March of Priam" (line 1), "Epitaph" (line 3), "Had You Loved Me" (line 4), "Samian Epitaph" (line 3), "Melancholy Hours" (line 8), and "Melancholy of Jason, Son of Cleander, Poet in Commagene; A.D. 595" (line 6). While Cavafy's sense of the word does not possess the "sadomasochistic" dimension of suffering found in Swinburne, the note of spiritual pain and melancholy anguish is no less intense than that foregrounded by the Victorian poet.

25. On John Cavafy's published poems, see G. Savidis (1991, 126). John published a volume of poems in 1896. See also L. Savidis (1983, 144–147). Liddell notes that "John wrote post-Shelleyan English verse with a good deal of facility. . . . [In the 1880s] John might still be called the more accomplished writer" ([1974] 2000, 40).

26. See Ekdawi (1997, 224), who argues that the poem "Darkness and Shadows," usually attributed to Constantine, was actually written by John. See also Cavafy (2003a).

27. Only the title of this poem survives; it contains a typographical error—"Σαμλίδικη Ωραιότης" ("Samlacian Beauty"). See G. Savidis (1987, 73). Hermaphroditus, the son of Hermes and Aphrodite, was loved by Salmacis, the nymph of the fountain in which he bathed. As he continued to ignore her entreaties, she embraced him and prayed that the gods make them one body. Swinburne's verses on Salmacis read, "Yea, sweet, I know; I saw in what swift wise, / Beneath the woman's and the water's kiss / Thy moist limbs melted into Salmacis" (2004, 105).

28. On Browning's influence on Cavafy, see Ricks (2003) and Tombrou (2004).

29. This Baudelairizing would find a sympathetic ear in Cavafy, who early in his career would compose a poem titled "Correspondence according to Baudelaire" (1891). See chapter 2 and Walder (1976, 7–19).

30. The persona and sad plight of the painter Simeon Solomon come to mind here; his canvases express this very tension between Hebraic holiness and Hellenic hedonism—religious absorption and physical beauty, as Elizabeth Prettejohn (2007, 87) defines it. A member of the Pre-Raphaelite circle, Simeon saw his reputation in the art world sink after his arrest in 1873 on charges of sodomy. Although it would be tempting to trace a line of influence here, there are no indications that Cavafy was familiar with Solomon's work or would have had occasion to view it. Yet Solomon's synthesis of the religious and aesthetic dimensions overtly infused with the homoerotic anticipates Cavafy to an uncanny degree. See Cruise (2005 and 2010) and Prettejohn (2007, chap. 3).

31. For the popular caricature of Wilde as a sunflower in *Punch*, see Spencer, who argues, "To Wilde is owed the ultimate distinction of turning Pre-Raphaelitism into a *fin-de-siècle* movement" (1972, 98–99).

32. The *Poet and Image* canvases were inspired by William Morris's poem "The Earthly Paradise." As Cooper writes, "Burne-Jones approached this classical legend through the intermediary of Morris's medievalizing poetry rather than Ovid's original tale in the *Metamorphoses*" (2003, 103). See also chapter 3 in Jenkyns (1991).

33. Cavafy's obsessive fixation on minute details—historical as well as aesthetic—is well attested to. As Liddell writes,

> He had a passion for accuracy of detail. In the poem "Alexandrian Kings" Caesarion was *Dressed in pink tinted silk*. "I dressed him in pink silk," he said, "because at that time an ell of that sort of silk cost the equivalent of so-and-so many thousand drachmas." And he was of course aware that the Roman world knew Coan silk, long before the silk of the mulberry-leaf-fed worms of China was known to the west. He was reproached by the eminent botanist Yannis Sareyannis for the unseasonable roses at Pella, on the table of Philip V of Macedon on the day when he heard of the defeat of Antiochus at Magnesia, a battle which took place in December. Sareyannis reminded him that important news travelled quickly at that date, for there

were various kinds of telegraph, extensively described by Polybius; Philip's dinner must therefore have been in December or early January. Cavafy replied: "It's a historical possibility. It's the case of a king with much wealth at his disposal, for whom the means of having these flowers in winter was easy. Apart from this, there was a winter export of flowers from Egypt. We know Egypt exported roses to Italy in the winter. In the first century Italy became independent, through the improvement of agriculture, and had its own *rosae hibernicae.*" ([1974] 2000, 123–124)

34. "Endymion is particularly famous for having aroused love in the goddess Diana, in her guise as Selene (the Moon). After Diana discovered the beautiful shepherd asleep, she asked Jupiter to keep him dozing forever so she might find him every night" (Aghion, Barbillon, and Lissarrague 1994, 118). In other versions of the myth, Endymion receives eternal youth from the gods and the gift of sleeping for as long as he wishes. It should be noted that Watts painted various interpretations of this theme.

35. "The Fleshly School of Painting" was the title of an article in the *Contemporary Review* (October 1871) in which Robert Buchanan attacked the Pre-Raphaelites, Rossetti in particular (Hares-Stryker 1997, 237–247).

36. One could hypothesize that the neomedievalism of the times, which, pace Ruskin, showed a considerable interest in Byzantine aesthetics—however dimly understood—ignited Cavafy's lifelong fascination with medieval Byzantine themes. In 1877, the cornerstone of London's St. Sophia Cathedral was laid (Dowling 1915, 87); according to Alexander Ionides, Burne-Jones offered his services to decorate the interior of the completed Byzantine edifice with Byzantine frescoes—free of payment— but the faction of the community that came from the island of Chios voted down the offer (A. Ionides 1927, 48). On Burne-Jones and Byzantium, see Bullen (2003, 118–158); on Burne-Jones and religious themes, see Waters and Nahum (2009).

37. Powell writes that "Burne-Jones, and perhaps Swinburne as well, must have seen parallels in the Laus Veneris theme to their own experience. . . . In her languor, Venus was both the tragic rejected goddess of Swinburne's poem and the fatal woman of the artist's own experience. She was a dangerously erotic figure for the critics, who found her enervation symptomatic of a disease that would become the epidemic of Decadence in the following decade" (1992, 231, 234). See also Maliaras (1992), who analyzes the various images of Zambaco in the painter's work. As Swinburne comments in his "Notes on Poems and Reviews," the Laus Veneris tale centers on the "immortal agony of a man lost after all repentance—cast down from fearful hope into fearless despair—believing in Christ and bound to Venus—desirous of penitential pain, and damned to joyless pleasure" (quoted in Powell 1992, 225).

38. There are indeed numerous parallels in the aesthetic principles of the Pre-Raphaelite poets and Cavafy's poetry (in addition to those of Swinburne mentioned above). As defined by David Latham, Pre-Raphaelite poetry is "characterized by its choice of genre—ballads, songs and sonnets; by its literary characters from medieval tales and popular ballads; by its jarring juxtaposition of vivid details that produce grotesque transgressions of decorum through an indeterminate focus that shifts between the spiritual and the sensual; and by its concern with the mutable moment that arises from 'the desire of beauty, quickened by the sense of death' [Pater] and that leads to a pervading sense of degeneration from an idealized past" (2003, 22). It should be noted that Cavafy's earliest poetic compositions in the 1890s included more than ten sonnets. His foray into ballads and folklore would shift into a Greek "laographic" (folkloric) mode in the 1880s (see Jeffreys 2002, 224–229).

39. See Cavafy (2003c) for these essays and the unpublished essay on Browning. Cavafy's notes on Ruskin appear in Tsirkas (1971, 223–265). Cooper (2003, 73–11) provides a relevant overview of these prominent themes and legends in Pre-Raphaelite art.

40. Interestingly enough, the balled "Auld Robin Gray" was painted in 1873 by the Pre-Raphaelite artist John Melhuish Strudwick, who apprenticed with Burne-Jones and exhibited regularly at the Grosvenor.

41. For Tennyson's influence on Cavafy, see Jusdanis (1982).

42. Savidis notes that an Italian translation of the libretto to *Lohengrin* existed in Cavafy's library (Cavafy 1993, 167). When the Wagners came to London in May 1877, they stayed with Hariclea Ionides and her husband, Edward Dannreuther, passionate Wagnerians (Wildman and Christian 1998, 204).

43. "The decade 1878–89 saw the progressive appropriation of Burne-Jones's then-known work by the Parisian Symbolists and Decadents" (Wildman and Christian 1998, 28). Moreau's work has been labeled "symbolist" because of his emphasis on the imagery of death (Bryant 1996, 121) and stylized withdrawal into the self's inner world of dream and sleep (Des Cars 1998, 35). See chapter 3 for a discussion of Moreau's influence on Cavafy.

44. The work of J.F. Lewis, an Orientalist often associated with the Pre-Raphaelites (Bate 1905, 91), was representative of the odalisque genre. On the connection between this tradition and Cavafy's poem "Dünya Güzeli," see Jeffreys (2002).

45. Cooper writes, "As Henry James pointed out, aesthetic appeal is more important in this painting than historical accuracy. *The Times* agreed that 'It is a work which has no counterpart in the actually existing order of things.' It is full of ambiguity, not least in the choice of the title. The mill itself is relegated to the background, while the viewer's attention is drawn instead to the pacing girls. Their restrained actions belie the picture's erotic tension" (2003, 160).

46. On Pre-Raphaelite typology and allegory, see Hönnighausen (1988, 28–82). *The Soul's Prison House* is the title of a painting by the Pre-Raphaelite artist Evelyn De Morgan (née Pickering), which was exhibited at the Grosvenor in 1888 (Newall 1995, 68).

47. Whistler's inscrutable paintings were ridiculed by Ruskin and his camp for their unfinished quality (Merrill 1992, 220), a criticism that calls to mind the Greek poet Kostis Palamas's scathing comment about Cavafy's poems being "notes that resemble reportage from past centuries" (quoted in Peranthis 1970, 213).

48. See Alexander Nehamas's commentary on the poem, in which he writes that its last line "confirms Cavafy's aestheticism" (Leontis 2002, 99). Lena Arabatzidou's Greek monograph on Cavafy and aestheticism (2013) appeared while this study was virtually finished, and although timing prevented me from engaging with it critically, I note its presence and importance as a parallel study on the topic.

49. This is my alteration of Sachperoglou's phrasing "aesthetically appealing, to the point of passion." My rendering conveys the more precise correspondence of the Greek word "αισθητικός" with the tenets of aestheticism, along with the acute sensitivity of the aesthete (both the beholder and the beheld in the poem) who suffers for beauty.

50. Burne-Jones's *Love among the Ruins*, which featured Maria Zambaco, comes readily to mind here.

51. On Whistler's influence on Wilde, see Bruder, who writes, "Wilde's debt to Whistler (among others) in his aesthetic formulations is indisputable" (2004, 169).

2. Translating Baudelaire

1. See Clements (1985, 76). She writes, "The most striking feature in an account of Baudelaire's posthumous literary life is that he has by so many poets, novelists, and critics of art and literature been regarded as a progenitor" (3).

2. Cavafy's poem "The City" may be read as an inversion of the flânerie dynamic whereby the city haunts the flâneur rather than the flâneur the city. See Turner (2003), in which he notes the connection between flânerie and cruising: "Cruising is a practice that exploits the ambivalence

of the modern city, and in doing so, 'queers' the totalizing narratives of modernity, in particular, *flânerie*" (46).

3. The year 1891 marks the date of Cavafy's official affiliation with the Alexandrian newspaper *Τηλέγραφος* (*Telegraph*). Prior to this, he had published two brief articles in the newspaper *Κωνσταντινούπολις* (*Constantinople*): "Το Κοράλλιον υπό μυθολογικήν έποψιν" ("Coral from a Mythological Perspective," 1886) and "Οι απάνθρωποι φίλοι των ζώων" ("The Inhumane Friends of Animals," 1886.

4. On the prose poem as a precursor of free verse, see Clive Scott, "The Prose Poem and Free Verse" (1976, 349–368). Cavafy's poetry was initially criticized as unpoetic by his initial detractors, who took their cue from his rival Kostis Palamas.

5. Edward Kaplan writes, "Realistically speaking, Beauty can only alleviate anxiety or *ennui*—not cure it—as it sanctifies the possible" (1990, 9). The opposite of spleen or ennui, the ideal is related to beauty in Baudelaire's poetic universe. As Jonathan Culler notes, "The *ideal* is . . . most generally whatever provokes effort and aspiration, including the world of ideal forms and beauty itself. It is thus both opposed to spleen and, in its inaccessibility, a cause of spleen" (1998, xvii). See also Jamison (2001), who writes, "Most famously, *Les Fleurs du mal* records his creative travels between opposing poles he styles 'Spleen' and 'Idéal': between the modern and classical, the temporal and eternal, the venal and immaculate muse (256).

6. Brix (2001, 11–12).

7. Cavafy's poems involve the urban aesthetic of love "at last sight"—the quintessentially Baudelairean "eternal farewell" noted by Walter Benjamin (2006, 185).

8. Cavafy reiterates this principle in his own "Philosophical Scrutiny" years later, which reveals how enduring this poetic philosophy would remain:

> Moreover let us consider the vanity of human beings, for this is a clearer way of expressing what I have called "the worthlessness of effort and the inherent contradiction in every human utterance." For few natures, for very few is it possible to— after accepting it—act accordingly, that is refrain from every action except such as subsistence demands. The majority must act; and though producing vain things their impulse to act and their obedience to it are not vain, because it is a following of nature, or of *their* nature. Their actions produce works, which can be divided into two categories, work [*sic*] of immediate utility and works of beauty. The poet does the latter. As human nature has got a craving for beauty manifested in different forms—love, order in his surroundings, scenery,—he purveys to a need. (2010, 117)

Cavafy's emphasis on the importance of beauty, along with the acknowledgment of vanity in conflict with the dutiful effort to compose, aligns him with Poe.

9. Elizabeth Prettejohn traces this trajectory from Poe through Gautier, Baudelaire, Swinburne, Pater and Wilde:

> The practice of repeating the words of a previous writer, with or without acknowledgement, would become a distinctive characteristic of Aesthetic writing. . . . Perhaps, too, this corresponds to the ubiquitous practice, in Aesthetic painting, of repeating the styles and motifs of other artists, both past and present. The practice may seem to verge on plagiarism, in the case of verbal texts, or on derivative imitation, in the case of paintings. But the closeness of the repetition makes possible a distinctive relationship between the Aesthetic work and its predecessor, one that marks appreciation or reverence for the predecessor while at the same time transforming it into a new work of art. (2007, 54)

10. On the centrality of Baudelaire's sonnet for symbolist poetry, see Balakian (1977, chap. 3). Cavafy's translation of the sonnet is analyzed in detail by Dimitris Pandelodemos, who points out

that the translation preserves neither the sonnet structure nor the rhyme scheme of the original (1983, 1501). See also Tsoutsoura (1993, 84), who argues that the translation is faithful and original. For Cavafy's relation to aesthetic poetry, see Jusdanis (1987, 33–37).

11. The term "mystic nourishment" (*le mystique aliment*) comes from Baudelaire's poem "L'Ennemi" ("The Enemy").

12. See Heintzelman (1956) on Legros's illustrations of Poe. Baudelaire describes these in "Painters and Etchers" as "those few pages in which Edgar Poe finds himself translated with a harsh and simple majesty" (1965, 220).

13. In his review "Exposition Universelle, 1855," Baudelaire writes, "The poor man is so Americanized by zoocratic and industrial philosophers that he has lost all notion of the differences which characterize the phenomena of the physical and moral world, the natural and the supernatural" (1964, 83).

14. As Margueritte Murphy writes, Baudelaire takes issue "with the broader conception of history behind the contemporary notion of progress, for which technological innovation and industrial production serve as bellwethers. Baudelaire admits that progress can occur—specifically, in questions of morality, in the careers of individual artists from year to year, in the price and quality of goods. But he objects to the belief in the inevitability of progress, seeing this as both a constraint on liberty and a delusion" (2008, 33).

15. In his essay "Shakespeare on Life" (1891), Cavafy writes "I do not care for excessive dogmatism" (2010, 27).

16. The Baudelairean dimension of "Builders" was noted by George Savidis (1991, 116). The poem was criticized by the editor of the *Attic Museum* for its French style of enjambment (Cavafy 1983, 94). In his unfinished poem "In the Sixth or Seventh Century" (1927*), Cavafy's speaker expresses an interest in the status of Hellenism in Alexandria before the onslaught of the Arabs and boasts that it is only natural that those who reestablished Greek speech in the city should be interested in such matters. The fact that this is no longer the case less than a century after the poem was written is an example of Cavafy's ironic sensibility, which seemingly operates both proleptically and retroactively.

17. On the particular reading tastes and demographics of this audience, see the important studies of Papaleontiou (1998), Daskalopoulos (1990), and Droulia (2005). The Greek poet Tellos Agras notes that "translation constitutes an organic part of our literature" (Papaleontiou 1998, 13).

18. On the Greek language issue, see the seminal works of Tziovas (1986b), Mackridge (1985), and Kopidakis (2000).

19. Cavafy's failure to achieve this is noted by George Savidis, who describes the purist prose as hopelessly "stiff" (1987, 183). Cavafy's encyclopedic speaking style remained one of his dominant character traits, as Timos Malanos argues in his introductory note to *Καβαφικά Αυτοσχόλια* (*Cavafy's Self-Comments*) (Lechonitis 1942, 11–12).

20. David Connolly (2002, 33) notes that this was case with George Seferis.

21. John Cavafy's translations of his brother's poems were published by Ikaros Press in 2003. Sarah Ekdawi (1997, 223–230) notes the similarity of the poems written by the Cavafy brothers.

22. Cavafy composed numerous notes to John expressing his disapproval over various word choices selected for the translations. His glacial pace in supplying E. M. Forster with poems and his ultimate withholding of authorization for the Hogarth Press's proposed English edition of the poems is one of the great enigmas of the poet's promotional behavior. See the introduction to Jeffreys (2009).

23. On Dimaras's term "δημοσιολόγος/demosiologos," see Ourania Polykandrioti (2005, 170). Emmanuel Roidis and Dimitris Vikelas were both Greek men of letters whose prose style and cosmopolitan tone certainly influenced Cavafy. Dimiroulis (2005, 48) notes that Roidis was considered a foreigner and outsider by many Greek critics who took issue with his urbane sarcasm, polemical antiromanticism, and heretical pessimism, qualities that would later become Cavafy's own.

24. See Stillman (1891), a much-discussed essay in which he divides men into "journalists and eternalists, ephemera and immortals" and criticizes journalism for having become "an agency for collecting, condensing and assimilating the trivialities of the entire human existence." He warns young men who desire to follow literature that "our present journalism" is "the enemy" of all the "finer things": "A noble literature implies the ambition of immortality, and the truth alone is immortal" (688). Stillman was an American painter, journalist, and photographer who served as a correspondent for the *London Times* and married Marie Spartali, part of the London Greek circle that included the Cavafy family.

25. Cavafy (2003c, 14).

26. Ibid., 15.

27. Cited in G. Savidis (1983, 12).

28. See Sachinis (1981) on the influence of aestheticism on the Greek prose writers of the late nineteenth and early twentieth centuries. Although absent from this study, Cavafy was similarly impacted by the same foreign influences that acted upon his Greek contemporaries, influences that included Poe, Baudelaire, Ruskin, Swinburne, Pater, Whistler, Huysmans, and Wilde.

29. As noted by Daskalopoulos (1999, 48).

30. Edward Kaplan (1990, 38) uses the terms "aesthetic fables," "fables of the human condition," and "fables of the artistic quest" to categorize Baudelaire's prose poems, terms that apply equally to Cavafy's prose poems.

31. "I will look upon these clothes and will remember the great celebration—which by then will be completely finished" ("Garments").

32. It would not be an exaggeration to claim that the reclusive poet was distilling into his poetry "drop by drop" (to quote Seferis) the conscious cosmopolitanism he acquired during his apprentice years as a journalist; his present international appeal and growing global audience are clearly indebted to the journalistic demands made upon him by his bourgeois Levantine readership. During his mature phase, Cavafy surely sensed that he was writing for a world audience, a position explored by Damroch (2003) and Jusdanis (2003).

33. Tsirkas (1971, 217). Cavafy's earliest writings in English include the travelogue "Constantinopoliad—an Epic" (1882) and eight unpublished articles and fragments.

34. On the cult of Victorian prose, see Levine and Madden (1968). See chapter 4 for Walter Pater's influence on Cavafy.

35. See Haas (1982).

36. For the centrality of folklore in the formation of modern Greek culture, see Herzfeld (1982).

37. On Papazis, see Tsirkas (1958, 135–138, 464–465).

38. For Cavafy's relation to the occult, see Haas (1984).

39. See George Savidis's commentary on this unpublished essay, where he notes that the list made by Cavafy was implemented by the Educational Association of Egypt (1987, 218–219). Savidis has, to date, offered the most incisive and thorough readings of Cavafy's prose, most of which appear in his two volumes of collected essays (1985, 1987).

40. Cavafy (2010, 42). For a full appreciation of Cavafy's museum ethos, see the commentaries and illustrations in Leontis (2002).

41. Cavafy (2010, 40).

42. As early as 1883, Cavafy expressed an interest in becoming a professional journalist, but he appears to have received discouraging advice from his family, namely his aunt Amalia Papou (Daskalopulos and Stasinopoulou 2001, 24). Although officially affiliated with the *Telegraph* from 1891, he began working as a paid employee at the Third Circle of Irrigation in 1889. The year 1901 marks the date of Cavafy's last journalistic submission for the *Telegraph*.

43. Liddell ([1974] 2000, 81). Liddell observes that in the Elgin Marble essays, "his attitude throughout is more 'Philhellenic' than anti-British—it is symptomatic of his growing Hellenism" (ibid.).

44. For the Greek text of this letter written by Cavafy to Marika Tsaliki, see L. Savidis (1983, 317).

45. On Lucian and Greek performativity, see Goldhill (2002b). In his monograph *The Invention of Prose* (2002a, 12), Goldhill notes the sophistic rhetorical technique of displaying and showing off knowledge (*apodeixis* and *epideixis*), a strategy likewise employed by Cavafy in his journalistic writings. Cavafy was enamored of the sophists, especially their approach to language as art and artifice.

46. In what appears to be another curious coincidence, Moréas published his important document on symbolism—a letter to the *Supplément littéraire* of *Figaro,* which became the manifesto for the symbolist movement—in 1886, the year Cavafy published his first poems. Although a full consideration of the influence of Moréas on Cavafy is beyond the scope of this book, it is a topic that deserves additional exploration.

47. On Moréas's relation to Baudelaire, see Butler (1967, 52–53). On Moréas's new evolution beyond symbolism, see Shryock (1998).

48. Butler (1967, 39) notes that the first truly decadent volume of poetry was Moréas's *Les Syrtes* (1894).

49. See note 30. Cavafy's debt to Poe via Baudelaire is explored by Lavagnini (2003), Athanasopoulou (2003), and Katsigianni (2000). Athanasopoulou notes the prevalence of the doppelgänger in Poe's work and offers a reading of "In Broad Daylight" based on Poe, interpreting the ghost as a double of Alexander A. (Katsigianni 2000, 663). See also Nanos Valaoritis (1983, 651), suggesting that Cavafy's interest in Antiochus IV Epiphanes might have its source in Poe's short story "Four Beasts in One: The Homo-Cameleopard."

50. Rhonda Garelick notes the paradoxical social predicament of the flâneur: "Decadent Dandyism is paradoxical in that it turns sharply away from the external world while nonetheless being deeply aware of the new, changing and largely urban landscape" (1998, 43). On a related note, Kirsten Macleod (2006, 29–31) points out the connections between dilettantism and the decadent sensibility, connections applicable to Cavafy's ambivalent feelings toward journalism in the 1890s. On the dialectical tension between journalism and decadence, see David Frisby (1994, 93, 95), who elaborates on Walter Benjamin's assertion that "the social foundation of *flânerie* is journalism" and makes interesting connections between flânerie and the short prose form, gambling, hunting, detectives, and werewolves. Cavafy, it should be noted, penned an unfinished narrative on the subject of lycanthropy in 1882 that documents his early interest in issues of marginality. On Poe and the flâneur tradition, see Werner (2004).

51. As Rosemary Lloyd notes, "The word Baudelaire used for his feelings in early 1848 was intoxication, *ivresse*, a term he would take up again in a prose poem ["Enivrez-vous"] in which he urges his readers, if they do not want to be the martyred slaves of time, to remain always intoxicated, on wine, poetry or virtue as they choose" (2008, 77).

52. Cavafy's piece echoes Baudelaire's prose poem "La quelle est la Vraie?," which concludes with the line "I found myself caught, perhaps forever, in the burial-place of the Ideal" (1989, 161).

53. The prose poem's foregrounding of the voyage motif will later be refined in "Ithaka."

54. Anna Katsigianni (2000, 86) notes the poem's autobiographical element in the tension between the poet's experience and the public's censorship.

55. Scott (1988, 116). As David Scott writes, "The poet, like the painter, was a maker of marks on the white page" (37). On the interchangeability of the prose poems and paintings, see Shattuck (1983, 29).

56. See Connolly (2003) and Kostis (2006).

57. The panic could also be read as an illustration of Sedgwick's gay gothic "homosexual panic" (1990, 189).

58. The combination of gambling and ghosts foregrounded in the story recalls Baudelaire's prose poem "Le Joueur généreux," which involves an encounter between a "generous gambler" and the devil.

59. On Cavafy's rings, see Malanos (1957, 63). Much of the story is set at the Casino of San Stefano, one of Cavafy's regular Alexandrian haunts.

60. In the *Book of Thoth*, the scribe and magician Nefrekeptah is told by a priest that he might find the Book of Thoth (who is the Egyptian god of writing) in the middle of the Nile at Coptos, guarded by snakes and scorpions and a great serpent that cannot be killed. It is contained in an iron box, in which there is a wooden box, in which there is an ivory box, then an ebony, then a silver, and finally a golden box in which lies the Book of Thoth. On Cavafy's connection to the esoteric movement, see Haas (1984). Khaled Fahmy notes that "the theme of hidden treasures was a common one in much of the popular literature of Egypt in the second half of the nineteenth century" (2004, 302). It should be noted that Cavafy possessed a copy of H. Rider Haggard's *King Solomon's Mines,* a book that foregrounds a perilous quest for treasure. Poe's "The Gold-Bug" also involves a treasure hunt and the discovery of an iron-banded treasure chest containing gold and jewels.

3. Pictorialist Poetics

1. Technically speaking, the Parnassians included those poets who published in *Le Parnasse contemporain: Recueil de vers nouveaux*. As Philip Stephan notes, "Of the four poets commonly associated with symbolism, Baudelaire, Verlaine, and Mallarmé all had poems in at least one of the three editions of the *Parnasse contemporain* (1866, 1869–71, 1876), and Rimbaud submitted verse to it, which was refused, in 1870. So they deserve to be called Parnassians as well as symbolists" (1974, 1).

2. Schaffer (1929, 56). As Robert Denommé writes, "In rejecting the excessive effusion of Romanticism, the Parnassians vowed to champion the tightly constructed and more impersonal lyricism steeped in the ready observation of concrete reality rather than in any carelessly devised and vaguely defined metaphysical attitude" (1972, 22). Pace Gautier, art is created by painstaking craftsmanship and not romantic inspiration (Grant 1975, 134). For the theoretical indebtedness of this group to Gautier, see Schaffer (1929, 34, 37) and Majewski (2002, 21–43).

3. "A Parnassian in his attitude towards his art and in his technical perfection, Baudelaire was, notwithstanding, something of an interloper in the Parnassian camp. . . . The symbolists, genetically, were thus the direct offsprings of the Parnassians. . . . Verlaine and Mallarmé, the prophets of their two principal groups, began as Parnassians" (Schaffer 1929, 230–231). Philip Stephan argues for a more expansive appraisal of their contribution to poetry: "The lesson of the Parnasse, that objective description, while apparently an end in itself, could actually serve to express the poet's emotional reactions" (1974, 111).

4. I am indebted to David Scott (1988) for this term. See his engaging study for a thorough exploration of this phenomenon.

5. Sonya Ilinskaya (1983, 35, 48) notes the early influence of the Greek romantic poets of the Athenian school, notably D. Paparrigopoulos and M. Stratigis. See Dimaras (1982) for an overview of Greek romanticism. Schaffer avers that Parnassianism was "the phoenix which arose from the ashes of the Romanticism of 1830" (1929, 155).

6. Politou-Marmarinou (1983) outlines the valorization of Greek art and Hellenism by the Parnassians—especially Leconte de Lisle and José-Maria de Hérédia, whose emphasis on the exotic, history, philosophy, and formal perfection was highly influential on Cavafy. Yiannis Rigopoulos (1991, 44) argues that Cavafy is, in general, more visual (painterly) than tactile (sculptural) in his ekphrastic poems.

7. See Prettejohn (2007, 5–6) for a history of the art for art's sake movement which she traces back to Kantian aesthetics. Pierre Michelle states that Gautier's *Emaux et camées* is "the end product of the poet's intimate affinity with the techniques of the painter rather than those of the sculptor" (quoted in Denommé 1972, 54).

8. As Rosemary Lloyd writes, "Gautier's sense of color and shape, and his exuberant vocabulary, as well as his enthusiasm for artists whose work reflected the passions and predilections of Romanticism, exercised an important influence on the young Baudelaire" (2002, 189).

9. See Stephan (1974, 21–22), who notes that Gautier's "Notice" to the 1868 edition of *Les Fleurs du mal* "inaugurated an exclusively decadent interpretation of Baudelaire's poetry."

10. See Kelley (1994), Lloyd (2002, chap. 10), and Krieger (1992).

11. See chapter 1, note 9.

12. Kathryn Gutzwiller writes that "Cavafy's use of ecphrastic elements in his poetry shows striking similarities to Meleager's innovative eroticizing of the ecphrastic tradition in epigram. For both poets, the canonical ephebic beauty of Greek statuary is the standard by which to measure a beautiful body, seen and desired" (2003, 75).

13. Gautier's use of the term "romantic" would be further developed by Baudelaire in his "Salon of 1846," where he writes, "Romanticism is the most recent, the latest expression of the beautiful" (1965, 46). As Lloyd points out, "For Baudelaire, Romanticism was the expression of modern society, the vehicle of modern art, which he defined as 'intimacy, spirituality, color, aspiration to the infinite, expressed by all the means that the arts contain.' Romanticism is also an integral part of that great sense of melancholy that Baudelaire sees pervading modern life, a 'high and serious melancholy' conveyed for instance in Delacroix's paintings." (2002, 195–196). See Wakefield (2007), who identifies Dante, Ossian, Lamartine, Chateaubriand, Hugo, Byron, and Scott as authors who had the greatest impact on French painting. As Philip Stephan notes, decadence was "both a revolt against one kind of Romanticism and a continuation of another, Romanticism's perversely deliberate choice of what is unpleasant." (1974, 18).

14. "Baudelaire's openness to works of the plastic arts, his cult of images, his friendships with artists, particularly his relationship with Delacroix, and above all his determination not just to understand his reactions to works of art but to give those reactions a resonant written equivalent—this is what makes him the most powerful and suggestive art critic of his time" (Lloyd 2002, 202). Richard Grant notes that Gautier's art criticism tries to make us "see" the painting, "to sense its dramatic composition, while at the same time making sure the reader recognizes the critic's wide literary and artistic knowledge. This impressionist treatment appealed widely to the public of Gautier's day" (1975, 51). On Gautier's influence on Baudelaire, see M. Spencer (1969, 96–102).

15. "This discreet adaptation of images . . . is symptomatic of a more general tendency in Baudelaire and other nineteenth-century poets . . . for it was often *unacknowledged* pictorial images—in particular drawn from etchings and engravings—that were to provide the richest and most varied sources for transpositional poetry" (D. Scott 1988, 60). A similar syncretic approach occurs in the novel, as Henry James observed in 1884: "The analogy between the art of painting and the art of the novelist is, so far as I am able to see, complete" (quoted in Kahn 1987, 2).

16. Baudelaire writes, "Delacroix, always respectful of his ideal, is often, without knowing it, a poet in painting" (1965, 56). Delacroix himself insisted that he "was painting not objects but thoughts" (Wright 2001, 1). J. A. Hiddleston makes the following relevant comparison: "Instead of being associated with life, health, exuberance, fulfillment, and procreation, love in Delacroix's painting as in many of Baudelaire's poems is linked to the unhealthy underside of things and to the anti-values of waste, despair, diminution, and death" (1999, 63). One could argue that love functions similarly in Cavafy's poetry.

17. Delacroix held a unique place in the history of Philhellenism. His paintings on the Greek revolution of 1821 (*Greece Expiring on the Ruins of Missolonghi, The Massacre at Chios*) were featured prominently in the exhibition of 1826 in aid of the Greek War of Independence (Wakefield 2007, 196). He reinvigorated the tradition of monumental painting and, as Dorothy Johnson notes, "has no rival in the Romantic period for his vast range and consistently innovative treatment of historical subjects" (2001, 118). His mantle was taken up by Gustave Moreau, who radically rethought history painting by elevating it to the level of allegory and symbol.

18. Cavafy's unpublished "Before Jerusalem" (1893*) certainly owes something to this Orientalist genre and perhaps even to Delacroix's melodramatic presentation of crusaders: "Now they've gotten to Jerusalem. / In their ecstasy and in their fixed devotion / they've forgotten their quarrels with the Greeks, / they've forgotten their hatred for the Turks. // [. . .] they tremble like little children / and like little children cry, all cry, / beholding the walls of Jerusalem" (Cavafy 2001, 217). On the theatricality of gesture and posture in Delacroix, see Hiddleston (1999), 90.

19. As Henry Majewski writes, a transposition d'art is "at the same time a description, a poetic re-creation, and a symbolic interpretation of the painting observed or imagined. The painting's function is to be a point of departure or impetus for the poetic impulse and ultimately a source of signification in the text. The painting-in-the-poem provides a presence or spiritual essence that gives the work its center, its ideal value" (2002, 43).

20. Other identifiable examples from Baudelaire's poems and prose poems include "Les Phares" and "Les Bohémiens en voyage" (based on works by Callot) and "Lola de Valence" (Manet), while other works allude to paintings or borrow pictorial effects: "Les Plaintes d'un Icare" (Brueghel) and "Duellum" (Goya) (Majewski 2002, 52).

21. This poem was originally categorized under the heading "Prisons." See also the unpublished poem "The Four Walls of my Room" (1893*).

22. In a self-commentary note, Cavafy writes that the "person intended is entirely symbolic, and we must rather take him to be an artist or man of learning" (2009b, 273). *Ovid among the Barbarians* was painted by Delacroix on one of the domes in the Chamber of Deputies (Palais Bourbon), Paris, in addition to being painted numerous times on free-standing canvases.

23. See Huyghe (1971) for a thorough catalog of these paintings, as well as Constans (1996). The Ionides family owned two Delacroix paintings, *The Shipwreck of Don Juan* and *The Good Samaritan,* as well as numerous etchings.

24. This Hellenocentric perspective is more characteristic of Cavafy prose writings, for which see chapter 2. See Schaffer (1944, 136–181) for a thorough overview of Parnassian Hellenism, and Dallas (1984, 345–353) on ekphrasis and the Second Sophistic.

25. Yiannis Rigopoulos (1991, 55) notes that Edouard Schuré might have been Cavafy's source for the painting's description. Other possible sources include an 1864 salon critique by Maxime du Camp and Alexandre Dumas's *L'Ami des femmes* and *Les Idées de Madame Aubray,* texts that include descriptions of Moreau's painting. I am indebted to Katerina Ghika for this information.

26. Regarding the term "translation," Michel Brix writes,

> Baudelaire uses this word on many occasions to signify that the major value of a work of art resides in the original impression the author is struggling to reconstitute. "A beautiful picture is faithful to the dream which brought it into being." . . . In other words, a picture representing a landscape is beautiful in so far as it succeeds in awakening in the viewer the very feeling which made the painter find it beautiful. Thus, it is not the subject matter which counts in painting ("the beauty of a painting does not depend on the things represented there"), but the moral fruitfulness, the power of suggestion of the picture, its capacity to translate the feelings experienced by the artist in regard to that which he is painting. (2001, 12–13)

This very process animates Cavafy's impressionist meditation on Whistler in his poem "Sea of the Morning," as discussed in chapter 1.

27. See Pieris (1992, 95–99) and Rigopoulos (1991, 51–61).

28. See Showalter (1990, chap. 8) and Dijkstra (1986).

29. On the underlying affinities between the writings of Huysmans and the art of Moreau, see Grigorian (2004). Cavafy would likely have seen Moreau's *The Apparition* at the Grosvenor in 1877. Huysmans, it should be noted, also wrote art criticism (see Kahn 1987).

30. The opening lines of Philostratus's *Imagines* are worth quoting: "Whosoever scorns painting is unjust to truth; and he is also unjust to all the wisdom that has been bestowed upon poets—for poets and painters make equal contributions to our knowledge of the deeds and the looks of heroes" (Philostratus and Callistratus 1931, 3). It bears noting also that Callistratus's *Descriptions* involves a series of ekphrases on statues.

31. Showalter (1990, 151). See Gilbert (1983, 154), noting that Herod's burst of revulsion when ordering Salome's death at the end of the play relates to Wilde's own reaction to the implications of Salome's challenge to the world of art, the "outright attack upon the mediating function of culture and art." Like Dorian Gray, who found Sibyl Vane interesting again only after her death ("a wonderful tragic figure"), Cavafy's Sophist has little interest in Salome while she is alive. Only after her death will she become an icon of depravity. See Zagona (1960) for a thorough overview of the treatment of this theme in the nineteenth-century literature.

32. On Moreau's Orientalism, see Lacambre, who notes that "two dominant strains of style shaped Moreau's choice of motifs: Hellenic and Hindu" (1999, 19). Moreau's canvases *The Triumph of Alexander the Great* and *The Peri* also feature this hybrid Greco-Indian aesthetic. Cavafy's Orientalist poem "Dünya Güseli" (1884*) was clearly influenced by Orientalist painting, as I argue elsewhere (Jeffreys 2005, 58–61).

33. On the fascination with gems shown by many fin de siècle writers, see Humphreys (2003).

34. Adapted as stanzas from William Rees's prose translation (1990, 121–124). Cavafy's poem "Blue Eyes" (1892*) was likely inspired by Gautier's "Caurulei oculi" ("Eyes of Blue"). See Gautier (1968) for the accompanying works of art associated with Gautier's poems.

35. See chapter 1 for the connection of this poem to the Pre-Raphaelites.

36. Hollinghurst comments that in Rodenbach's fourth collection of poems, *La Jeunesse blanche*, "the mysterious accord between the soul and the city, explored in a mood of lonely withdrawal and silent contemplation, is established" (2005, 13). This relates to the tradition of the flâneur explored in the previous chapter.

37. See Hanson (1997), examining the dialectic of shame and grace and the numerous conversion narratives penned by decadent authors.

38. See Cavafy (2009b, 506) (translator's note).

39. See the relevant discussion in chapter 2.

40. See Knight (1986, 81, 72), who notes that Gautier, in his preface to *Mademoiselle de Maupin*, evokes flowers as an analogy for art: "Like art, they are 'useless' but indispensable because of their beauty" (32).

41. Kopidakis (1983, 631–632) cites Plutarch's "Life of Demetrius" as a relevant intertext.

42. See *À Rebours*, chapter 8, for a catalog of natural flowers that look like fakes.

43. See Cavafy (1993, 167) (editor's note).

44. On the influence of Huysmans's floral tropology on the decadent movement, see Knight (1986, 228–232).

45. "Indeed the transformation in the poetic rhetoric of flowers in nineteenth-century France can be seen not only as a prefiguration of modern literary sensibility but as one of the major conditions for its development. . . . For where Romantic flowers had spoken of the mysteries of life and death or of the poet's understanding of nature's language, the flowers of the Symbolists speak of the mysteries of language itself" (Knight 1986, 246).

46. Theodore Ralli (1852–1909), an Orientalist who studied with Jean-Léon Gérôme in Paris, exhibited regularly at the salons in Paris as well as at the Grosvenor. His painting *The Prayer before Holy Communion at Megara* (Paris Salon, 1890) sold for €863,000 in 2008, setting a record as the fourth most expensive painting by a Greek artist. (I thank Michelle Iatrou for bringing this information to my attention.) He executed a number of Orientalist paintings that could have served as sources for Cavafy's poem "Prayer" (Liddell 1997, 95). See Andreadi (2003) for the possible influence of Orientalist canvases on Cavafy, and Jeffreys (2005), 58–61.

47. The highly pictorialist poems Cavafy originally grouped under the Parnassian title "Ancient Days"—"The Tears of Phaethon's Sisters," "The Death of the Emperor Tacitus," "The Funeral of Sarpedon," "Horace in Athens," "The Footsteps of the Eumenides," "The Horses of Achilles" and "The Tarentines Carouse"—all share a common salon aesthetic that ultimately derives from the academic tradition of history painting, the genre that favored characters from the Bible, national history, and classical mythology.

48. The other locus classicus of this tradition is Plutarch's statement (attributed to Simonides of Ceos) that painting is "mute poetry" and poetry "a speaking picture" (Steiner 1982, 5). See also Cheeke, who writes that Plutarch's famous apothegm "sows the seeds of a whole tradition of thinking about the meaning of what each art lacks in relation to the other: the silence of paintings . . . and the pictorialism of poetry: the way poetic language may strive to produce pictures or images for the mind's eye" (2008, 20–21).

49. Thomas Couture's painting *The Romans of the Decadence* caused a great sensation when exhibited at the salon of 1847. It bore a warning subtitle from Juvenal: "Luxury has fallen upon us, more terrible than the sword, and the conquered East has revenged herself with the gift of her vices" (Gilman 1979, 93). This very Orientalist dialectic is central to Cavafy's presentation of the Hellenized East, a topic I explore at length (Jeffreys 2005).

50. See Pamela Fletcher, who devotes an entire chapter to the phenomenon of the "problem picture," an almost-forgotten genre to which Collier contributed in large measure: "Collier's problem pictures of the early 1900s recast the moralizing traditions of Victorian genre into a form of public modern art that engaged viewers in the discussion of contemporary moral, social and aesthetic questions" (2003, 4).

51. As Jean Hagstrum writes, "When artistic imitation came to be understood as a rendering of natural objects, social details, and psychological effects, then *enargeia* became an important term in literary criticism. But it originated in rhetoric, where it was used to describe the power that verbal visual imagery possessed in setting before the hearer the very object or scene being described" (1958, 11). In this sense, Cavafy's poem falls fully into the tradition of ekphrastic rhetoric.

52. Cavafy (1983), 116. For Horace's connection to decadence, see Barrow (2007, 50–51), who notes that Horace provided the Victorians with an exemplum of decline and that Horatian lines were appropriated as catalog quotations to accompany a number of paintings.

53. Philostratus, as Arthur Fairbanks reminds us, often wrote ekphrases on paintings that were figments of his imagination. He was a "sophist who developed the descriptions of paintings as a form of literary art" (Philostratus and Callistratus 1931, xxvi).

54. "Sarpedon, the son of Apollo and Bellerophron's daughter Laodamia, was a Lycian chieftain allied with the Trojans . . . who was killed by Patroclus, whereupon the gods, who were fond of him, sent Sleep and Death to carry him back to his homeland and build his tomb there" (Aghion 1994, 261).

55. The poem was revised in 1908 and republished in *Nea Zoe* (*New Life*).

56. The death of Sarpedon was featured on ancient Greek vases from the end of the sixth century BC, the most famous example being that depicted on the Euphronius Krater (c. 515–510 BC). See Lathia (1978) for an interesting discussion of the influence of Greek vases on Cavafy's poetry.

57. See note 50 on the genre of the problem picture.

58. "I am the Empire at the end of its decline / Which awaits the Barbarians fair and tall / While composing acrostic in an idle scrawl / To which sad sunshine lends its golden shine" (quoted in Stableford 1990, 95).

59. See Jagot (2008, 588), who notes that, for the French, these paintings problematize the themes of the German peril (post 1870) and the degeneration of the Frankish dynasty (588). Classic examples of this subgenre include Delacroix's mural *Attila and His Barbarians Overrunning Italy and the Arts* (Hemicycle of the Library, Palais Bourbon) (figure 6), *The Sack of Rome by the Barbarians* by Jean-Noël Sylvestre, *The Halt of the Merovingian Hordes* by Evariste Luminais, and

Germanicus before the Remains of the Legions of Varus by Lionel Royer. Similar depictions were also found on Roman sarcophagi, most famously the *Portonaccio Sarcophagus* and the *Piccolo Ludovisi*. See Rivière, (2008a, 166–169).

60. See Catsaouni (1983) on Cavafy's theatrical presentation of history.

61. Boletsi (2013) and Dimiroulis (1983) offer summaries of various critical readings of the poem. See also Tziovas (1986a) and Vassiliadi (2008, chap. 5), who presents an interesting chart with analogous poems by Panayiotis Synadinos, Paul Verlaine, W. B. Yeats, Valeri Bryusov, and George Seferis (108–111).

62. Poggioli (1983) offers a standard decadent interpretation of the poem.

63. See the excellent essay by Aillagon (2008, 42–53).

64. G. W. Bowersock (2009, 197–198) notes the "rising tide of relativism in historical interpretations of the Roman Empire" and the "Gibbonian view of decline and fall" yielding to a model of "transformation."

65. G. Savidis (1991, 135). The Ralli paintings Cavafy saw at the 1897 salon were *Le Parvis du Saint-Sépulcre, à Jérualem* and *Devant le mur de Salomon, à Jérusalme*. The painting *The Supplication* (figure 7) was painted in 1893 and would likely have been seen by Cavafy during a visit to Ralli's Cairo studio. I am indebted to Katerina Ghika for researching the dates and exhibition history of the Ralli paintings.

66. John Duffy (1995, 88) notes that the Byzantine empress Zoe possessed a miraculous icon of Christ that predicted the future by changing color and complexion when asked questions.

67. Cavafy (2003c, 90). The passage goes on to mention Paparrigopoulos's historical analysis of the miraculous deliverance of Constantinople from the Avars in 626 owing to divine intercession through the medium of the wonder-working icon of the Virgin Vlachernitissa. This event is commemorated in the religious poem *The Akathist Hymn*, one of Byzantium's great hymnographical compositions.

68. Fifteen Tsarouchis sketches also accompany a 1983 Italian translation of Cavafy's poems by Nicola Crocetti. The painting (figure 8) was included in a 1951 British edition of Cavafy's poems.

69. Hockney's *Kaisarion with All His Beauty* (1961) predates the *Illustrations for Fourteen Poems by Cavafy* (1966), which are rather free interpretative renderings of the Stangos-Spender translations. As Christopher Sykes notes, "The etchings . . . rather than being exact illustrations of each poem, were largely intended to parallel them, suggesting to the reader an experience similar to that described" (2011, 173). For further commentary, see Webb (1988, 73–76).

70. The Tate Britain Museum display caption identifies the figure on which Kassarion stands as the artist himself, next to whom is a stylized Egyptian portrait of Hockney's mother. http://www.tate.org.uk/servlet/ViewWork?cgroupid=999999961&workid=21038&searchid=9630.

4. Paterian Decadence

1. Particularly apt are G. W. Bowersock's comments: "Cavafy was one of the few modern admirers of ancient Alexandria to prefer the late antique period to the Hellenistic one. The city's cultivation of Greek culture and its lively conflict between polytheism and Christianity on the eve of the Arab conquest were more congenial to a Greek of the late nineteenth and early twentieth centuries than the proud and confident Hellenism of the capital of the Ptolemies" (1996a, 263). Marguerite Yourcenar, who divided Cavafy's poetry into cycles, notes that "the Fall of the Hellenistic Monarchies—Triumph of Rome [cycle is] the largest, since it includes at least two dozen poems and the ones most charged with pathos and irony" (1984, 166). See also Bruce W. Frier, who points out that "from about 1900 until the end of this life in 1933, Cavafy would write and publish or circulate some 40 poems concerned in one way or another with the political ascent of Rome in the Mediterranean" (2010, 6).

2. The phrase comes from J. B. Bullen (1991, 157). Gregory Jusdanis (1987, 82–83), Michalis Pieris (1992, 53–62), David Ricks (2001, 25), Martha Vassiliadi (2008, 91), and Panagiotis Roilos (2009, 9, 74, and 197) touch upon Cavafy's relationship to Pater. See also Richard Dellamora's (2010, 121–142) discussion of Pater and Sappho in connection with Greek desire and Cavafy.

3. See Lesley Higgins (2002, 39), who notes that Wyndham Lewis, T. S. Eliot, and Ezra Pound, although bent on excluding Pater from the Modernist canon, were each indebted to him in significant ways. Eliot's comments are representative of the New Humanists of the 1920s and '30s for whom Pater represented "that inexhaustible discontent, languor, and homesickness . . . the chords of which ring all through our modern literature" (Seiler 1980, 41).

4. See Cavafy's marginal notes on John Ruskin (Tsirkas 1971, 223–265), in which he similarly refutes the moral bias of the Victorian critic. Of particular interest is Cavafy's repudiation of Ruskin's comment "The artist who *represents brutalities and vices*, and not for rebuke of them is absolutely condemned," which he counters with his own Baudelairean retort: "The true artist does not have, like the hero of a myth, to choose between virtue and vice; both will serve him and he will love both equally" (Liddell [1974] 2000, 117).

5. "Swinburne introduced Pater to Gautier's writings; Gautier, Mürger, and Baudelaire, constitute the formative trio of French authors whose criticism shaped Pater's understanding of romanticism" (Higgins 2007, 428). On Pater's unacknowledged but pronounced debt to Baudelaire, see Clements, who writes, "Pater transferred, from Baudelaire's account to his own, essential material for his presentation of the aesthetic critic, the constituent elements of aesthetic criticism itself, an idea of abstraction in art, a theory of the relationships of the arts to one another, a repertoire of metaphorical relations, and a conception of modernity" (1985, 105).

6. As Elisa Bizzotto writes, "Pater's imaginary portraiture stands out as the epitome and codification of English *fin-de siècle* short fiction," and she counts Joyce's *A Portrait of the Artist as a Young Man* and Woolf's *Orlando* among works directly influenced by Pater (2002, 222–223).

7. Although none of Pater's writings presently survive in Cavafy's library, Michalis Perides noted their presence back in the forties, and it may be assumed that Cavafy owned and read Pater's works both in bound form and in the Victorian periodical press.

8. They were restored to the third printing of the book in 1888, albeit in a somewhat edited form. Typical of the negative reactions were those expressed by W. J. Stillman, Sarah Wister, and Agnes Repplier, all of whom believed Pater's influence to be morally subversive (Seiler 1980, 5). Although Pater repudiated charges that he was a decadent hedonist and corrupter of youth, his connection to literary decadence was unmistakable. As William Buckler writes,

> [*The Renaissance*] is thus a superb example of the literature of decadence in more than one sense. It brings an idea to birth, magnificent gestures, and a worthy close; it shows how an age was born, flourishes, and decayed; it studies how the generations succeeding the great Renaissance found in art solace for their culturally depleted state; and it adds to our literary experience a fine example of how a critic who is both intellectually rigorous and imaginatively sympathetic can treat a subject of critical decay with constructive dignity rather than attitudinal harshness or sentimental lament. (1987, 102)

Ellis Hanson adds to this decadent categorization by noting that Pater is a "decadent writer, not only because of his tortuous and exquisite style, his fascination with the *objet d'art* and the fragment, but also because of his preoccupation with death and decay" (1997, 184).

9. The infamous concluding paragraphs were not originally written to end *The Renaissance*; they were initially penned as the final few paragraphs of Pater's 1868 review essay "Poems by William Morris," which was later reworked as "Aesthetic Poetry" (1889), writings that, as Brake (1994b, 47) notes, were immediately associated by reviewers with "degeneracy, rhapsodizing, and affectation."

10. See Pieris (1992, 55), who was one of the first critics to explore Pater's influence on Cavafy.

11. See in particular the preface to *The Renaissance,* where Pater outlines the function and aesthetic end of pleasure. Cavafy's "Sophist Leaving Syria" (1926) is another example of a Paterian-inspired meditation on a beautiful youth: "To have Mevis / just for two or three days, they often give / as much as a hundred staters. I said in Antioch; / but in Alexandria as well, in fact in Rome even,/ you can't find a young man as attractive as Mevis" (1992, 143).

12. See Mellor (2008) for an excellent overview of this relationship. Horace's line from *Epistles* 2.1 remains the locus classicus for this perverse cultural relationship: "Graecia capta ferum victorem cepit et artes intulit agresti Latio" ("Captive Greece captured her savage conqueror and brought the arts to rustic Latium"). For a different take on the privileged status of Hellenism in Rome, see Cavafy's essay "Greek Scholars in Roman Houses," an appreciation of Lucian's essay "On Salaried Posts in Great Houses," which recounts the pathetic plight of a Greek tutor in Rome.

13. The story resonates with language reminiscent of "In the Month of Athyr": "'*Full of affections*,' observed, once upon a time, a great lover of boys and young men. . . . And yet, amid all its littleness, how large his sense of liberty in the place he, the cadet doomed to leave it—his birthplace, where he is also so early to die—*had loved better* than any one of them!" (Pater 1986, 343, 345, emphasis added).

14. See Dellamora's (1994) intriguing reading of the story, in which he analyzes how it involves the "conscious effects of Spartan-model pedagogy in nineteenth-century England" and the way Pater invokes Dorianism's warrior model and the "sacrificial logic" to the state that makes "a seductive appeal to subjects of male-male-desire. Such men are subliminally offered an exchange: their lives for validation of their desires for other men" (45).

15. As William Shuter writes, "Nowhere, in fact, does Uthwart seem more like a work of Greek sculpture than when he is finally deprived of all capacity of motion, for the same aesthetic necessity that shaped his beauty requires his early death" (1997, 38). Shuter notes the related Paterian motif of the uncovering not only of the remains of the dead but also of antique artifacts (97–98).

16. "The diaphanous type embodies the youthful Pater's utopian dreams of a homosocial society that reinstated the ethics and aesthetics associated with the spirit of Hellenism, and in particular 'the care for physical beauty, the worship of the body' that he celebrates in the Preface to *Studies*. His description in 'Diaphaneitè,' it is evident, like his characterization of Marius, is on one level, an attempt to sublimate the painful, sometimes exquisite sensitivity that, as a man who loves other men, he feels as he confronts life in 'the adulterated atmosphere of the world'" (Beaumont 2010, xii).

17. Pater published regularly in the *Westminster Review* during the 1860s, the *Fortnightly Review* during the 1870s, and *Macmillan's* during the 1880s (Brake 1994b, 32). The quarterlies of this period published essays characteristically possessing both the qualities of a "review–like essay" and an "essay-like review" (Brake 1994b, 25), both elements of which are prevalent in Cavafy's own prose writings.

18. Pater's "plundering from the *Curiosités Esthétiques* and *L'Art Romantique* is one of the best cases we have of what Richard Ellmann calls an 'authoritative larceny'" (quoted in Clements 1985, 78).

19. See Debaisieux (1997), Sachinis (1981), and chapter 2.

20. William Buckler notes that "Pater's *Appreciations* was one of the two most influential volumes of literary criticism the nineteenth century produced, the other volume being Matthew Arnold's *Essays in Criticism*" (1987, 107).

21. See Tufescu (2008), where she notes that plagiarism constituted a decadent tradition that deliberately sought to undermine romantic notions of fecundity and originality: "Pater stole from Baudelaire, who stole from Poe, who stole from Coleridge; and their thefts begot Wilde" (15). On Cavafy's creative encounter with Wilde's writings, see Ekdawi (1993a) and Boyiopoulos (2012).

22. Pater comments on "that terror, the seeking for which is one of the notes of romanticism in Shakespeare and his circle. The stream of ardent natural affection, poured as sudden hatred upon the youth condemned to die, adds an additional note of expression to the

horror of the prison where so much of the scene takes place. . . . With that instinctive clinging to life, which breaks through the subtlest casuistries of monk or sage apologising for an early death, he welcomes for a moment the chance of life through his sister's shame" (1986, 502–503). This idea resonates throughout Cavafy's essay, which emphasizes Claudio's terror at the thought of death and his ardent desire to live. Filippo Maria Pontani (1991, 155) notes the liberties taken by Cavafy when translating passages from *Measure for Measure,* which he terms a "free translation."

23. Cavafy also engages with the topic of vanity in his essays "A Night in Kalinderi," "Thoughts of an Aging Artist," and "Philosophical Scrutiny," as well as in the poem "Dareios" ("a certain insight into the vanities of greatness" [1992, 107]). Alkis Thrylos (1924, 157) was one of the first critics to comment on Cavafy's broad focus on vanity.

24. Cavafy cleverly concludes the essay by conflating the notions of measure and vanity:

> We Greeks have the vanity or the aspiration of always wanting to bring the measure of our own things to all we do. Owing in part to this habit, and motivated in part by the analogy of thought, I will conclude my article by copying a few lines from Lucian's 'Dialogues of the Dead': *Diogenes:* . . . . I must interrogate this most reverend senior of them all.—Sir, why weep, seeing that you have died full of years? Has your Excellency any complaint to make, after so long a term? Ah, but you were doubtless a king. *Pauper:* Not so. *Diog:* A provincial governor, then? *Pauper:* No, nor that. *Diog:* I see; you were wealthy, and do not like leaving your boundless luxury to die. *Pauper:* You are quite mistaken; I was near ninety, made a miserable livelihood out of my line and rod, was excessively poor, childless, a cripple, and had nearly lost my sight. *Diog:* And you still wished to live? *Pauper:* Ay, sweet is the light, and dread is death; would that one might escape it! (2010, 30).

25. Marcus Aurelius, a practitioner of the New Cyrenaicism, begins his oration with the following lines: "The world without and within me flows away like a river, therefore let me make the most of what is here and now. The world and the thinker upon it, are consumed like a flame, therefore let us turn away our eyes from vanity; and renounce; and withdraw ourselves alike from all affections" (Pater [1885] 2008, 131).

26. Marius concludes his journal with "Dared one hope that there is a heart, even as ours, in that divine *Assistant* of one's thoughts—a heart even as mine, behind this vain show of things" (Pater [1885] 2008, 276).

27. Lucian's dialogue "Hermotimus or Concerning the Sects" is a sustained attack on philosophical schools in which the skeptic interlocutor succeeds in undermining the structure of philosophic idealism. "The Halcyon" is a spurious work attributed to Lucian.

28. Cavafy's essay, published in the Ottoman Greek newspaper *Constantinople* in November 1893, relies heavily on and acknowledges James Russell Lowell's essay "Shakespeare Once More" (*Among My Books)*. It should be noted that Cavafy's cousin Pantelis Cavafy published Greek translations of Shakespeare's *The Tempest* (1874), *Two Gentlemen of Verona* (1874), and *Twelfth Night* (1881) in Constantinople (Tsirkas 1958, 150, 489).

29. See Dowling (1986, chap. 3) on the fatal "golden book" (164). Decadent texts in this outré tradition include Apuleius's *The Golden Ass*, Shakespeare's *Sonnets*, Huysmans's À *Rebours*, Pater's *Marius* and *The Renaissance,* Gautier's *Mademoiselle de Maupin,* and Wilde's *A Picture of Dorian Gray*.

30. See Bassett (1999, 255) on Pater's rather ineffectual attempts to correct the "poisonous" effects of *The Renaissance*.

31. Moran adds, "While ostensibly adhering to the standard structure of a Christian narrative genre, Pater covertly establishes a heretical alternative in which the self becomes the standard of all things, its cultivation into a type of perfection becomes religious practice. . . . The narrative structure of Pater's historical conversion romance also differs from its predecessors in its

tendency to synthesize rather than oppose contending systems of belief" (2002, 178). Cavafy aspires to achieve a similar synthesis in his presentation of Christianity.

32. Goldhill adds that "the genre starts to appear in strikingly increased numbers in the 1870s, and during the 1890s fully forty new volumes were published in England, and from 1900 until the end of the First World War another 60" (2011, 156). See also Vance (1997, chap. 9).

33. Goldhill (2011, 231) aptly labels this mixture the "popular sublime." Liddell ([1974] 2000, 125) makes the important point that Cavafy, "in his way, wrote historical fiction."

34. See Easson (2004) on Bulwer-Lytton's visit to Pompeii, especially the excavations at "The House of the Tragic Poet," which inspired his description of Glaucus's house: "Bulwer implies the decoration is Glaucus's choice, imported direct from Greece" (107). Curiously, in 1863, Bulwer-Lytton was offered the throne of Greece after the abdication of King Otho, perhaps because of his diplomatic service in Corfu (Bulwer-Lytton [1871] 2005, 217 [editor's note]).

35. On Bulwer-Lytton's interest in magic and the occult (another possible line of influence on Cavafy), see Seed (2005, xxxv). On his influence on Poe, Wagner, and Victorian writers, see Christensen (1976, 222–234).

36. Cavafy possessed a copy of *Devereux* in his library and quoted from *Zanoni* in his essay "Misplaced Tenderness."

37. See Spawforth (2012), where he explores the complex relation between Rome and the decadent influences of Orientalizing Alexandrian Hellenism conceptualized as Asian by Roman writers and poets.

38. Mowbray Morris was identified as the author by Christine Bolus-Reichert, who notes the centrality of Charles Kingsley in this tradition: "If Hellenistic Alexandria and Victorian Britain were indeed parallel in their cultural, political and religious development, then British imperialism would of necessity reach an end as complicated—and as inevitable—as the literary culture it had produced. . . . However, as Kingsley's critics complained, if the analogy between Roman Alexandria and Victorian Britain holds, then 'he seems to anticipate for Europe a social dissolution like that of the lower empire' in which the purity of Christian Europe is lost" (2009, 187–188).

39. As Sarah Ekdawi notes, Cavafy "adopts the word 'Alexandrian' as latter-day homosexuals have taken up 'queer,' and used it to denote 'homosexual' in a wholly positive way" (1996b, 36). See also David Ricks (2004, 341), who points out that Cavafy, while fully aware of the term's decadent connotations, was also conscious of a countervailing movement to define the term more positively as "an age of difficult and delayed germination."

40. This is precisely the point made by Bowersock (1981, 103), who writes that, for Cavafy, Christianity—particularly a permissive brand that permitted a delectable life—"did not preclude being pagan in the old sense." Cavafy's unique blend of austere sensuality was not lost on Nikos Kazantzakis, who labeled him "the hermit chieftain who subjugates curiosity, ambition and sensuality to the austere order of an ascetic Epicureanism" (1975, 74). Coincidentally, E. M. Forster (2004, 97) notes the presence of a "dull colossal statue of Marcus Aurelius" in the Alexandrian Museum, a frequent haunt of Cavafy, who wrote a review of the museum and its holdings in 1892. On Cavafy's thematic chapter "The Beginnings of Christianity," see Haas (1983a), whose study of religion in Cavafy overlooks the presence and influence of Pater.

41. This critique of the Roman fetishization of Hellenism is also present in *Marius*, particularly in the banquet in chapter 20, where Marius finds himself reacting with indifference to the rhetoric and the dramatic performance (*acroama*), and is ultimately underwhelmed by his meeting with Apuleius. See Ricks (2004) and Trapp (2004) on Hellenism's association with luxury and excess during the late-antique period.

42. I am indebted to Ellis Hanson for the Paterian categories of comradeship and mourning. Hanson goes on to note that "virtually *every* representation of love between men in Pater is haunted by the grave—and the stronger the suggestion of homoerotic desire, the more eagerly Pater seems to want to see one of the two men dead" (1987, 184).

43. Marius is arrested and assumed to be a Christian at the end of the novel. After bribing the guards to release Cornelius, he is left to die at a Christian farmhouse, where he is given a secret Christian burial as a martyr.

44. Dellamora (1990, 165) notes the implicit valorization of the male body as the object of masculine desire in Pater's move towards Christianity. He also points out how Anglo-Catholic parishes in England "provided spaces in which men of different classes who were sexually attracted primarily to other males could mingle in an open and respectable way. By the 1890s, these congregations afforded homosexuals a measure of visibility and tacit accommodation" (149).

45. This point is made by Moran (2002) (see note 31). Cornelius, Hanson argues, is more than simply a religious touchstone for Marius: "More than Flavian, he is a spiritualization of the male body, his physical beauty qualified by a military *ascesis* and idealism that the pagan sensualist lacked" (Hanson 1997, 213). Brake (1994b, 42) makes the important point that *Marius* chronicles the failure of pagan religions to cope with death.

46. "Another of the men reputed to have been the first homosexual mortal, Thamyris, was also a wonderful poet. He made the hubristic mistake of challenging the Muses to a contest; as a consequence of this impertinence, he was deprived of the powers of sight and sound" (Woods 1998, 2).

47. Jusdanis notes the poem as an example of how literature functions to "defamiliarize the routine of daily life, to uncloud our vision with unexpected vistas, to sharpen our perceptions. This poem forces readers to look at Christianity anew by returning us to a time when it was a mere cult" (commentary in Leontis 2002, 132).

48. See Keeley's interpretation of the poem, in which he argues that, with "Myris" "the poet had arrived in his last years at a tragic sense of life—and the controlled expression that best evokes it—which was sufficiently profound and universal to permit him in his best moments to translate his hedonistic bias and his special view of history into poetry of the highest order" (1976, 141). The mythical and historical writing strategies that Keeley identifies in Cavafy likewise comprise the dominant mode in Pater, to whom Cavafy is thoroughly indebted for his method. As Gerald Monsman writes, "Prior to the publication of 'The Child in the House,' Pater had written in *The Renaissance* of historical personages mythically; he had also written in his Greek studies of mythical figures historically. But in 'The Child in the House' he created his first *imaginary* portrait—a weaving of history and myth around an imaginative motif" (1977, 72). On the equally plausible and curiously similar possibility of Paterian influences on Marguerite Yourcenar (although emphatically repudiated by the author herself), see Bann (2004a, 3).

49. Cavafy's "Prayer" offers a similar presentation of a superstitious religious practice, although here the Christian icon is sympathetic, whereas the heathen idol exhibits a rather comical cultural hostility toward the prayers of a Christian convert.

50. See Cavafy's comment on the poem, noting that he deliberately omitted mention of the bestowal of titles on the two Cleopatras: "I describe what I think the Alexandrians chiefly rushed to see" (G. Savidis 1985b, 201).

51. On recently discovered antique depictions of Kaisarion, see Frier (2010, 29–30).

52. Noted by Dimaras (1982, 138), who also comments on the poem's purely descriptive "Parnassian quality." Savidis contrasts the demotic style of the verse with the highly purist diction of the epithets describing Kaisarion's costume (G. Savidis 1985b, 208), details that were clearly meant to emphasize the aesthetic dimension of the poem.

53. On Cleopatra's shrewd strategy regarding titulatures, see Bingen, who notes that it was her "Macedonian aristocratic ancestry" that she highlighted in her new titulature: "*Philopatris* refers implicitly to her ancestor, the Macedonian Ptolemy, who first reigned in Alexandria over a vast empire where Egypt was not a homeland but a strategic base; she invokes the Macedonian blood of both the Ptolemies and the Seleucids" (2007, 78).

54. See Vassilis Lambropoulos's fine analysis of the poem, in which he notes how it problematizes decadence: "Surely the contrast is meant to foreground a sense of decline, comparing ancient glory to current corruption and the painful belatedness that follows every classicism. Instead of flattering continuity, the poem ridicules the Hellenic pretenses of worthless authors, court sycophants, and rotten leaders. As the second century B.C. was drawing to a close, an entire world was coming to its pathetic end with the Roman conquest, and just as was happening in 1922 to the Greek presence in Asia Minor despite irredentist delusions promoted by servile artists" (2003-4, 73). See also Cavafy's "The Dynasty" for a sarcastic catalog of dynastic nicknames.

55. Cavafy, taking Pater's cue, treats Heinrich Heine's theme of the gods in exile directly in "Ionic." See also Vassiliadi (2008, 155).

56. Mendelsohn astutely notes how

> Cavafy's choice of his sculptor's subjects is hardly casual, and indeed is highly suggestive in its implied comment on the relationship between Roman and Greek culture, and on certain political ironies. Aemilius Paullus and the two Scipios, all three famous for their philhellenism, presided over Rome at the zenith of its consolidation of power throughout the Mediterranean, at the expense of the Hellenistic kingdoms whose culture the three so admired; Marius was responsible for a political development that would lead Rome herself into her Imperial phase; and Caesarion represents, in his parentage and his very person, the failed dream of a truly Greco-Roman political and dynastic unity. (2009b, 389–390 [translator's note])

57. See Giannakopoulou (2001, 88–89), who discusses the influence of Pater's Winckelmann on Cavafy's conceptualization of the sculpted male body.

58. Malanos claims, "In the 17 years that I knew him [1916–1933] he never bought new books and any that he borrowed were historical works necessary to his poetry. . . . His curiosity is of a kind that refers to the past. . . . The past is the necessity of life to his poetry, the 'atmosphere' of his imagination" (Liddell [1974] 2000, 123).

59. Joyce (2007, 15). The current literary revival of Victorianism—Neo-Victorianism—is highly relevant here for assessing Cavafy's own residual Victorianism. As Julie Sanders writes, "The Victorian era proves in the end ripe for appropriation because it throws into sharp relief many of the overriding concerns of the postmodern era: questions of identity; of environmental and genetic conditioning; repressed and oppressed modes of sexuality; criminality and violence; the urban phenomenon; the operations of law and authority; science and religion; the postcolonial legacies of empire" (quoted in Heilmann and Llewellyn 2010, 24). See also Ho (2012), arguing that "the return to the Victorian in the present offers a highly visible, highly aestheticized code for confronting empire again and anew; it is a site within which the memory of empire and its surrounding discourses and strategies of representation can be replayed and played out" (5).

5. Cavafy's Byzantium

1. Quotations in Angelov 2003, 8–9. Hegel's comments are highly reflective of western Europe's disparaging view of Byzantium: "Its [Byzantium's] general aspect presents a disgusting picture of imbecility: wretched, nay, insane passions, stifle the growth of all that is noble in thoughts, deeds, and persons. Rebellion on the part of generals, depositions of the Emperors by means or through the intrigues of courtiers, assassinations or poisoning of the Emperors by their own wives and sons, women surrendering themselves to lusts and abominations of all kinds" (in Angelov 2003, 9). See Vasiliev (1958, 6), with an introduction that offers an overview of western European scholarship up through the mid-twentieth century. For more recent appraisals, see Stephenson (2010), and Haarer (2007).

2. See Stephenson (2010c) for a useful overview of the work of Freeman, Gregorovius, and Schlumberger, in which he notes that these pioneers of popular Byzantine history "reintroduced Byzantium, as medieval Greece, in a positive light to a popular audience" (462).

3. See Christodoulou (2010) for a thorough overview of the contributions of Zambelios and Paparrigopoulos to modern Greek attitudes on Byzantium. Diana Haas (1996) explores Cavafy's debt to Paparrigopoulos's redaction of Byzantine history. See also Kitromilides (1998) on Paparrigopoulos and Byzantium.

4. Steven Runciman was J. B. Bury's one postgraduate student (Stephenson 2010c, 476), a connection that aligns him with Cavafy's revisionist trajectory.

5. The phrase "la aute idéale de roses" comes from "L'Après-midi d'un faune" ("The Afternoon of a Faun"); Baudelaire's phrase comes from his definition of decadent dandyism in "The Painter of Modern Life" (1995, 29).

6. Spirit, citing Wilde, notes that Byzantium combined two artistic traditions: "'Greek art, with its intellectual sense of form, and its quick sympathy with humanity; Oriental art with its gorgeous materialism.'" Such a union allowed a replaying of the Romantic use of the 'East' to augment 'Western' imagination. At Byzantium, the pagan and primitive associations of the Orient mingled with images of a Christian hierarchical and ordered society to provide a heady alternative to Victorian culture" (1995, 157). On Cavafy's connection to the Orientalist tradition, see Jeffreys (2005).

7. See Reed (2004, 69), who explores Roger Fry's notion of a "proto-Byzantine modernism": "Bloomsbury imagined modernism as a form of Byzantinism" (71). Reed also has an intriguing chapter on the *Borough Polytechnic Murals* (1911), painted by Duncan Grant, as expressing "the modern ideal of homoerotic democracy" (81). It should be noted that both Vanessa Bell and Duncan Grant painted canvasses of Byzantine empresses (81–86).

8. "The foundations of Byzantine studies as a scholarly discipline were laid in France during the seventeenth century. It was in this period, for example, that the grandiose project for the publication of the collected works of the Byzantine historians, 'the Paris corpus,' was undertaken. Furthermore, Byzantium captivated the minds of the French monarchs, who took a personal interest in it and patronized the study of its civilization" (Angelov 2003, 8). As Patrick McGuiness writes in his introduction to *À Rebours*, "Many artists of the period [late nineteenth century] invoked the decline and fall of the hyper-civilized Roman Empire as the most resonant 'culture rhyme' for modern France. Certainly there were grounds for such views: a sense of historical decline symbolized by a humiliating defeat at the hands of the Prussians" (2003, xv). Rémy de Gourmont offered the following appraisal of the vogue of Byzantinism: "Having seen with its own eyes the death struggle of Byzantium, Europe coupled these two ideas, Byzantium—Decadence—which became a commonplace. . . . From Byzantium, this association of ideas was extended to the whole Roman Empire, which is now, for sage and respectable historians, nothing but a series of decadences" (quoted in Thornton 1983, 17).

9. In a letter dated July 31, 1880, praising Huysmans's *Croquis Parisiens,* http://homepage. mac.com/brendanking/huysmans.org/reviews/croquisrev/croquis2.htm. See also my discussion of Huysmans's connection to Gustave Moreau in chapter 3. For the pictorial dimension of this Byzantinizing aesthetic, see note 32 in chapter 3.

10. Andrew D. White (1959, 288) records seeing Bernhardt perform Theodora at the Zizinia Theatre in 1889. I am grateful to Katerina Ghika for bringing this to my attention. In England, Sardou was preceded by Philip Watt's *Theodora: Actress and Empress* (1866), which offered a "heady mixture of potent beauty undermined by corruption and death" (Spirit 1995, 160).

11. Cited in Spirit (1995, 162). See also Bullen (2003, chap. 5), for a thorough exploration of Ruskin and Byzantine Venice. Bullen notes that "Ruskin added a new ingredient to the current treatment of Byzantine art and architecture: sensuous pleasure, and an ability to articulate that

pleasure in mesmerizing prose. His pleasure may be contained within a firm moral structure, but it is pleasure nonetheless" (122).

12. *Theophano* was dedicated to J. B. Bury. In his article "An Update on the Elgin Marbles" (1891), Cavafy thanks Harrison on behalf of the Greek people and all humanity for advocating the return of the Elgin Marbles to Greece (2010, 26). Harrison's essays, with which Cavafy would have been familiar, were reprinted in *The Meaning of History* (1900). See also A. N. Rambaud, who, in "Empereurs et Impératrices d'Orient" in *Revue des Deux Monde* (1891)—a review of Shlumberger's book on Nicephoros Phokas (1890)—refers to Theophano as "une Fleur de décadence" (822).

13. Diehl's *Études byzantines* (1905) and *Byzance: Grandeur and Décadence* (1919) were also known to Cavafy. Malanos (1957) was one of the first critics to document Cavafy's significant debt to Diehl.

14. Regarding Byzantine law, military prowess, and architecture, Harrison writes,

> The most signal evidence of the superior civilisation of Byzantium down to the tenth century, is found in the fact that alone of all states it maintained a continuous, scientific, and even progressive system of law. . . . It was a strange error of the older historians, into which Gibbon himself fell, that the Byzantine armies were wanting in courage, discipline, and organisation. On the contrary, during all the early Middle Ages they were the only really scientific army in the world. . . . And when justice is done to its [architecture's] constructive science, to its versatility, and at the same time to its severe taste and dignity, this Byzantine type is one of the most masculine and generative forms of art ever produced by human genius. (1900, 24, 22, 30)

15. Philippe Jullian (1971, 151), while highly indebted to Praz, also includes a chapter on Byzantium that makes mention of Cavafy.

16. See Kaldellis (2010a) for a list of the major Byzantine historians. We cannot say for certain which Byzantine historians Cavafy read, as his surviving library contained no primary sources. We know that he borrowed books and made regular use of libraries for his scholarly reading. For his legendary command of Byzantine history, see Ftyaras (1983), who, having studied with Diehl at the Sorbonne, ranked Cavafy above the French Byzantinist: "He [Cavafy] gave us the spirit of the period in great detail" (547). Ftyaras records that Cavafy once told him "I am four-quarters Byzantine and three-quarters Alexandrian" (546).

17. These poems include "Leaving Therapia" (1882), "Beizades to His Love" (1884), "Dunya Guzeli" (1884), and "Nichori" (1885). "Constantinopoliad an Epic" (1882) is a curious amalgam of diary entries, literary reflections, commonplace notes, and memoir.

18. Karl Krumbacher (1856–1909) was a pioneering German Byzantinist whose work *The History of Byzantine Literature* played an important role in reversing the predominantly negative view held by European scholars of Byzantine literature as derivative and second-rate. Cavafy was greatly indebted to Krumbacher for reinstating Byzantine literature in the canon of world literature and thus assisting nineteenth-century Greek intellectuals in establishing a line of continuity between modern, medieval, and ancient Greek literature.

19. See Ghika (2009), an article that illustrates the lengths to which Cavafy went to research the heraldic designs of his family crest, particularly the helmet motif. See also Kakavas (2002) for facsimiles of the crests of various Greek families who gave to the community of Saint Sophia in London.

20. Two poems that were not destroyed are "Before the Gates of Jerusalem" and "I Prefer Death to Living."

21. On the matter of rendering Cavafy's abbreviation "Ευδ."in the title, which could refer to either the empress Eudocia (Athenais) or Eudokia, see Haas (1996, 38) and Ekdawi (1996a, 23). The praise due to her likely comes from Gibbon, chapter 32. Among the most notorious of empresses, she would have drawn Cavafy's interest for being both a poet and a tragically abandoned woman. See Diehl (1963, chap. 2).

22. See Savidis (1985a, 96), where he refers to them as "historical vignettes or anecdotes, versified with care but rather frigidly, without the inimitable dramatic or ironic mastery which Cavafy was gradually to discover." While Cavafy clearly moved on from formal Parnassian conventions in his poetry, Savidis overstates the movement away from decadent Byzantinism, although Cavafy clearly matured into a more nuanced and, on occasion, ironic view of Byzantium, as is true with all his mature approaches to his subjects.

23. Haas (1983b, 77) sees Paparrigopoulos as the source of inspiration for these poems and follows Savidis's view that Cavafy read Gibbon after reading Paparrigopoulos.

24. Ekdawi (1996a, 21) writes, "The subject-matter and Western orientation of these poems have been lifted almost wholesale from the *Decline and Fall of the Roman Empire*." Cavafy most likely read A. N. Rambaud's "Empereurs et Impératrices d'Orient," published in the *Revue des Deux Mondes* in 1891.

25. Hirst (2003, 63). Ekdawi (1996a, 28, 31) insists that by virtue of the intended disruptive proximity of the poems "In the Church" and "Manuel Komninos" (according to Cavafy's thematic arrangement, which introduces what Hirst calls a "complex interplay"), the poem resonates with an unmistakably ironic view of Byzantinism.

26. For a compelling study of Byzantine aesthetics, see Pentcheva (2010).

27. As Hanson (1997, 219) notes, Pater's description of Chartres Cathedral in *Gaston de Latour* prefigures Huysmans's *La Cathédrale* in its passion for ritualism, vestments, and holy relics. See chapter 4 for Cavafy's indebtedness to Pater's aesthetic view of Christianity and the tension between the sensual and spiritual aspects of Christianity.

28. Interestingly enough, Thrylos (1924, 171) was one of the first critics to fully appreciate Cavafy's decadent turn of mind, although she overstates his sui generis poetic originality by neglecting to connect him to the literary decadence out of which he was working.

29. See Haas (1983b, 79–80), where she furthers her point by making apt textual connections between the instances of the possessive "our" used by Cavafy in many of his Byzantine poems. Haas notes that Cavafy's use of the term "Byzantinism" follows Ferdinand Gregorovius by unapologetically acknowledging the Asiatic component of Byzantine civilization (73–74). As Bowersock writes, "'Our Byzantinism' was a startling thing to say in 1912 and would have been almost any time until recently. Yet Cavafy saw the Hellenism of the Byzantine Empire not as a corruption of the Greek polytheist past, but as an affirmation of it, to which he willingly linked himself" (1996b, 250). See also Angelov (2003, 11), who notes that in the French and Italian traditions, Byzantinism has a slightly different meaning: "It is described as the propensity to discuss subtle and trivial matters, perhaps by analogy with the petty religious disputes of the Byzantines, and is also a synonym of decadence and verbal intricacy."

30. Nietzsche's influence on Cavafy has not been adequately studied. See Pagoulatos (2010) and Tziovas (1986a). To a large degree, Cavafy shares Nietzsche's identification of decadence as "a representative and essential condition of humanity" (Silk 2005, 602); his notion that one has to work one's way further into decadence in order to find a way to revalue, transform, and cure it (J. Scott 1998, 74); and the philosopher's critique of Christianity as irredeemably decadent (Benson 2008, 133).

31. Here we find the title of Cavafy's poem "Of Colored Glass" quite likely suggested by Huysmans's catalogue of ecclesiastical kitsch.

32. Kostis Palamas had this intertextual strategy in mind when he faulted Cavafy's poems for being "reportage from the past ages." The prose passages from Byzantine history fuse rather seamlessly with Cavafy's notoriously "prosaic" verse, another aesthetic reason why these historical prose texts appealed to Cavafy and another reason why the Athenian school of Greek poets found his poems lacking in conventional poetic qualities.

33. See Kaldellis (2007), where he argues, "the Second Sophistic fundamentally shaped the perception and reception of Hellenism in Byzantium and in early modern times. . . . As in the second century, we will witness in the twelfth the rise of showmanship in performance to

complement the emphasis on panegyric and the emergence of authorial egos of epic proportions, yet all this in the context of a Christian society and (often) ecclesiastical careers. Komnenian Byzantium . . . fully deserves the label of a 'Third Sophistic'" (40).

34. Kaldellis (2010b, ix). He notes in his excellent introduction that *The Secret History* expresses Prokopios's outrage over Justinian and Theodora's oppressive reign on many levels: "At home, the regime inaugurated an era of bigotry, repression, corruption, and injustice. Those viewed as sexual and religious deviants were targeted and persecuted while funds, often illegally obtained, were funneled to the priests of the only approved faith. Religion was made an instrument of government to a hitherto unprecedented degree" (vii).

35. "The anonymous author who wrote the preface to her husband's [Bryennios] *History* had given them a mythical and exaggerated bloodline, tracing them back to a cousin of Constantine the Great" (Laiou 2000, 11).

36. "It must be admitted that these tears are somewhat excessive, and that, no matter how sincere, they end by being rather irritating. Besides, there is every reason to believe that in the account of her misfortunes, as with everything else that concerned herself, Anna Comnena, whether consciously or not, exaggerates, and depicts events under a light that is more tragic than true. . . . And no matter how sad, how melancholy may have been Anna Comnena's last years, it must not be forgotten that she herself was to blame, rather than destiny " (Diehl 1963, 192–193).

37. Hirst offers the following apt comments on the poem: "What we have in Cavafy's 'Anna Comnena' is a text which locates itself within a historical debate and, though it seems to lean in one direction [i.e., Anna's less than sincere sorrow over Bryennios's death], does not finally come down on that side, but remains suspended in its own unresolved tension; and in consequence is able to go on reverberating in our minds, justifying its existence as a poem" (2000, 61–62).

38. This point, which has been largely overlooked by critics, renders the poem less unresolved and ambiguous in its tensions. As Thelma Gouma-Paterson writes, "All three imperial women, Anna, Irene and Anna Dalassene, ultimately derived their power through their relationship to Alexios, their father, husband, and son respectively. The difference, however, between Anna and her maternal prototypes is that she, in old age, reclaimed that power as author and historian, that is through her intellect, long after her father's death, when she lived as a virtual exile totally removed from the circles of imperial power" (2000, 119).

39. The highly dramatic displays of abjection and hieratic performances by Cavafy's Byzantine royal women introduce a coded but unmistakable element of high camp to his presentation of their respective plights, inspired no doubt by Sarah Bernhardt's legendary camp interpretations.

40. Kristeva writes that Anna "was able to describe events from the perspective of both a military strategist and a depressed psychologist. She examined every thread and knot of this ongoing set of conflicts that were endlessly breaking down and reconstructing themselves; but she did it in a way that also revealed things about her own Byzantine soul. Any historian would admire her" (2006, 81). Kristeva is less sympathetic on the matter of Byzantinism: "'Our values,' wrote Kristeva, 'have been delayed for two thousand years in us.' According to her, the Orthodox individual is incapable of adapting to modern society, a fact that became especially apparent after communism's fall" (Angelov 2003, 5).

41. According to Henry Maguire, "Ceremonial presented an image of *taxis*, the harmonious order that was thought essential for the proper functioning not only of the court but also of the whole empire. *Taxis* was opposed to *ataxia*, the disorder abhorred by the Byzantines and considered characteristic of barbarians and heretics. The court's framework was an elaborate hierarchy of offices and titles, reaching from the emperor downward" (1997, 184).

42. Hirst (2000, 63), where he also notes Kostis Palamas's opinion that the poem was a joke (62).

43. See Spatharakis (1976, 184–189). Diehl emphasizes the drama behind the staid appearance of the official portrait-like tableau: "For Anna Dalassena it was a splendid revenge for the cruel deception she had suffered in 1059. She had dreamt then of becoming Empress, and now her

dreams had come true. For some twenty years her son permitted her to rule the Empire jointly with him; and in justice to her it must be admitted that she governed well" (1927, 324).

44. Hirst (2000, 71), who sees the brevity of the poem—the "collapsing three chapters of the *Alexiad* into a few words"—as deliberately insolent and an indication of Cavafy's mockery, overlooks the decadent pictorial aesthetic that informs the poem, specifically Cavafy's attempt to imitate the static two-dimensional flatness of Byzantine monumental art.

45. See Magdalino (1993) for an overview of perspectives on Manuel's decadence, which, he notes, began with Choniates and were picked up by Gibbon and Finlay. They saw the emperor as "the incarnation of a decadent twelfth-century *ancien régime*—an extravagant, hedonistic anachronistic *roi soleil* who ruined what was left of the only progressive element in Byzantine society, its embryonic middle class" (15).

46. See introduction to Hanson (1997).

47. Choniates, Magdalino notes, "is out to show not only that Manuel fell short of the ideal image projected in the encomia, but also that the image itself is a dubious ideal. . . . It is clear that Choniates associated the imperial image developed in the encomia for Manuel with the type of imperial misrule which, in his view, caused the empire's decline in the late twelfth century" (1993, 478). On the prophecy concerning Manuel's madness and his near lapse into heresy during his final years, see Choniates (1984, 124–125). See also Haas's (1996, 413–441) analysis of the poem in the context of Cavafy's overall religious sensibility.

48. Kantakuzinos wrote four books collectively titled *Historiai*, as well as treatises attacking Islam and Judaism. As Nicol notes, his decree (*Tomos*) of the Council of 1351 declaring Gregory Palamas and hesychasm to be fully in keeping with the Orthodox faith was perhaps the most monumental of all his achievements: "It became and remains binding truth for the whole Orthodox church" (1996, 112).

49. On Kantakuzinos's leniency, see Nicol (1996, 82).

50. Irini Assan was the granddaughter of Irini Palaiologos and Tsar John III Assan of Bulgaria. She entered into monastic retirement as the nun Eulogia. See Nicol (1994, chap. 6).

51. In "The Patriarch," Cavafy eviscerates John Kalekas as arrogant and ungrateful for the kindness shown to him by Kantakuzinos.

52. Mendelsohn (Cavafy 2009b, 363). For a different reading, see Hirst (2003, 79), who is of the opinion that Cavafy viewed Kantakuzinos negatively and held an "underlying hostility towards the fourteenth-century emperor." Hirst's rather fanciful view that the name Kantakuzinos conceals that of Eleftherios Venizelos (65) falls flat when we consider that the Byzantine emperor never traveled to the West, unlike the Greek prime minister, whose career was made negotiating his country's future with the Western great powers.

53. Numerous critics have made compelling connections between the dates of these Byzantine poems and the tragic events of the Greek campaign in Turkey following World War I that resulted in the Asia Minor catastrophe. See G. Savidis (1985b, 352–354), Christidis (1958, 22), Hirst (2003, 65), and Mendelsohn's editorial note in Cavafy (2009b, 366–368).

54. Interestingly, T. S. Eliot selects virtually the same Greek phrase for the opening epigraph of *The Wasteland* (a quote from Petronius's *Satyricon*), in which the Sybil cries "αποθανείν θέλω" ("Would that I were dead").

55. See Jeffreys (2005, 7–13) for a parallel reading of Cavafy's and E. M. Forster's mutual appropriation of the Plethon legend.

Epilogue: Decadence's Gay Legacy

1. Regarding Max Nordau's notorious definition of decadence as a degenerate disease, Regenia Gagnier comments, "Taking the disease literally, Nordau institutionalized the pathologization of the artworld that would progressively desublimate art in the twentieth century. Culture

could henceforth be attacked as an index of the social diseases of modernity. Specifically, health, muscularity, and masculinity were opposed to a decadent feminine Art" (2010, 88).

2. Gay men, as Susan Sontag famously claimed in her "Notes on Camp," "constitute themselves as aristocrats of taste" (Sontag 1964, 529). Rictor Norton (1997, 222) notes that Wilde's famous defense during his trial for acts of gross indecency "should be seen in the context of a queer cultural elitism that was an important factor in some branches of the gay emancipation movement in the 1890s."

3. Regarding this period, Dellamora writes, "In part, a struggle was carried out over whether literature, indeed poetry, was a better discursive site for articulating same-sex intimacy than sexology, criminology, and anthropology" (2010, 121–122).

4. Kaye (1995, 2); Denisoff (1995, 189). In terms of the twentieth century, Gregory Woods maintains that "homosexuality is in essence a construct of the (late) nineteenth and twentieth centuries; *as* an essence it is just as distinctively a characteristic of modernism as are atonalism in music, Cubism in painting, or interior monologue in the novel" (1998, 5). As Gagnier argues, "Decadence is also a category of Taste, the construction of a private canon or gesture that defines the self through its choices, as in Nietzsche's Hellenism or Pater's highly idiosyncratic Renaissance that reaches from twelfth-century France to eighteenth-century Germany" (2010, 90).

5. Christopher Robinson (2005, 267–268), while acknowledging Cavafy's debt to the fin de siècle, argues that he refrained from suppressing the direct representation of same-sex desire, or "coding" it, as did many French and British decadents.

6. As Peter Christensen writes, "The overall tone of the entire [Cavafy] canon is one of acceptance of gay male sexuality and a recognition that personal and artistic creativity can spring from what the bourgeois world may consider decadent or unrewarding encounters" (1995, 151). The decadent poetry of Cavafy's German contemporary Stefan George (1868–1933) offers an interesting point of comparison, on which see Woods (1998, 184–185).

7. On the great "unrecorded history" of Forster's gay life, see Moffat (2010), and chapter 6 specifically on the influence of Cavafy on Forster's sexual liberation and fiction: "But Cavafy proved there was a different path: by exercising authorial control he forged a homosexual culture. Sublimely detached from the dictates of the public, he refused to encounter the world on any other than his own terms" (144). On Cavafy's homosexual reputation as a factor in establishing his reputation outside Greece, see Bien (1990).

8. Vidal offers the following take on Auden's reading of Cavafy: "A troubled, sometime Christian, even puritan, Auden suspected that the passionate encounters Cavafy describes are largely one-sided because the poet no doubt paid for them" (2001, xvii).

9. See Chauncey (2009, 281), who acknowledges Cavafy's exceptional status in the heyday of homosexual abjection. Regarding this particular pre-Stonewall strain of "maladjusted sentimentality," Halperin cites D. A. Miller on the related "queer affects" of the gay cult of the Broadway musical: "the solitude, shame, secretiveness by which the impossibility of social integration was first internalized"; and "the excessive sentimentality that was the necessary condition of sentiments allowed no real object" (2012, 94–95). The legacy of this rejection of shame in favor of pride is equally problematic for Halperin: "Instead of transcending the secret shame and solitary pleasures of our sentimentality, as we would like to think, we have assiduously closeted them" (95).

10. "Beauty holds out the possibility of transcending shame, escaping a community of the stigmatized, acceding to the rapt contemplation of pure physical and aesthetic perfection, leaving behind all those sad old queens, forsaking irony for romance, attaining dignity, and achieving true and serious worth, both in your own eyes and in other people's" (Halperin 2012, 207–208).

11. On Cavafy's relation to ancient Greek eros, see Alexiou (1983), Yourcenar (1984), and the essays in *Classical and Modern Literature* (2004, 23:2). For queer-theory-based readings of Cavafy, see Syrimis (2003) and Papanikolaou (2005). Papanikolaou (2014), a monograph on Cavafy and homosexuality, was published after I completed this study.

12. Andrew Holleran's novel *The Beauty of Men* (1996) is a prominent example of fiction that problematizes the post-Stonewall dilemma of how gay men remain defined by their bodies and obsession with youth.

13. Gregory Woods takes issue with Lilly: "Cavafy . . . is so explicitly writing about sexual desire that his insistence on visual beauty is entirely consistent with every level of his thought" (1998, 189).

14. As noted by Keeley (1992, 246n). Margaret Alexiou points out that "what is relevant is not actual past experience, but the recreation of intense physical sensations which can be fully realized only in art" (1983, 53).

15. Nikos Stangos, art critic and poetry editor at Penguin, and director for Thames & Hudson, was an early translator of Cavafy into English. With edits from Stephen Spender, his translations accompanied David Hockney's volume of Cavafy etchings (Plante 2009, 127).

16. David Plante reads Auden's kitsch comment in the context of fantasy: "Cavafy allows the reader to indulge in sexual fantasy, and at the same time, by his undercutting, he lets the reader know that this *is* fantasy" (2009, 134).

17. Although Cavafy falls well short of abjection in the emotional portraits of his poetic personae, one does encounter traces of the maladjusted sentimentality Halperin describes in his study of queer subjectivity: "Once upon a time, gay culture was rooted in 'the aestheticism of maladjustment,' as Daniel Harris calls it. With those roots in social rejection and marginalization now definitively severed, traditional gay culture is certain to wither away. . . . 'The grain of sand, our oppression, that irritated the gay imagination to produce the pearl of camp, has been rinsed away,' Harris explains, 'and with it, there has been a profound dilution of the once concentrated gay sensibility'" (2012, 117).

18. Christopher Isherwood's seminal definition of high and low camp appeared in his novel *From the World in the Evening* (1954).

19. See Holliday and Potts (2012), Dorfles (1969), and Nerdrum (2011) for excellent overviews of the concept.

20. As Dennis Dutton notes, "Some late-nineteenth Pre-Raphaelite work, with romantic fantasies of a medieval golden age, lies on the boundary of kitsch, while saccharine evocations of Classical themes by such painters as William-Adolphe Bouguereau and Lawrence Alma-Tadema often cross the line" (2009). Certainly the popularizing sentimental strains in Cavafy's work that lend it to kitsch are rooted in these painterly influences.

21. As Nerdrum (2011, 27) argues, kitsch came to signify "the antithesis of modern art." He goes on to note that there are high forms of kitsch that include the work of Wagner and Tchaikovsky: "Kitsch became the nickname for all those who didn't go along with the new century: Sibelius, Ilya Repin, Zorn, Tchaikovsky, Rachmaninov, Gershwin, and many others" (31).

22. Scruton adds that "serious artists are inevitably aware of kitsch: they fear it, are constantly on guard against it, and if they flirt with kitsch it is with a sense of risk, knowing that all artistic effort is wasted should you ever cross the line" (1999). See also Clement Greenberg's classical essay, "Avant-Garde and Kitsch" (1939), where he writes (apropos of Cavafy) that the "precondition for kitsch, a condition without which kitsch would be impossible, is the availability close at hand of a fully matured cultural tradition, whose discoveries, acquisitions, and perfected self-consciousness kitsch can take advantage of for its own ends. . . . This is what is really meant when it is said that the popular art and literature of today were once the daring, esoteric art and literature of yesterday."

23. Olalquiaga equates the kitsch object to souvenirs: "Emptied of experiential dimension, remembrances are hardened, take second place to an extrinsic function—being educational or ornamental—and lose their singularity upon entering the market as exchangeable items. . . . . Like these 'human aquariums,' kitsch is nothing if not a suspended memory whose elusiveness is made ever more keen by its extreme iconicity" (1998, 76, 28). Cavafy's presentation of the classical world

in an often ersatz manner is not unrelated to this quality identified by Olalquiaga; his poems function like so many imaginary souvenirs from a virtual antiquity, as is also noted by Yourcenar: "Consequently the gesture of the poet and of the lover handling his memories is not so different from that of the collector of precious or fragile object, shells or gems, . . . beloved objects" (1984, 181).

24. See Fred Kaplan's study, in which he connects sentimentality to the "cherished Victorian belief that human beings are innately good, that the source of evil is malignant social conditioning, and that the spontaneous, uninhibited expression of the natural feelings . . . is admirable and the basis for successful human relationships" (1987, 7). On the Victorian use of sentimentalism to negotiate sexual taboos and disguise eroticism, see Purton (2012, chap. 6). Cavafy's portrayal of marginalized gay men who suffer unnecessarily aligns him with this dominant facet of sentimentalism (Chapman and Hendler 1999, 9). He certainly wishes to provoke our emotional sympathy for the plight of his lovers.

25. On sophisticated parodies of kitsch, Scruton writes, "Preemptive kitsch sets quotation marks around actual kitsch and hopes thereby to save its artistic credentials. The dilemma is not: kitsch or avant-garde, but: kitsch or 'kitsch.' The quotation marks function like the forceps with which a pathologist lifts some odoriferous specimen from its jar" (1999).

26. As Goysdotter writes, "The theatricality of staged photography can be said to be a resurrection of the narrative that had been repressed under modernism's straight photographic depiction of the world of objects" (2013, 80). She goes on to note how staged photographers like Michals embrace the sentimental, unlike Ansell Adams and other purists (93).

27. In his afterword, Yeros writes, "I thought that the best models for this work would be people from the world of letters and the arts, people who knew and admired Cavafy's poetry" (2010, 157).

28. Tempelsman added the following lines: "And now the journey is over, too short, alas too short. / It was filled with adventure and wisdom, laughter and love, gallantry and grace. / So farewell, farewell."

29. Regarding Jacqueline Kennedy Onassis's lauded taste, Christopher Hitchens comments on her lowbrow appreciation for the Lerner and Loewe lyric from their musical *Camelot* ("Don't let it be forgot, that once there was a spot, for one brief shining moment that was known as Camelot"): "Odd, when you reflect upon it, that her first instinct was for the popular, the kitsch, and the second rate" (2011, 2).

30. "Certainly, Warhol is well-known for his consumer imagery and frankly commodified aesthetic. . . . Cultivating a queer style that embraces the erotics and aesthetics of the commodity, . . . Warhol brilliantly abstracts and desexualizes the 'essence' of Marilyn as object of exchange, subject to endless repetition and fetishistic fragmentation" (Glick 2009, 160, 139–140).

31. The phenomenal explosion of Cavafy translations in English is a subject that warrants a full book-length study. The poet's popularity owes much to the tradition of the "North American Translation Workshop" (see Gentzler [2001, chap. 2]), in which translators with little to no fluency in the poem's original language work from cribs or previous translations that function as cribs. In the age of computer-aided and machine translations, one wonders about the impact of this linguistic commodification and mechanical reproduction of Cavafy and its unmistakable popularizing relation to kitsch—translation kitsch, as it were.

32. See Lugg (1999) on the role of kitsch in American politics and the Kennedy legacy of "Camelot" in particular (64–66).

Acknowledgments

I am extremely grateful to my editor Peter J. Potter and the editorial staff at Cornell University Press for their patience, guidance, and expertise. The comments of the two anonymous external readers have proven invaluable to the book's progress and expansion. The production editor Sara Ferguson and copy editor Jamie Fuller have worked diligently to improve the final text, and the design team graciously accommodated my choice for a Tsarouchis image on the front cover, producing a stunning design.

This book has benefited along the way from the support and insights of numerous colleagues and friends. The rich contents of the Cavafy archive were made available to me by its former owner and curator, Manuel Savidis, to whom I owe a debt of gratitude, along with the archivist, Katerina Ghika, who has been unstinting in her assistance with biographical and historical material essential to completing this study. Suffolk University has provided me with scholarly support in the form of travel grants, course releases, and a sabbatical leave; I wish to thank the former chair of my department, Tony Merzlak, along with the former dean, Ken Greenberg, for backing this project.

There are many readers to whom I am indebted for taking the time to critique chapters at various stages of the book's composition. The late and dearly missed Peter Caputo offered commentary and encouragement on every level. Critical feedback was given by Gregory Jusdanis, Maria Moschoni, Ann Antippas, Maria Koundoura, Katerina Ghika, Bruce Frier, Sarah Ekdawi, and Dimitris Tziovas. The final text is immeasurably richer owing to the generous critical responses provided by these readers.

I also wish to thank the following friends, scholars, librarians, artists, art curators, and students who have contributed to this project in ways both great and small: Voula Shone, Marianna Xenidou, John Heropoulos, Michael Tandoc, Rhea Lesage, Peter Hawkins, Vassilis Lambropoulos, Theresa Maronna, Angelica Jeffreys, Charles Savery, Maria Katsanaki, Ioanna Moraiti, Violetta Koronaiou, Efi Agathonikou, Michelle Karampine-Iatrou, Hilary Nanda, Melissa Rich, Kyle Sullivan, Eric LaPre, Alekos Fassianos, George Economou, Dimitris Yeros, and Cory Furtado.

Grateful acknowledgment is made for permission to reprint the following excerpts and translations. An earlier version of chapter 1 appeared in *The Journal of Modern Greek Studies* 24.1 (copyright © 2006 The Johns Hopkins University Press). An earlier version of chapter 2 appeared in *Imagination and Logos: Essays on C. P. Cavafy* (Harvard University Department of Classics, 2010). *The Complete Poems of Cavafy,* translated by Rae Dalven (Harcourt Brace/Hogarth Press, 1961, 1989), is used by permission from Houghton Mifflin Harcourt Publishing and Random House Group Ltd. *C. P. Cavafy: Collected Poems,* translated by Edmund Keeley and Philip Sherrard © 1975 (Princeton University Press, 1992), is used by permission of Princeton University Press, copyright © C. P. Cavafy, reproduced by permission of the estate of C. P. Cavafy c/o Rogers, Coleridge, and White Ltd, 20 Powis Mews, London W11 1JN. *C. P. Cavafy: 154 Poems,* translated by Evangelos Sachperoglou (Athens, 2003), is used by permission from the translator. *C. P. Cavafy: Sixty-Three Poems Translated by J. C. Cavafy* (Athens: Ikaros, 2003) is used by permission from Manuel Savidis. *Complete Plus: The Poems of C. P. Cavafy in English*, translated by George Economou with Stavros Deligiorgis (Emersons Green, UK: Shearsman Books, 2013), is used by permission of the translator. "Cavafy Anthology," translated by George Valassopoulo, in *The Forster-Cavafy Letters: Friends at a Slight Angle,* edited by Peter Jeffreys (Cairo: American University in Cairo Press, 2009), is used by permission of Laura Lightbody.

INDEX

Note: Italic page numbers refer to figures.